LEGLESS IN GINZA

LEGLESS IN GINZA

Orientating Japan

ROBIN GERSTER

MELBOURNE UNIVERSITY PRESS

Melbourne University Press
PO Box 278, Carlton South, Victoria 3053, Australia
info@mup.unimelb.edu.au
www.mup.com.au

First published 1999

Text © Robin Gerster 1999
Design and typography © Melbourne University Press 1999

This book is copyright. Apart from any use permitted under the *Copyright Act* 1968 and subsequent amendments, no part may be reproduced, stored in a retrieval system or transmitted by any means or process whatsoever without the prior written permission of the publisher.

Designed by Guy Mirabella
Typeset by Designpoint in Bembo
Printed in Australia by RossCo Print

National Library of Australia Cataloguing-in-Publication entry

Gerster, Robin, 1953– .
 Legless in Ginza: orientating Japan.
 ISBN 0 522 84863 X.
 1.Gerster, Robin, 1953– . 2.Gerster, Robin, 1953– Views on Japan. 3. College teachers—Japan. 4. Japan—History—1952– . 5. Japan—Relations—Australia. 6. Australia—Relations—Japan. I. Title.
952.049

TO DEBORAH & BENJAMIN

CONTENTS

	Acknowledgements	ix
	Author's Note	xiii
	Prologue: Lunch at Bill's	1
1	Into the Inferno	7
2	Riding Santa's Surfboard	39
3	Fault Lines	79
4	The Big Smoke	111
5	Out of Edo I	157
6	Out of Edo II	181
7	Boomerang Japan	211
	Notes	238

ACKNOWLEDGEMENTS

I have several people to thank for their contribution—practical, unwitting or otherwise innocent—to this narrative. Among people living in Japan, I am grateful in particular to Toshiko Ellis for her immense efforts on my behalf, in helping me firstly to survive and then to enjoy my two years at Tokyo University. William Gater was a wonderful colleague and friend throughout my time in Tokyo. While almost everyone else seemed likely to succumb to terminal ennui, he got on with living and working in a city he had come to consider his home. His local knowledge was invaluable to me. Michael and Christine Hinds were boon companions and kindred spirits both in Japan and beyond. I am especially indebted to Michael for keeping me abreast of events in Japan since my departure, and for his prodigal wit and perceptiveness, both of which I have shamelessly plundered in making this small picture of contemporary Japan.

ACKNOWLEDGEMENTS

Others to whom I am in debt include Sachiko Tamai, the Senior Cultural Officer at the Australian Embassy in Tokyo, Yoichi Kibata at Tokyo University and Yasue Arimitsu at Doshisha University in Kyoto. Out in Kemigawa, we enjoyed the hospitality of Teruaki Fujishura immensely and often. In our apartment block, Akemi and Koichi Sato and Yuki and Osamu Chinone were model neighbours—welcoming, friendly, ever-helpful. We will never have better.

While I was in Japan, Peter Fitzpatrick, Peter Pierce, Lindsay Van Jager and my parents Margaret and John Wyenberg kept me informed of what was happening at home, while receiving and responding to my lengthy and occasionally demented missives, parts of which I have drawn on in writing this book. Others who helpfully participated in the Australian background to this narrative include Michael Ackland, Gay Baldwin, Jan Bassett, Carol Boas, Michael Carmen, Kevin Foster, Ian Jackson, David Osborne, Lenore Stephens, my brother Peter Gerster and brothers-in-law Lawrie and Jonathan Zion. I must particularly express my gratitude to Barbara Zion for her dexterity in administering our other 'lives' in Australia during our absence.

At Melbourne University Press, Teresa Pitt was a superbly supportive commissioning editor, while Mary Ellen Jordan and her production team did an excellent job in turning a drab manuscript into a good-looking book. On the manuscript itself, Jenny Lee proved to be a perspicacious, challenging and creative editor. It was a pleasure and a relief to work with such thorough professionals.

Finally, thanks to Deborah Zion for agreeing to join me in the Japanese adventure, maintaining her equilibrium while I went crazy, mopping up when I made a mess of things, and

ACKNOWLEDGEMENTS

ensuring that our time together in Tokyo was memorable and productive in all kinds of ways.

And to Ohara-san, wherever you are, cheers!

AUTHOR'S NOTE

This is a work of non-fiction. In three minor cases, however, I have changed the names of actual people in order to spare them any embarrassment. One character is a composite, the embodiment of several persons (and their words, attitudes and experiences) rolled into one. I leave it to the reader to guess who that character is.

For the sake of uniformity I have eliminated all macrons, the short horizontal lines used to indicate long vowels. Japanese words and phrases are italicised unless they have become so much a part of spoken and written English as to make their italicisation absurd (for example, 'sumo', 'sushi', 'tsunami'). Japanese names appear in the conventional Western order (which is increasingly used by the Japanese themselves when rendering their names in English)—that is, given name followed by family name.

Parts of chapters 2 and 3 have already appeared, respectively, in the journals *Quadrant* and *Meanjin*.

GREATER TOKYO
1 : 450 000

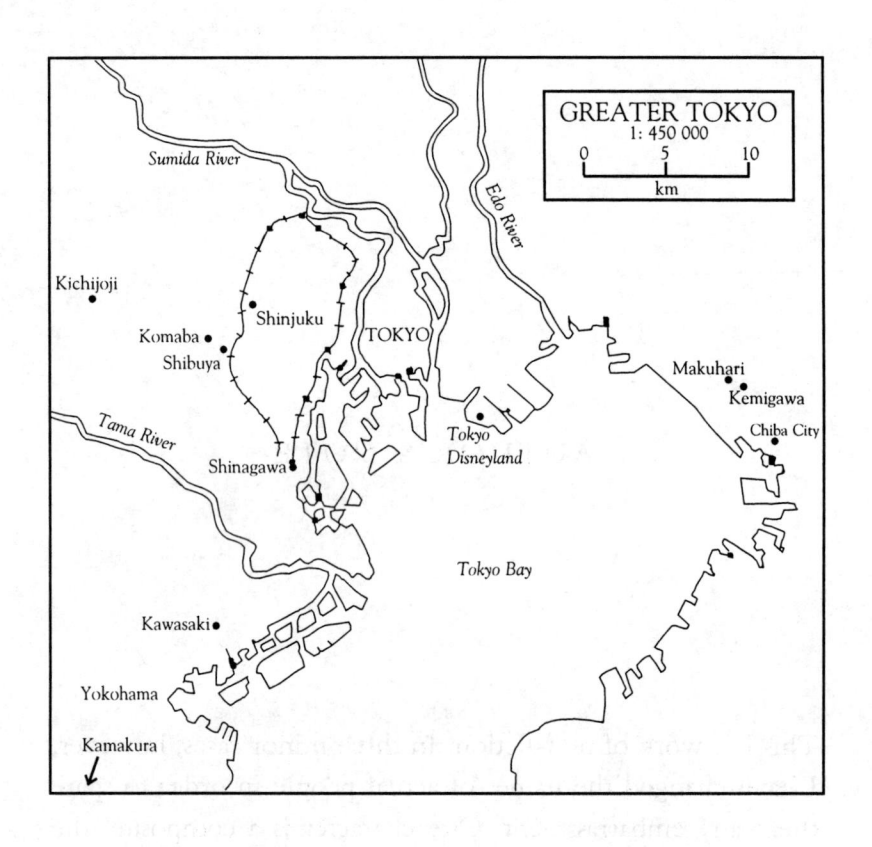

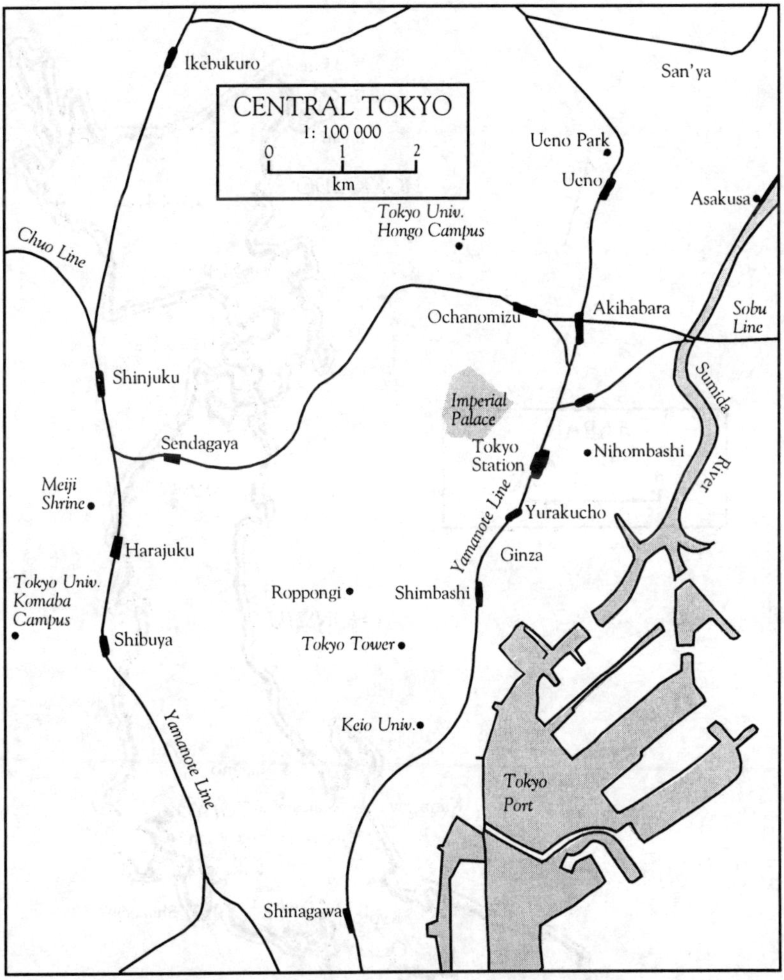

CENTRAL TOKYO
1: 100 000
0
1
2
km
Ikebukuro
San'ya
Ueno Park
Ueno
Asakusa
Tokyo Univ.
Hongo Campus
Chuo Line
Ochanomizu
Akihabara
Sobu
Line
Sumida
River
Shinjuku
Imperial
Palace
Sendagaya
Tokyo
Station
Nihombashi
Meiji
Shrine
Yamanote Line
Yurakucho
Harajuku
Ginza
Tokyo Univ.
Komaba
Campus
Roppongi
Shimbashi
Shibuya
Tokyo Tower
Keio Univ.
Yamanote Line
Tokyo
Port
Shinagawa

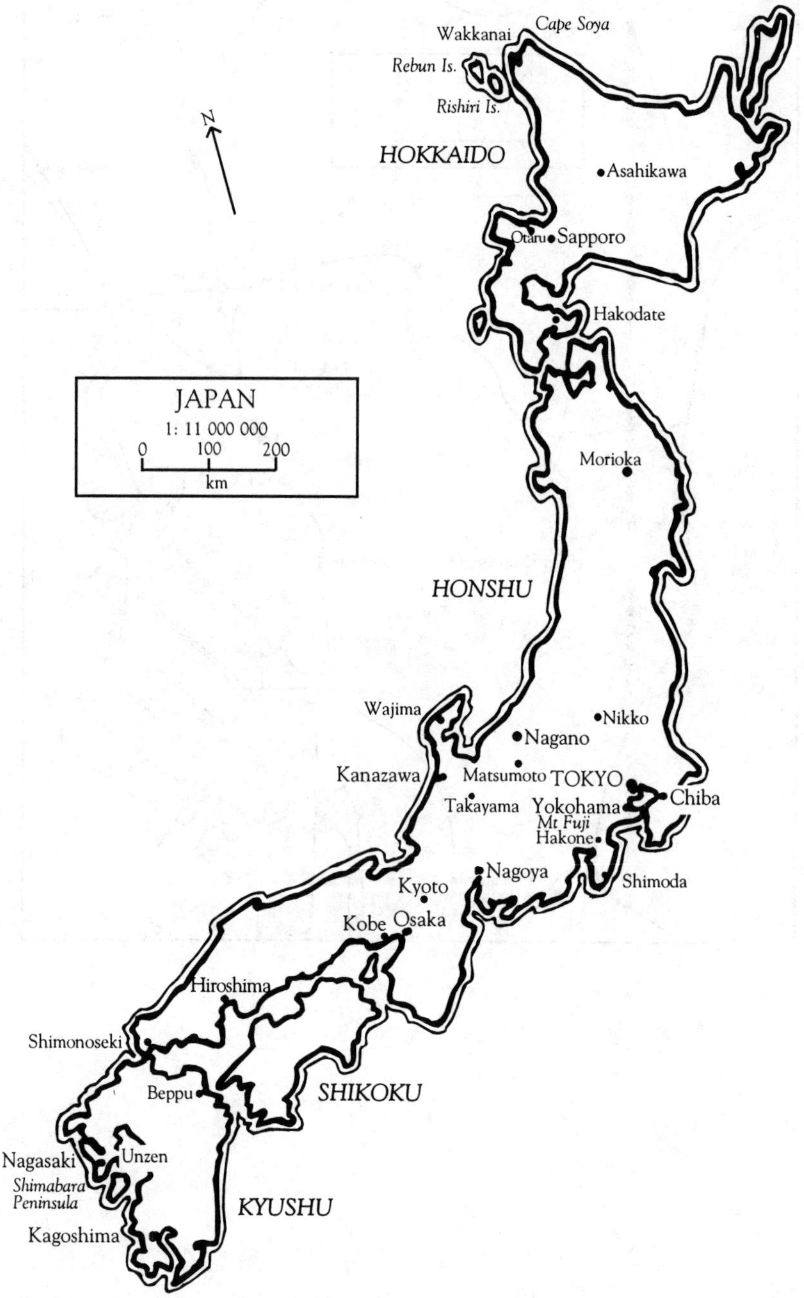
JAPAN
1: 11 000 000
0
100
200
km
N
Cape Soya
Wakkanai
Rebun Is.
Rishiri Is.
HOKKAIDO
Asahikawa
Otaru
Sapporo
Hakodate
Morioka
HONSHU
Wajima
Nikko
Nagano
Kanazawa
Matsumoto
TOKYO
Chiba
Takayama
Yokohama
Mt Fuji
Hakone
Nagoya
Shimoda
Kyoto
Kobe
Osaka
Hiroshima
Shimonoseki
Beppu
SHIKOKU
Nagasaki
Unzen
Shimabara Peninsula
KYUSHU
Kagoshima

A legless body is my kingdom's map,
Limping in folly, halting in distress . . .

    Thomas Middleton,
     'The Wisdom of Solomon Paraphrased'

The man who says, 'I've got a wife and kids' is far from home; at home he speaks of Japan.

    Paul Theroux,
    The Great Railway Bazaar

⌘ ⌘ ⌘

PROLOGUE: LUNCH AT BILL'S

It was not a picture-postcard view. By a vacant lot near the *pachinko* parlour next to the railway lines beneath the flyover stood a bivouac of prefabricated shelters, as unwelcoming as the Nissen huts where 'New Australians' were deposited in the Melbourne of my childhood. About a hundred metres away, squatting in a garden of rusting bicycles, was a grey concrete building that looked like an enormous pillbox. Here during World War II, according to the district's mythology, Tokyo Rose broadcast her seductive messages out over Tokyo Bay and into the great blue Pacific, an Oriental siren luring thousands of American GIs to demoralisation and death. I suspect the local legend is an invention. Legends are few and far between in Kemigawa, an undistinguished suburb among scores of other undistinguished suburbs in the south-eastern corner of Japan's colossal capital. But I was moved to believe it on this, my first day in the place where I was to live for the next two years.

In one of the makeshift dwellings lived a Canadian *émigré* whom I shall call Bill, for that indeed was his name. Bill cut a handsome figure. Tall, dimple-chinned and possessed of the vivid blue eyes of a young child, he must once have been blond but now, deep into middle age, had gone almost completely bald. A dashing dresser given to conversing in French, Bill roamed Kemigawa's modest streets and lanes with all the insouciance of a Parisian *boulevardier*. And why not? He worked and socialised downtown, but he *lived* out here in the suburban wilderness. A resident of Japan for nearly a quarter of a century, most of them as a teacher of English language at Tokyo University, Bill considered Kemigawa his home. He liked it; he didn't think it was ugly at all. In any case, his present accommodation was temporary. His old house had recently been demolished, and a brand new one—in the helter-skelter fashion of Japanese urban redevelopment—was in the process of being erected.

I too was to work at the university, as the visiting professor in Australian Studies, and Bill had been dragooned into serving as my minder. He had met me at Shin-Kemigawa station to direct me to the apartment that my wife Deborah and I had been allocated for the duration of our stay. Apparently it was in a large block leased by the university and situated opposite its sporting fields, part of which contained a small golf course. This last detail had been communicated to me as a sweetener (golf courses being akin to sacred sites in Japan) to make up for the fact that we were being put up in an area that my map revealed to be countless railway stations and nearly thirty kilometres from downtown Tokyo. Go much further south from the Big Smoke and you'd end up in Okinawa. Originally we had been offered a large flat in Shinagawa, a prized area in the city, but just before our departure I was informed that it had been double-booked. This was a finessing of the truth. One of my future Japanese colleagues had pulled rank—or that is what I was inclined to think in my more disillusioned moments during the following few months. Some people call it Japanese obtuseness, dissimulation, lack of frankness. But others would point to my own hypersensitivity, the paranoia typical of thousands of foreigners in Japan who imagine a slight in every Japanese gesture, word and action. Whatever, Kemigawa was not Shinagawa, and Tokyo Rose had another notch on her belt.

Situated in Chiba Prefecture, Kemigawa was in what locals—hopefully summoning glamorous associations with San Francisco—liked to call the 'Bay Area'. But the sound of waves could not be heard, just the incessant noise of numberless trains and the creak of the great Japanese social-industrial machine grinding on. Somewhere in one of his books Ian Buruma, one of the more sensible foreign Japanologists, describes the suburbs that stretch from Tokyo to Chiba City as 'dismal'. This seemed a charitable description. Even on bright, sunny days the dominant colour of Tokyo is grey, but on the bleak, bone-numbing early April morning when I ventured across the Edo River towards my new home, words like 'Stygian' sprang to mind. At least Deborah was still in Melbourne, attending to last-minute arrangements before flying out the following week. I would have plenty of time to prepare her for the worst. In the local *pachinko* parlour, visible immediately I descended the steps at Shin-Kemigawa station, players sat grimly at their machines, watching the little metal balls hurtle and spin. The parlour was called 'Kimagure', meaning 'caprice' or 'whim'. The very name mocked, taunted, jeered: what strange and unaccountable fancy had moved me to this place?

Bill's back was bad. Insisting that the apartment block was a short step away, he ignored the taxis idling by the railway station and blithely led me through long, narrow streets while I struggled with two excruciatingly heavy suitcases and the shiny new leather briefcase I had purchased to celebrate my Tokyo appointment. We walked and we walked and evidently became quite lost. That 'short step' was in danger of becoming a death march. My arms ached, my legs turned the consistency of tofu, my mood soured. I ordered Bill to a halt in order to gather what was left of my strength. A bilingual sign outside some kind of municipal office told me that we had come to rest by a 'Disaster Evacuation Area', a designated place for people to congregate in the event of some major natural catastrophe. An earthquake, in other words.

Like many newcomers to Tokyo—I had landed at Narita just three days earlier—I was preoccupied by fears of earthquakes, especially of the dreaded 'Big One' that would destroy the metropolis and shake the world to its financial foundations. Back in the central city waiting for the apartment to become vacant, I had already felt a tremor or two. But now, although I had no desire to die in Kemigawa, I felt so tired and fed up that I could not have cared less if the Big One had hit there and then. Sensing my frame of mind, Bill took stock of the situation and suggested that I wait where I was while he sought guidance. This seemed like a good idea, and he ambled off.

The impassive, leaden sky suddenly started to weep rain. I felt like crying myself. I wanted to go home. Violence seemed the next best thing, so I scoured the landscape for a Japanese to strangle by way of revenge for the dreadful treatment meted to Our Blokes during the war. Then Bill came back into view, perched in the passenger seat of a car, which screeched to a halt beside my saturated pile of luggage. OK, he would do. In fact,

PROLOGUE: LUNCH AT BILL'S

it was Bill I especially wanted to throttle. But it did not come to that. Grinning broadly, Bill introduced me to the driver, a woman who knew the location of the apartment block. She cheerfully deposited my bags in the boot, and we drove off.

The Todai *apato* turned out to be a relatively new building, hardly elegant but hardly hideous either, across a busy road from a large green belt containing the promised golf course. A pity I'd given up the game. After meeting the diminutive concierge, who'd been alerted to the imminent arrival of a foreigner but seemed psychologically unprepared for it, I was led to my apartment. It contained a living room, bathroom and shower, small kitchen and three bedrooms, including the 'Japanese room' (tatami matting, paper screens) that is customarily featured in contemporary Japanese domestic living so that the locals can keep in touch with their roots. I appreciated the traditional touches, but was less impressed by the fact that the apartment was without any form of furnishing at all. Nothing to cover the windows, nor a single light bulb; only the toilet to sit on. Bill's face took on a worried look. I had already been presented with a telephone by Toshiko Ellis, a Japanese colleague, and had arranged to purchase a phone line from my Australian predecessor in the Tokyo University job. I plugged the receiver into the outlet. At least I now felt connected to Planet Earth.

Meanwhile, the flat was filling with women, my new neighbours—amusing, resourceful and attractive women, the wives of undeserving, insecure and narcissistic men (so I liked to think)—who began cleaning and 'fixing' the flat, stocking it with soap and shampoo, lugging in lamps, getting on to the gas company, setting up a futon on the tatami, installing heaters and inviting me to tea. Things were looking up. Bill's sunny smile returned, his blue eyes shone and he suggested lunch.

LEGLESS IN GINZA

So off we went to his Nissen hut in the clearing late morning, through streets that now seemed full of exotic charm. I observed 'Japanesey' houses, many of them wooden, with exquisite little gardens; small public squares where noisy children played, watched by their doting mothers; a few kimono-clad women clomping their way toward the station on some important social outing; bakeries and coffee bars and restaurants serving *sashimi* and *yakitori*; stores selling cloth or stationery or *sembei*, the Japanese crackers that are a Chiba speciality; liquor stores stocked with sake and beer and wine from all over the world. I did not realise it at the time, but I was showing disturbing signs of entering the first emotional phase that Arthur Koestler many years ago identified as the common experience of foreigners in Japan[1]: the 'colourful haze of euphoria' famously experienced by the Greek–Irish–American writer Lafcadio Hearn, who went weak at the knees at the wonder of all things Japanese when he wandered around Yokohama on his first, tediously celebrated day in the country.

Phase One, however, did not last long. Koestler's second and third phases—mounting exasperation sometimes verging on hatred, then general acceptance and understanding—followed swiftly, later that very afternoon as I recall. That the three phases were liable to hit me in rapid succession, and out of their designated order, was to become one of the most disorienting things about living in Japan. Yet, if I never became Lafcadio Hearn, I never again turned into the aspiring Jap-basher stamping his feet and contemplating murder outside the Kemigawa 'Disaster Evacuation Area' either.

Bill and I arrived at his place, and I played with his black cat Kuro while he uncorked a bottle of wine and prepared a meal. I was away.

⌘ ⌘ ⌘

1 INTO THE INFERNO

Ohara dragged greedily on his cigarette—he had perfected the Japanese way of smoking, which is to extract and exhale the maximum quantity of noxious fumes—and said, 'Don't you think your situation in this place is a bit like Dante in the *Inferno*?'

'How come?'

'Because you know you're in hell, but you also know you'll eventually leave.'

Ohara was a colleague. An American from a city somewhere in the Midwest, he was fond of quoting the self-definition of the travel writer Bill Bryson: 'I come from Des Moines. Somebody had to.' He had lived in Japan for what he described as 'an eternity'. In a fit of idealistic passion he had married a comely, sweet-natured Japanese girl, but she had turned out to be a dragon and they had divorced long ago. Away from work, he told me, he now grazed contentedly in fields so luxuriant with attractive unattached women that he could tolerate the most tormented of professional environments. Dead fluent in Japanese—he taught the novels of Junichiro Tanizaki to his students in their native language—Ohara had few illusions about the University of Tokyo, or indeed about Japan itself, but had reached some kind of rapprochement with both. He had even dropped the apostrophe from his moniker (as in 'Scarlett'), transforming it into a not uncommon Japanese family name, which means something like 'big field'. A very large man, so large he could barely perform a 360-degree turn in the average Japanese room, Ohara thought this a huge joke.

He had quickly and correctly identified the response of a functionally monolingual Australian to an institution, a city, an entire country that for much of the time seemed to offer a version of hell on earth. I appreciated the broad point of the Dantean allusion, but rushed to the hallowed text itself to see if Ohara had anything 'deeper' in mind. I had only come across Dante through studying Eliot's *The Waste Land* as a student, and the borrowing I remembered—about death having 'undone so many'—seemed a bit much to apply to working at Tokyo University. But, reading Dante's great epic—not all of it, as I gave up somewhere near the cusp of Paradise—I saw what Ohara was driving at. It is not difficult to find apposite Dantean tags to illustrate the experience of teaching at Tokyo University.

'Todai', the common conflation of 'Tokyo Daigaku' (university), is a sort of educational embodiment of the Great Buddha at Kamakura. It reposes serenely in the knowledge of its unchallenged and indeed unchallengeable position as the most prestigious tertiary institution in Japan. This, in a country where there are almost as many universities as noodle bars:

1 INTO THE INFERNO

more than 550 at last count. The imperial university, Todai is the source that nourishes the upper echelons of the nation's omnipotent bureaucracy, generation after generation, and therefore occupies an exalted place in Japanese society. Mere mortals look up to it in awe and wonder, struck dumb by the very mention of its name.

The university has two campuses, named Hongo and Komaba after their Tokyo locations. Less grand than its stately sister, the Komaba campus where I was based makes up for its modest dimensions by the surrealistic enchantments offered by its landscape. Neo-classical buildings vie with Stalinist work-blocks. Huge, blackly glistening crows shriek and sashay through the rank vegetation that strangles the college grounds. Discarded furniture gathers mould, accumulated rubbish—old tins and boxes, bicycles, electronic equipment—is everywhere. A hen picks its way along the barren ground by the bookshop; a goat dreamily grazes in the long grass by a derelict dormitory; cats scrounge for scraps by the entrances to staff offices. Like the progeny of some Indochinese hill tribe, small children frolic in the few square yards of bare earth that surround a dilapidated wooden shack located in a far-flung corner of the campus. This is the Komaba day-care centre. In the heavy snows of early 1998 the campus took on the appearance of a Soviet gulag. Then, during the humid *tsuyu*—the rainy season of June and early July—it became some sweltering South-east Asian POW camp, buried deep in the heart of the Tokyo jungle.

Standing at the urinal in the most malodorous lavatory in the known world—on the second floor of Building 9, in which my office was housed—I could look down and across at a slowly disintegrating wooden chair inexplicably positioned on the roof of the building next door. There it stood, through the bitter snows of winter and the ferocious heat of summer, an ironic Daliesque reminder of the scholastic purpose of this singular institution. Also adjacent to Building 9 was a swimming pool that evidently had not been cleaned for years. In this miasmic pond mosquitoes teemed and frogs croaked, their antediluvian din drowned out only by the dozen or more wretchedly inept student saxophonists who practised in the arcaded dressing sheds, individually playing Beelzebub's music all day, week after week, month after month, year after unending year. Was there ever, I wondered, a place less conducive to contemplative intellectual endeavour than the University of Tokyo, Komaba, Meguro-ku 153, Tokyo, Japan?

'We have come now', says Virgil to Dante on his journey through hell, 'to a place where . . . You will find the people for whom there is only grief: Those who have lost the benefit of the intellect'. 'To-dai'—to die, then, and to be sent down to hell. One had to pity the students, who had triumphantly negotiated the notorious 'examination hell' endured by Japanese school leavers and had gained entry to the Elect, only to be confronted by conditions that gave the appearance of being deliberately designed to stymie study. Or so it seemed . . .

The students were probably too shattered by the process of physically getting there to notice the roughness of the conditions. 'Commuter hell' is another of the hells on offer in Tokyo. Travelling to Komaba from Kemigawa is one of those travel experiences that stays with you—the unforgettable sensation of being swept up in the raging torrent of people that gushes through the city's labyrinthine transportation system, men and women on their way to and from another day of toil, tormented spirits yearning for the comforts of home, the womb that all-too-briefly protects them from a demanding world.

1 INTO THE INFERNO

And the clamorous crowds of the city itself, flowing across the huge intersections in Ginza or surging through Shinjuku, buffeted by infernal gales in summer and by icy blasts in winter, affronted by mephitic vapours and unnerved by continual seismic shudders and jolts. Ah, the quakes, the quakes, real and anticipated. That 'murky countryside', Dante writes of one of the circles of hell, 'trembled so much, that even to think of it/ Still leaves me terrified and bathed in sweat'.

Writing in fear and loathing of what post-war Tokyo had become, Hal Porter in 1968 demonised the city as 'groaning, shrieking, roaring, clashing, squealing and thundering like a satanic factory'.[1] The noise is unremitting—trains, traffic, sirens, street vendors, buskers, brilliantined hustlers, a cacophony of human voices both living and recorded. Deafening messages from railway platforms or huge video screens declaim and exhort, shop assistants in department stores offer shrill, robotic welcomes, the people who bump into you on the pavements mutter their beg-pardons. And then there are the innumerable *pachinko* parlours. At least one could hurry by the metallic roar that emanates from these appalling smokehouses. I wondered how the players inside were able to survive. Impersonators of the damned in a Sartresque limbo, Koestler called them.[2]

Reeling from Tokyo's torments, I started dreaming of the clean, spare spaces of Norway, and spent some of my precious research time inventing escapist, middle-of-the-road tunes such as might in madder moments be attempted by the ageing crooners one sees on Japanese TV. My personal favourite, my very own 'My Way', was called 'Easy Living':

Easy livin' . . .
You know that's the way you need to go—
Just take it easy, just take it slow.

Don't do it four times,
Just do it the twice.
Four times is OK,
But twice is twice as nice.

Yes, it's easy living,
And that's the way you have to go—
Just take it eeeasy, just take it s-s-slow.

⌘⌘⌘

So why had I, 'halfway along the road we have to go', willingly submitted to this ordeal? During a mildly acrimonious public contretemps over my review of a collection of essays that dealt in part with matters of Australian and Asian cultural relations, the Melbourne-based editor of the volume argued that I had gone to Japan for 'fun and profit'. This was a presumptuous assertion. Certainly I had not dragged Deborah and myself to Japan to be miserable or go broke, though both fates occasionally seemed likely during our stay. But to put the reasons for a Japanese sojourn down to such motives is itself to fall prey to Orientalist fancies of the gorgeous East, and goes to show how Japan, that paradigm of the 'politically incorrect', continues to stump even the most zealous post-colonialist.

Yet I cannot claim noble motives. Quite simply, I saw Japan as a change as well as a challenge. In *Tokyo World*, Humphrey McQueen's account of his own experience as the Australian Studies professor at Todai, he records that, when one of his students asked why he had gone to Japan, he had replied, 'To see Australia better'.[3] I had no such laudable ambition, though it is true that certain things about my homeland became more blindingly obvious while I was away. But I had wanted to get away from the place, mentally as well as physically. This was clearly a wrong-headed notion—after all, I was employed to teach Australian Studies, and so had to reflect upon Australia intellectually and 'explain' it to students, to some of whom it was as remote as Mars, or even Korea for that matter.

In any event, it proved impossible to escape Australia. It was in the news all the time, and almost all the news was bad. Very soon after my arrival the massacre at Port Arthur in Tasmania catapulted Australia on to the Japanese front pages and put this unsettled newcomer's whinges and brittle dejection into perspective. In the *Japan Times* account of the ensuing trial six months or so later, the paper published a photograph of the killer, Martin Bryant, bearing the simple caption **'AUSTRALIAN'** in bold type. Socially and politically, Australia seemed to be regressing, and the Japanese press was there to record every backward step. The 'stolen generation' story, the Howard government's opposition to the Wik judgment, even the prime minister's refusal to meet a travelling troupe of sumo wrestlers (a special PR disaster in Japan), all were given detailed attention. So was the decline in Japanese tourism; an Australian survey widely reported in Japan explained that Japanese visitors found the Great South Land 'underdeveloped', 'dirty' and 'boring', and its inhabitants 'ill-mannered'.

Then there was Pauline Hanson, who became so well known in Japan in 1997 that her name appeared in the headlines in the way usually reserved for heads of state. (Meanwhile John Howard had to make do with being identified as 'Aussie PM'.) Hanson was a name one just could not avoid. Even one of my Todai colleagues was called Hanson. To make matters worse, a pubescent American vocal trio of that name was particularly popular in Tokyo at the time, and all over the city their pimpled visages and lank golden locks stared out at me on giant billboards daubed with the word 'HANSON', stinging like an accusation.

Naturally I attempted to explain the political phenomenon in cool, logical and reasonable terms. Something along the lines of: '. . . the Hanson backlash, to magnify a minor Queensland parliamentarian into a figurehead for the numbers of Australians of Anglo-Saxon or Anglo-Celtic origin who feel themselves disempowered and diminished by the globalisation of the market economy and by the cosmopolitanisation of contemporary Australian life itself, is merely the latest if perhaps the most furious manifestation of anxiety at the hotly contested process of "Asianisation" of the past twenty or so years, as the nation has reoriented itself away from its European origins toward an economic, political and cultural future in the Asia–Pacific region'. Such a diagnosis might go over all right in middle-class urban Australia, where 'cultivated' people (some of whom privately agree with some of Hanson's views but none of whom would ever want to be associated with her) hate to think that the country really is irredeemably racist and as insecure about its geo-cultural identity as it always has been. My Japanese colleagues and students were politely sympathetic; indeed, they couldn't understand why Australia should be so desperate to be 'part of Asia' anyway. Australia's neck was as red as ever. So be it. My Western colleagues, especially the disdainful Englishmen, were not impressed. They knew better—Australia had reverted to type. I was constantly apologising for my homeland. In the end I gave up; they were probably right.

1 INTO THE INFERNO

⌘⌘⌘

The news about Japan was not much good either.

It seemed that I had swapped a comfortable existence in Australia for some frightful dystopia on the brink of collapse. The apocalypse was at hand; all that was required was the coming of the Big One to signify Japan's descent into abject ruin. That at least, was the impression given by some sections of the Western press, and not merely the tabloids either. Towards the end of 1996, in the 'comfort' of my Todai office (by then I could mentally transform the cacophony outside into something resembling a muted muzak), I innocently began reading *Japan—Behind the Lines*, the professional memoir of Ben Hills, a highly respected Sydney journalist who was the Tokyo correspondent for the *Sydney Morning Herald* and the Melbourne *Age* from 1992 to 1995. What I read made me want to dash for Narita and flee the country, quick smart. Hills' alarming and not entirely inaccurate version of Japan is of an environmental nightmare; a 'democracy' whose hapless citizens are at the mercy of corrupt politicians, venal businessmen and an implacably powerful bureaucracy; a society whose obsession with sameness drives its young people to commit suicide in droves; a place where you can pick up AIDS and a lethal dose of *E. coli*, get gassed in a subway (if you don't get crushed to death first), killed in an earthquake, ripped off, taken for a ride and left high and dry, all on the same day.

The great Japanese success story was unravelling, and how people everywhere were enjoying the spectacle! Barely able to contain their smugness at the torpid state of the Japanese economy and the glaring weaknesses of its financial system, Western political leaders (most egregiously the British prime minister, Tony Blair, while visiting Tokyo in early 1998 on a mission to beg for increased Japanese investment) started lecturing the country on how to lift its game. In the media, the rampant gloating was only contained by the realisation that Japan's economic woes spelt potential trouble for the rest of the world. After the financial crises that hit many Asian countries in the latter part of 1997 and early 1998—a currency 'meltdown', to use the apocalyptic trope in favour at the time— Western countries looked to Japan to retrieve the situation. When Japan seemed incapable of doing so, it copped the blame for being (true to form) irresponsible and self-interested.

Ultimately, however, the temptation to snigger proved greater than the urge to lecture. This was nowhere more apparent than in the response of the BBC and CNN satellite news services to the sobbing public apology of Shohei Nozawa, the president of the huge brokerage house, Yamaichi Securities, when it went bust in November 1997. This was a moment of some pathos—Nozawa was pleading to the public not to allow the company's employees to 'walk the streets', unwanted, unemployed—but his words were not translated in the Western TV coverage. All that was left was the faintly comic image of yet another humiliated, self-pitying Japanese crook, and the news presenters could hardly conceal their mirth. The breakdown of Japan's vaunted lifetime employment system and the prospect of the numbers of jobless rising to hitherto unimaginable figures were presented less as the stuff of social tragedy than as an opportunity for ridicule. 'DEATH OF A SALARYMAN', punned *Time* magazine in its feature story on the aftermath of the Yamaichi debacle.[4]

The explosion of negative reporting was not confined to caustic foreigners. The Japanese press was equally critical. The rotten state of Japan was dissected in article after article in the

1 INTO THE INFERNO

English-language newspapers the *Japan Times*, the *Daily Yomiuri* and the *Asahi Evening News*, to which my reading was necessarily restricted. Often reproduced in translation from the vernacular press, these stories featured titles such as 'FAILURES CATCH UP WITH JAPAN' (on the government's inability to push through basic administrative and fiscal reforms) and 'CONDUCT ILL BEFITTING JAPAN' (on institutionalised political impropriety). Scathing editorials headlined 'THE BUCK STOPS AT THE BOARDROOM' and 'ARROGANCE, HYPOCRISY AND CORRUPTION' sought to shame the nation's political leadership out of its complacency.

There was plenty to be critical of and angry about. Japan's incestuous corporate, financial and political worlds were in disgrace. Financial institutions teetered and crashed while dodgy politicians dissembled and ran for cover; political parties disassembled and regrouped. Venerable companies were discovered making corrupt pay-offs to the *sokaiya*, corporate racketeers so shady one could barely make out their features in the grainy mug shots on the front pages. And, horror of horrors, senior bureaucrats, those men whose arrogance only ceases to amaze when one realises just how much power they possess, were discovered to be on the take. Their shame was put on show for everyone to see.

One notorious case involved a certain Nobuharu Okamitsu, the former Vice-minister of Health and Welfare, who was found to have been diverting public welfare expenditures in Saitama Prefecture to a private nursing-home conglomerate in return for lots of loot and favours, not least the inevitable golf club membership. Okamitsu lied and lied and lied about his misdeeds until he could lie no more; at last he was driven off in the back of a police car under the glare of the television arc lights, his face giving nothing away. In one form or other that scene was repeated night after night on TV while I was in Japan, as regular as the weather report: stony-faced shysters being taken into custody, men who all appeared to have emerged from the same womb, already in their smart blue suits, white shirts and dark ties.

The Japanese use the English-language euphemism 'wining and dining' to designate the enticements offered to bent bureaucrats and politicians, but 'gagging and shagging' would more accurately describe the inducements offered to grasping officials to keep quiet when things were amiss in their purview. I suspect a bit of deflected envy attended the outrage expressed by the Japanese man-on-the-street when TV interviewers asked his opinion of the venality that seemed endemic to Japanese public administration. This might explain the near-jubilation at the disclosure that senior bank inspectors from the powerful Ministry of Finance took bribes from banks to keep quiet about irregularities and warn of impending inspections. That particular scandal cost the Finance Minister his job and led to the suicide of a ministry official, Yoichi Otsuki. In January 1998, while awaiting questioning about his conduct, Otsuki hanged himself with a necktie in his apartment—an appropriate enough mode of departure, to be sure, for a disgraced member of Japan Inc., and a golden opportunity for *Time* magazine to regale its readers with further evidence of the turpitude of Japanese public administration. 'In Japan', it sneered, 'suicide means never having to say you're sorry'.[5]

Contrary to popular Western belief, however, the Japanese do not see life as some kind of dreary preamble to a spectacular act of self-destruction. The idea that suicide is a uniquely Japanese ritual began with the kamikaze legend during

1 INTO THE INFERNO

World War II and has been embellished down the years by such public performances as Yukio Mishima's shocking *seppuku* in 1970 and by films with a suicide theme that have found popular and critical success outside Japan, such as Takeshi Kitano's gut-wrenching *Hana-bi* (1997). The Japan-is-the-suicide-capital-of-the-world mob revelled in the casualties created by the financial scandals of 1997 and 1998, during which bankers and bureaucrats bumped themselves off at a distressing rate. The subject cropped up several times in *Time* magazine's feature on the Nagano Winter Olympics. There was mention of Japan's winning a gold medal 'just two days before a fourth person hanged himself in a government financial scandal'; even more gratuitously, *Time* remarked on the suicide of a Japanese marathon runner way back in 1968, four years after 'feeling he had let down his country' by failing in the Tokyo Olympiad of 1964.[6]

The suicides made good copy. Perhaps the most publicised suicide in Japan involved the Liberal Democratic Party lawmaker Shokei Arai. Facing arrest on suspicion of demanding illicit profits from a major securities company, Arai hanged himself on 19 February 1998 with a bathrobe belt tucked into an air-conditioning duct near the ceiling of his room in Le Meridien Pacific, a swish Shinagawa hotel. The demise of Arai—fifty, handsome, a Tokyo University graduate of Korean extraction who had once worked for the Ministry of Finance—brought to mind Peter Tasker's 1992 novel *Silent Thunder*, which begins with the body of a Finance Ministry official, a Todai alumnus of humble origins, hurtling towards a Tokyo pavement, suspiciously from the direction of one of the windows of a ritzy hotel. Around the time of Arai's death, the president of a failed auto-parts company and two of his business associates booked themselves into three separate rooms in a Tokyo hotel and individually hanged themselves with cloth belts attached to the ventilator grilles.

The crash of the 1980s bubble economy came as a tremendous surprise to a country where it had been complacently assumed that economic graphs only ever went up, never down. In his book *Lost Japan* (1996) Alex Kerr sardonically recalls that when the stock market nose-dived in early 1990, Japan's version of the *Wall Street Journal*, colloquially known as the *Nikkei*, found its typesetter's box did not contain the *kanji* for words such as 'drop', 'fall' and 'crash'.[7] The economic doldrums of 1997, while not as shocking as the bursting of that bubble, had a debilitating effect on public morale. As the yen weakened and the Nikkei stock index staggered and stagnated, so did Japan's national self-esteem and its sense of common purpose.

Ordinary people seemed to realise that Japan was undergoing a necessary process of adaptation, especially in terms of streamlining and internationalising its economy, but they didn't much like the new, 'different' nation that was emerging. The prime minister, Ryutaro Hashimoto, was caught between tenacious cultural traditions, subservience to vested interests, and the certain knowledge that change had to come. A thin-lipped spiv of a man with a viscous rocker's hair-do, Hashimoto walked the Japanese corridors of power with an exaggerated swagger that belied his short stature and rising desperation. With increasing stridency he started promoting a miscellany of imported economic rationalist practices and philosophies collectively known as the 'Big Bang', a label many Japanese found discomfiting. Japan, after all, had been the target of several 'big bangs' in its recent history. It didn't want an economic Hiroshima as well.

1 INTO THE INFERNO

Old certainties were gone or on their way out, but what would replace them? The press was always talking about the new generation who would undertake the remaking of Japan. So were American business leaders and politicians, whose insistent exhortations in late 1997 and early 1998 stung Hashimoto's supine government into remedial but ultimately ineffective economic action.

Meanwhile a measurable increase in seismic activity near Tokyo seemed to herald some impending cataclysm, even greater in scale than the one that shattered Kobe in January 1995. The Big One to match the Big Bang seemed to be just around the corner. I speculated about what would happen if it hit while I was riding the subway—as I usually was. No 'Disaster Evacuation Area' would be of much help then. When there is a tremor of any significance in the Tokyo area, the trains abruptly stop wherever they are on the line. I was once trapped in a stationary train tantalisingly short of my intended stop at Shibuya. The passengers around me were already reaching for their mobiles to offer excuses for their impending lateness when the intercom informed us that there had been a *jishin*, or earthquake, the Japanese word I most dreaded to hear.

I speculated about a lot of things on the subway, especially after a group of resourceful pickpockets took to tear-gassing train compartments. This was an unpleasant reminder of the murderous sarin gas terrorist attacks a couple of years before. (The members of the Aum Shinrikyo cult who perpetrated those attacks were on trial throughout my time in Tokyo, their case meandering interminably through the courts.) No wonder people were anxious. I know I was, often.

But making a run for the airport was risky as well. Opposition by local landowners to the extension of Narita

International Airport had turned violent. In early 1998 somebody or some group took to firing trench mortars from a vantage point behind the Holiday Inn—a happening that warranted only a small single-paragraph story on page two of the *Japan Times*. Even escape looked to be impossible.

Internecine bickering and disputation—that insidious foreign disease—was on the rise. The cracks in the economic monolith seemed to prefigure imminent social collapse. Indeed, a rash of familial homicides suggested that the most venerated of Japanese institutions, the family, was falling apart. No part of the archipelago was untouched. In November 1997, up north in Hokkaido, a young women was arrested for beating her 3-year-old son to death. The next January a 31-year-old trucker from Osaka was arrested for fatally bludgeoning his 11-year-old son (apparently the son was rebellious and the father 'wanted to make him behave'); on the same day a 49-year-old man in Shizuoka Prefecture, closer to the capital, was arrested for murdering his bed-ridden elder sister with a baseball bat. In Aichi Prefecture, a middle-aged salaryman butchered his family—wife, mother and two sons—before doing himself in. Throughout 1997 and into 1998 the list of episodes of atrocious violence grew and grew. Killings in Kyushu; family slayings in sleepy Shikoku, where they reckon nothing ever happens.

It is often suggested that the popularity of the Victorian murder mystery, with its customary focus on the murder of a household member, was a vicarious response to the suffocating constrictions of the Victorian family. In Japan the popularity of *manga*, the gaudy, S&M-saturated comics devoured by millions of salarymen as they wend their long way home, is usually explained away as an escapist release from the stifling decorum and unremitting pressures of Japanese life. Should the Japanese put down this repulsive, inane garbage and pick up Sherlock Holmes instead?

School violence was symptomatic of the same malaise that was affecting the Japanese family. An English teacher at a junior high school in Tochigi Prefecture north of Tokyo was stabbed to death by one of her students, a 13-year-old who took offence at being scolded and responded by plunging a hunting knife into her body several times. This appalling incident was followed by a spate of schoolyard knife attacks—or at least it appeared that way, such was the prominence given to them in the media. Japan had a become an odious parody of its 'glorious past': the samurai sword of hallowed legend had become a cheap instrument of absurd violence, wielded by disenchanted or disturbed children. Thirteen-year-olds were being stabbed to death by their classmates. Some students used knives to other destructive ends. Early in 1998 a 15-year-old boy, driven by what he described as an urgent need to fire a gun, stabbed a neighbourhood Tokyo policeman in order to secure his firearm. (He failed.) In response to mounting outrage, television stations started cutting scenes with knives from their dramas for fear of inciting further attacks, a policy that must have left gaping holes in their programming.

Controlled, constructive Japan was showing uncharacteristic signs of anarchy. After my departure in April 1998 a Todai colleague, Michael Hinds—a native of Omagh in Northern Ireland's Country Tyrone, a town famous at that time mainly for its madhouse, which you would think might have made him feel at home in Tokyo, but didn't—began sending me snippets from the Japanese papers to reassure me that the country hadn't come to its senses since I'd left. In Chiba a 17-year-old was sent to a reformatory for tormenting a 14-year-old who later hanged himself; in Osaka a 15-year-old high school student stabbed his father to death at the church of a religious sect. Just to remind me that teenagers had no mortgage on crime, Michael sent me reports of a rat poisoner at large in Akita Prefecture, and of a Mother's Day bandit disguised as a flower vendor relieving Japanese women of their money in *pachinko* parlours in northern Kyushu. And then in February 1999 came the ultimate proof that things were going horribly wrong in Japan. Michael wrote to inform me that a male Todai student at Komaba had stabbed a female fellow student on campus after an evening class—the result of a lovers' tiff between two cultists. 'Things fall apart' . . .

By far the most upsetting and horrifying incident during my two years in Japan was the murder of the 11-year-old Kobe schoolboy Jun Hase. On 27 May 1997 the sixth-grader's severed head was found at the front gate of a local high school; his torso was located on a nearby hilltop later the same day. These bald facts were bad enough, but were made even more unpalatable by the details that began to emerge. The boy's head, it was announced to a shocked public, had a message stuffed in its mouth, with words to the effect that the 'killing has just begun'. Within days a Kobe newspaper received a letter containing another warning—using codewords that no-one but the killer could know—suggesting that 'the game' was just 'beginning', and taunting the police for their incompetence. What 'great fun' it was to kill people, the note read.

Not surprisingly, the nation had assumed some adult maniac was on the loose, but perhaps the police should have guessed the age of the killer by the juvenile tone and language of the notes. There was palpable revulsion when, after some days, police pinned the crime on a local 14-year-old schoolboy who was already under notice for eviscerating cats. In his letter to the newspaper the killer had complained of leading 'an invisible existence', which he would remedy by taking revenge on the education system. Was this disturbed teenage killer an aberration, or horribly symptomatic of an entire social system that had sublimated individuality and perverted the natural means of personal expression? Was he—his name suppressed because of his age—a nameless, faceless harbinger of horrors to come? The legion of pontificating windbags who hog the Japanese newspapers and airwaves had a field day.

Poor Jun Hase's murder assumed a particular significance in my mind. As a schoolboy I briefly lived in Sydney around 1960, at the time of the kidnapping and killing of 8-year-old Graham Thorne, and I well remember that the public outrage was accompanied by a melancholy sense that this unconscionable crime—committed in *Australia!*—was a sign that the sunburnt country had somehow lost its innocence. To me Jun Hase, the photographed image of his plump, smiling form plastered all over the country, became Japan's Graham Thorne, martyred by a country become depressingly like everywhere else.

Yet the announcement of the teenage murderer's arrest was almost as appalling as the murder itself. I was watching TV when the news was first made public. Outside Kobe police headquarters the television reporter 'on the spot' struggled to convey the details of the arrest while being jostled and harassed by a uproarious horde of teenagers, mostly male, smirking, laughing, leering and preening before the cameras, on their mobile phones to their friends ('turn on the TV, quick!'), an ironic mockery of the story at hand. With their bad hair, antic attire and loutish, self-obsessed and senseless behaviour, these young idiots *were* the story—and the most demoralising sight I was to witness in Japan.

Nature itself seemed to be in revolt. In November 1997 people were complaining there was no snow on Fuji, and then El Niño threatened to scuttle the Nagano Winter Olympics. By the beginning of 1998 the snowfall in the Nagano area was less than half the average. Grass stood where snow should have been. Frantic Olympic organising officials looked to higher forces for assistance. A delegation headed for the ancient Zenkoji Temple on New Year's Day to pray for snow in a traditional Buddhist religious rite. The prayers were answered. Huge snowfalls in January saved the national honour, and the country looked forward to winning a few medals for a change.

Indeed, the winter of 1997–98 turned out to be a cold one, with a few exceptionally heavy snowfalls in Tokyo itself. The railway authorities sought to blame the bad weather for the clogging of the Chuo line, the aorta of the city's pulsating transportation network, and one on which I was dependent. (What could be a surer sign of Japanese decay than an inefficient rail system?) But the word soon got out. The culprit was not El Niño but the suicides. People were seeking simpler and cheaper, if messier, ways to end things than hanging themselves in overpriced hotel rooms.

Naturally, a great tribe of 'experts'—from the mildly plausible to the transparently lunatic—were invited to provide their opinion on this new phenomenon. One said that the poo-coloured Chuo line trains 'make people want to jump'. Another, the author of a book called, in translation, *Japan: A Musically Undeveloped Country*, opined that the jingles played over and over and over on railway platforms push people with suicidal tendencies over the edge.[8] It was hard, hearing and reading this stuff, to fight off the feeling that one had found oneself lost and alone in a very, very strange place.

1 INTO THE INFERNO

And all the while the ranks of the homeless swelled. The metropolitan government appeared to be uninterested in dealing with the emerging crisis, or else incapable of doing so. With public shelters virtually non-existent, homeless people took to creating cardboard shanty towns in shopping complexes, under flyovers, in public parks and by the banks of Tokyo's main river, the tumid Sumida. There was scarcely a corner of the city where one didn't come across the signature blue plastic sheeting they used as overhead covering.

The homeless were a constant, disarmingly stable presence amid the swirling sea of people rushing through Shinjuku station until a fire killed four people, prompting local authorities to take definitive action after months of attempting to move them on. Where did they go? Possibly to Ueno Park, where those blue sheets proliferated during 1997. By the time I left the city, the homeless had taken over the treed area adjacent to the National Museum, the repository of the cultural riches of Japanese history, their presence ignored by the thousands of promenading families who stroll through this most public of Tokyo's parks each weekend. The symbolism was pretty blatant.

There is a story by Yukio Mishima, 'Swaddling Clothes', in which the author (writing, I imagine some time in the 1960s) puts the plight of the Tokyo down-and-outer into a specific cartographic and socio-political context. The abject form of a homeless man, swaddled in newspapers, lies on a bench in Chidorigafuchi, the 'Abyss of the Thousand Birds', a narrow public park that borders the Imperial Palace in central Tokyo. Across its moat, the palace sits 'pitch dark and utterly silent'.[9] In its way 'Swaddling Clothes' is as powerful a statement about royal indifference to common suffering as Blake's 'London'. It is a story that some writer, even one without Mishima's obsessive, Rightist patriotism, could relocate in Ueno Park today, where present degradation sits cheek-by-jowl with past splendour.

⌘⌘⌘

A mere observer, insulated from the intense social and economic pressures to which Japan was being subjected, protected by my privileged position and my foreignness, I watched with increasing sympathy as Japan went through its latest round of tribulations; it has had a few, after all. And a strange thing happened: periodic fits of choleric hostility aside, I started to like the place. On good days, Tokyo seemed, if hardly heaven, then a tolerable and even fascinating kind of hell. I became defensive about Japan, standing up for it in conversation with my Australian friends and riled by the consistently negative way it is represented in the foreign media. And I bridled at the moans and whinges of the foreigners whose long list of complaints and suggestions for the country's 'improvement' dominated the letters pages of the English-language press. One correspondent wrote to the *Japan Times* in March 1998 to the effect that Japan was 'morally diseased, chronically dishonest and spiritually empty'. The nation, he continued, 'is a morass of selfish pride and materialistic cupidity'. Crikey! Had things really got *that* bad?

Almost certainly not. Japan's suicide statistics, for example, are nothing startling on the international scale—proportionally higher than those of the USA but dwarfed by those of countries such as Hungary and Finland—although it is true that the rate rose significantly in the period 1997–98,

1 INTO THE INFERNO

when the country slid into serious recession.[10] The crime rate remains enviably low: I felt more secure walking the streets and travelling the trains of Tokyo than I ever have in Melbourne, as did Deborah, who like most foreign women readily vouches for the city's safety. When a group calling itself the 'Guardian Angels' was set up in the mid-1990s to uphold law and order in the capital, the public reaction ranged from bewilderment to amusement. What did these urban vigilantes, who had evidently modelled themselves on the volunteer crime-fighters of New York, think they were going to do? Straighten the ties of drunken, dishevelled salarymen before they lurched on to the train home? You would see 'Guardian Angels' here and there in the metropolis, absurdly clad in combat attire of boots, paratrooper pants, bomber jackets and berets—testimony to the Japanese desire to emulate all things American.

Yet it is hard to ignore acts of random violence like the subway sarin gas attacks and the decapitation of schoolboys. So much media attention was lavished on these sensational and obviously worrying incidents that public awareness of crime, which is the same thing as a public appetite to read and hear about it, rose to an unprecedented level. The perception was that the crime rate was skyrocketing in tandem with the number of yen needed to purchase a US dollar.

Anxiety about rising crime is nothing new in modern Japan. After World War II two notorious sex killers, 'Bluebeard' Kodaira and Tsuji, mounted a reign of terror in the capital, each murdering more than twenty women in the course of a year. In his memoir *Foreign Devil* (1972), the Australian reporter Richard Hughes, who was based in Tokyo at the time, recalled the phlegmatic response of a Metropolitan Police Board inspector. The increase in sex crimes, he argued, was evidence of social conditions returning to normality after extreme privation: more sex crimes meant less poverty.[11] Such is the Japanese ability to rationalise iniquity. But sangfroid was in short supply in Japan in the late 1990s. Some people, foreigners not the least among them, dropped their bundles. Beneath the towering outrage of the aforementioned letter-writer to the *Japan Times* can be detected the same intensely personal disappointment that has marked Western responses to Japan since Lafcadio Hearn started lamenting the nation's fall from paradisal grace during the period of rapid 'modernisation' in the late nineteenth century. Japan has never been able to match the expectations and false standards that foreigners have imposed on it. In that sense, it has *always* been in a state of decline.

My time in Japan, in an age of racketeers and ruin, of knaves and knives, was, shall we say, 'interesting'. Interesting times are only a 'curse' if one is materially affected by all the social upheaval that is going on. I was not. A mere sojourner, I could relax and enjoy the spectacle; when I felt a bit depressed, I could lie back and think of Australia. The two years I was there, Tokyo positively *teemed*, not just with people but with ideas, intrigues, fears, phobias, visions and revisions. It rocked and reverberated with the shocks and after-shocks of political, bureaucratic, financial and social scandals. If things were falling apart, they clearly were also afoot. It seemed to me to be a good two years to be there. Then again, that's what everybody who's spent any length of time in that awful/fabulous, dreadful/enthralling city says.

⌘⌘⌘

1 INTO THE INFERNO

I had not come to Japan unprepared. I had read books; I had watched films; and I had remembered to ring Humphrey McQueen. He was able to furnish me with plenty of useful advice, though his recommendation, 'just don't fall ill'—portentously delivered near the end of our conversation—proved counterproductive. Sick with worry about getting sick, over the next two years I was to be assailed by a host of mysterious if thankfully minor ailments, mostly in the respiratory and digestive tracts. My anxiety was not alleviated by the spell-check on the computer I used in Japan, which kept on suggesting I replace 'Gerster' with 'gastro', nor by the fact that one of the big books about Japan in 1997 was a trenchant critique of Japanese medicine titled *Dying in a Japanese Hospital*. The annual Todai medical checks proved to be torrid affairs. A dozen nurses swarmed and buzzed around the clinic proffering specimen glasses and directing me into cubicles, then smirking over the results. They pressed and probed and pestered me with questions such as 'How many cigarettes did your grandfather smoke?' and, more affectingly, 'Ouchy?'—this last interrogative delivered wide-eyed by the young woman taking my blood as she plunged the needle in.

For my first few weeks in Japan, as McQueen correctly warned me, I would get everything wrong. The bungling was physical as well as intellectual and social. Unaccustomed to negotiating such Lilliputian spaces, I kept on bumping into things, in the apartment, in shops and on trains. Fortunately the words for 'excuse me' and 'very sorry'—*sumimasen* and *gomen nasai*—flowed effortlessly from my lips. In Japan, where conversation often seems mostly to involve verbal strategies of self-effacement rather than self-assertion, one can just about survive on these two expressions. Rather than the land of a thousand apologies, Japan is the land of just two, repeated endlessly, over and over, day after day.

Unfortunately those two expressions were almost the limit of my Japanese, despite an intensive six-week course taken in Melbourne before my departure. McQueen begins *Tokyo World* by remarking how he misused the words for 'please' and 'thank you'—'*dozo*' and '*domo*'—on his flight to Japan. It is an easy enough error for the innocent traveller to make. Even the linguistically savvy Ohara admitted to me one evening that the Japanese language had defeated him at first. In one of our favoured drinking haunts in what sometimes seemed to be shaping as the Land of the Rising Hangover—a bar run by a deracinated Bangladeshi in one of the dark and gloomy tunnels under the *shinkansen* tracks near Yarakucho station in central Tokyo—he drunkenly confessed to misusing those same fundamental words for the first few months of his stay.

Impressed by such Japanese usages as '*apato*', '*cardo*' and '*hotto doggo*', I embarked on my quest to become fluent in Japanese by simply adding the letter 'o' to English words to indicate my meaning. Admittedly this tactic had only limited effectiveness. (Evelyn Waugh adopted a similar approach to speaking Italian when he was stationed in Italy during World War II, and on this basis spread the rumour that the Yugoslavian guerrilla leader and later President, Marshal Tito, was a woman.) After a time, though, I learnt to recognise much of what was being said to me, even if replying remained a problem. Knowing a little proved to be more troublesome than knowing nothing at all, because it gave people the false impression that I could actually speak the language. Taxi drivers started chattering to me in Japanese, and some of them were offended by the apparent taciturnity of my responses. Having a haircut became an ordeal: half an hour

1 INTO THE INFERNO

stuck in a chair at the mercy of a garrulous Japanese hairdresser wielding scissors and flourishing razors, the sweat rising on my exposed forehead as he bombarded me with questions that I could not properly answer.

Another day, another *faux pas*. On one memorable occasion, while visiting my neighbour Koichi Sato and his wife Akemi, I engaged them in an earnest discussion (in English: they had spent a year in Nevada and had a beautiful little daughter called Reno) about the names the Japanese customarily give their pet cats. I innocently mentioned that a local shopkeeper, with whom I would occasionally have a rudimentary chat as I walked to the station, called his cat *Hako*, literally meaning 'box'. I wondered why Koichi seemed to gag when I volunteered this as a good name for a cat. I should have guessed something was up: the shopkeeper was an old bloke with a young man's leer and a luridly sexual sense of humour. It was months later, in a compendium of Japanese street slang, that I learnt that *hako* is a crude male term for vagina. 'Pussy', in other words.

At times communication breakdown threatened to trigger a nervous collapse, but I learnt to get by. The Japanese are nothing if not patient, and are more forgiving of linguistic incompetence than most. And one could always rationalise one's inability to talk the local lingo by deriving cheap pleasure from awkward Japanese usages of English. The sources of amusement were endless—a brand of cigarettes named 'Keith', an advertising brochure for a mobile pizza company bidding readers 'Good afternoon!', a sex bar in the nightclub district of Roppongi called 'Dick & Uprise'. (Kyoto boasts a bar called 'Pocket Billiards'.) A Western-style sit-down toilet at the Hongo campus of Tokyo University was designated by the sign 'STOOL' stuck to the door of its commodious cubicle.

There one could find 'Sistie' ('cistern?') toilet paper, which bore the legend on its plastic wrapping: 'Sistie says, fill your world with lovely flowers, and you're the best'.

Japanese advertising does tend to go in for little messages of the unbearably cute kind. An advertisement for a driving school on the tunnel wall in the Tozai line of the Tokyo subway, glimpsed night after night as I sped by on the train home, exhorted its potential customers to 'BE OUR JOLLY FRIEND'. The Beaux Arts chain of stores—specialising in the kind of useless knick-knackery one sees all over Tokyo—gave the promise: 'WE SELL YOU TASTY LIFE'. But for sheer poetry the Marond bakery stores could not be beaten. A habitué of the Kemigawa branch, I built up quite a collection of golden carry-bags emblazoned with the words:

> Women baking bread on Sunday. With flour-dusted cheeks they push up their sleeves. And at the breadboard knead with strong fingers, hands and bodies. Warm and yeasty, the kitchen is filled with promise.

Who needed the gruesome porn available everywhere in Japan when one could go and buy a couple of doughnuts at Marond instead?

The heedless Japanese recycling of English expressions could also be disconcerting. On the train into Tokyo one quiet Sunday afternoon I was sitting opposite a young woman aged about eighteen, pleasant-looking if nondescript, perhaps a shop assistant at Marond on her day off. Then I focused on the words spread in big red letters across her white T-shirt. 'FUCK OFF!' Was I, a foreigner, to take this message literally?

It sometimes seemed like it, especially on trains, when passengers would go to amazing lengths (such as electing to

1 INTO THE INFERNO

stand up) to avoid sitting next to me. The aloofness of the Japanese is axiomatic. Ever since St Francis Xavier journeyed to Japan in the sixteenth century, and maybe before, foreigners have felt the chill of Japanese contempt. 'The Japanese have a high opinion of themselves', Xavier complained, 'and so look down on all foreigners. They are very courteous to each other, but they do not show this courtesy to foreigners, whom they despise.'[12] Good luck to them, say I. Those missionary zealots had it coming. Anyway, contemporary Japan is much more open than it was. Probably. The young woman sitting opposite me had merely selected attire with a racy, foreign insignia. No doubt she'd heard the expression, left unsubtitled, a thousand times in American movies. If it was OK for Bruce Willis it was fine by her. No offence intended. (Probably.)

'FUCK OFF' had become a popular sartorial adornment in Japan. My colleague Michael Hinds, a connoisseur of the decadent, the grotesque and the merely risible aspects of Tokyo street life, was delighted to discover that the children's clothing franchise in the enormous Parco department store in Shibuya sported a large billboard with an angry-looking toy bear offering the selfsame unquivocal piece of advice. Michael reckoned the shop was doing a roaring trade.

Disorientation in Japan is literal as well as linguistic. It is often hard to know precisely where you are in Tokyo, and even harder to find your way to a particular destination. 'The streets of this city have no names.' So runs Roland Barthes' portentous introduction to his discussion of the urban toponymy of the capital. Street names, where they exist, count for little; the names that matter are those of wards, districts, blocks and the often inconsistently numbered buildings themselves. Way out in barbarous Kemigawa, the local cab drivers didn't seem to know what the street I lived in was called, although it was one of the major local thoroughfares and did have a name. Mention the name of the apartment block, however, and the taxi took off like lightning. Foreigners find what Barthes calls the city's 'domiciliary obliteration' maddening. Arthur Koestler thought it was evidence of Japanese resistance to the sensible strictures of Western logic; Barthes himself is more tongue-in-cheek generous, remarking that the Tokyo way of address, just one of the many facets of the city's lunatic semiotic system, 'reminds us that the rational is merely one system among others'.[13]

Certainly it could turn a simple night out into an adventure. One evening I suggested to a sceptical Ohara that we explore a self-styled 'Australian Wine Bar' called Uluru, located in Harajuku, a fashionable district that caters to the millions of teenagers who swarm through the streets of western Tokyo (if it is possible to 'swarm' when wearing footwear that appears to have been designed for a moon walk). Australian wine bars had become suddenly popular in Tokyo. I had been to one in Shibuya, a dive called 'Crocodile Army' that confined its Australianness to selling tinnies of XXXX and repeatedly showing a promotional video extolling the virtues of the Gold Coast: a kind of mini-hell. But Uluru was reviewed in the *Tokyo Journal* as the genuine article, with a vast selection of antipodean wines—an oasis for the homesick dreamer, for someone tired of sake and Asahi Super Dry who wanted to drink long and deep at the well-springs of the familiar.

I had looked for the Uluru in a desultory fashion a couple of times without luck, but decided that I'd find it in no time with Ohara as my tracker, habituated as he was to the mysteries of Japanese urban cartography. Armed with its address—set out in the Japanese form, just block and building numbers—

1 INTO THE INFERNO

we scoured the streets for an hour or more, searching for a place that seemed invisible, weaving in and out of Harajuku's hordes until we were legless with fatigue. Exasperated, I told myself that this was just another example of Japanese trickery. Ohara was amused; he enjoyed wild goose chases and didn't particularly want to drink plonk with names like 'Cockatoo Ridge' and 'Jacob's Creek' anyway. We asked dozens of local shopkeepers and their assistants for help; their directions conflicted. At one point we were directed to a discotheque that advertised a beach theme (presumably one leapt about to the beat of some aural horror on a heap of sand), which we discovered next door to a hairdresser's establishment called 'Slug'. This joint just had to be 'Australian'. It was not. Eventually in the gathering gloom we did find Uluru, which turned out to be a tiny place tucked down a dark and uninviting entrance driveway between shops selling oversized and overpriced military clothing. We had passed it a hundred times; it had been there all along. We went in and it was good. Even Ohara was impressed, though he politely allowed me to pay.

The real Uluru remains a mystery to me. Unlike many of my Japanese students at Todai, I have never been there; have never felt the desire. Homesickness had lured me to a bar merely because of the place it was named after, when I hadn't ever bothered to go to the place itself. Scholars of a post-modern bent interested in the travel phenomenon—by now so numerous as to represent an academic version of mass tourism—might make something of this. It certainly made *me* wonder about the possibilities of finding home itself in Japan. I had gone searching for Uluru in Tokyo, and what is more I had found it. Could this be a metaphor for the enlarging possibilities of living in Japan? Maybe. But that is to take the purely positive view. In 'Australian' wine bars and 'German' beer-halls and 'Mexican' cantinas, in love hotels fashioned after Greek temples and Gothic castles, in cultural monuments like its version of the Globe Theatre and replica of Disneyland, Japan offers the taste but not the substance of the outside world. Thus the world comes to Japan and at the same time the world is kept at bay. Searching for and finding an illusory paradise called 'Uluru' in Tokyo suggests the essential, irremediable, frustrating yet liberating vicariousness of the foreigner's experience there.

This is the great lesson Japan teaches its temporary residents: that 'home' is a kind of paradox. Tenuous, elusive, out of reach, it always exists, haphazardly but finally, Somewhere Else.

⌘ ⌘ ⌘

2 RIDING SANTA'S SURFBOARD

You may have come across him. (It is usually, though not always, a him.) Like some beast removed from his natural domain, he most stands out when he is in a foreign environment. I am talking of the pushy Australian professor abroad—the querulous big-noter, squealing like a stuck pig at the slightest inconvenience, complaining at the cost of everything, ogling the local talent and groping the female conference organisers while sussing out some cheaper accommodation, the button-holing boozer who leaves the bar just long enough to deliver a polished but vapid paper (like Tiananmen Square on a quiet day: vacant and windy); the crash-hot theorist, the intellectual titan, the would-be King of Critics who in reality is the academic equivalent of Prince Leonard of Hutt.[1]

I was thinking of this caricature while considering the persona of the Tokyo University professor, and more particularly my own position as a quasi-'official' professor of Australian

Studies. It could be a tiring job, and I am not talking about the hours of work. One was forever answering for Australia, defending Australia, explaining Australia, and struggling to overcome the hackneyed bush and ocker stuff that sticks to it like shit to a blanket. There were even days when I hated to utter the very word. Yes, I was touched when I was serenaded with a rendition of 'Waltzing Matilda' at my staff farewell party in March 1998, though for one wicked moment I thought of explaining to the assembled company that the jaunty melody is actually a suicide song—just to cross the cultural divide. (The song seemed especially incongruous in that setting, up on the fifty-fourth floor of a vertiginous skyscraper in Shinjuku, a bubble-economy folly called Tokyo Opera City. How, I wondered, would the structure stand up to a decent earthquake?) But I found it wearying that so many of my colleagues were unable to see Australia as anything but a set of folksy images, a barbarous backwater populated by ape-men and women with comical accents.

Predictably, such images were beloved by the Poms on the Todai staff, their native contempt for the colonies having ossified into rigid prejudice during their years living as self-conscious Englishmen in 'the East'. Several of the Japanese professors, especially those who imagined themselves as belonging to a branch office of Cambridge or Oxford (though on much better pay), were equally inclined to look on Australia with derision. That did not stop them from wanting to travel there as often as possible—on 'research', of course. One of my Japanese colleagues, a linguist, came back from Sydney with a postcard featuring an image of a bushwhacker spouting terms like 'strewth', 'you bewdy', 'fair dinkum', and 'I'll be buggered', and I was obliged to spend half an hour at his request trying to explain each term to him—a delicate operation. Evidently he was impressed, for he took to greeting me in the corridor with 'How they hangin', mate?'

Especially irritating was the local habit of mocking the tortured Australian vowel—as in 'to die' for 'today' and 'might' for 'mate'. I had to bite my lip when this happened, fighting off to desire to hit back at these teachers of English, some of whom were given to pronounce my first name as 'Lobin'. I had to bite my lip at other times too. At the first English Department staff meeting I attended, another Japanese colleague sniffed, upon being formally introduced to me, 'I hear you people eat kangaroo!' Ha, ha! Resisting the impulse to itemise some of the more curious Japanese eating habits, I sought refuge in my book. In fact, I took a book to all staff and faculty meetings, meandering conversations that could go on for hours, conducted underneath billowing cumulus clouds of cigarette smoke.

There were those of my Japanese colleagues, like Yoichi Kibata and Toshiko Ellis, who worked tirelessly to break down the stereotypes, and indeed to internationalise Todai more generally, through their involvement in an excellent foreign student exchange programme and in innovative course design. At the farewell party in Shinjuku, Professor Kibata announced that the next day there would be a symposium on Australia–Japan cultural relations, an event that we had worked long and hard to organise. Whereupon, egged on by a smirking Ohara (hailing from the Midwest, he understood the impact of the put-down, and richly enjoyed baiting me on such matters), a female Japanese professor with a monomaniacal specialisation in Wittgenstein giggled and asked with mock earnestness, '*Is* there any culture in Australia?' The effrontery of it aside, this wasn't an easy question to answer. As that postcard of 'Aussie lingo' signifies, Australia has marketed itself in a certain way, so perhaps one can't blame the Japanese or even the British for their assumptions, many of which aren't that wide of the mark.

Part of the problem with teaching Australian Studies abroad is that one is prone to play the parochial ocker in the expectation that that is what locals want. The really dispiriting thing is that, yes indeed, that *is* what they want. Even my friend Bill would encourage me to perform the Australian role; for my forty-fourth birthday he presented me with a copy of the Lonely Planet *Australian Phrasebook* to keep me up to scratch. This kind of pressure inclines one towards self-parody, and I found myself trading in antipodean idioms ('squealing like a stuck pig', 'sticks like shit to a blanket' and so on) more than I would at home.

At an annual Australia–Japan conference—titled 'G'day Australia'—sponsored by the embassy in Tokyo, the day's intellectual exertions ended with a repast of soapy 'Aussie Cheese' and crackers, washed down with bottles of Jacob's Creek, cans of XXXX and the gushy speeches that are a feature of such social occasions in Japan. I chatted to a group of young people who had been to Australia, or were to go, or would have liked to have gone. All cherished dreams of the wide open spaces, sun, surf, the whole bit. 'Why is the beer called "XXXX"?' one of them asked. 'Because it's brewed in Queensland,' I automatically replied, 'and Queenslanders don't know how to spell "beer".'

Dylan Thomas inimitably remarked upon the dangers of becoming too closely aligned with one's race or nationality. 'Professional Irishmen', he quipped, are 'very lepra-corny'. After two years of being, quite literally, a professional Australian, I understood what he meant.

2 RIDING SANTA'S SURFBOARD

⌘⌘⌘

Generally speaking, academics are a relentlessly stereotyped breed. Cornering me in the corridor of building 9, unpleasantly close to the lavatory in which someone had stealthily deposited the excreted remains of a particularly vile *bento* lunch not long before, Ohara offered me his opinion that universities are 'places where wankers congregate'. (Naturally he wasn't referring to *us*.) As they will be the first to tell you, academics are especially scorned and distrusted in Australia. Unloved and—increasingly—unemployed, they rate just above child-molesters on the cultural appreciation scale, and so tend to moan together in clusters, talking about nothing but themselves and their dreadful lot in life. That is when they are not bad-mouthing absent colleagues, some of whom may or may not be their friends. The 'cultural affairs bloke' at the embassy—an ex-army man—gave the distinct impression that he regarded academics as bullshit artists, a reasonable enough assessment, although we eggheads could offer the rejoinder that certain male Australian embassy types seemed to spend their careers engaged in one long act of becoming Sir Les Patterson.

Academics are treated with more respect in Japan than in Australia. The royal family even allows itself to be bored witless by them in an annual New Year ritual called *kosho hajime no gi*, in which celebrated scholars are invited to deliver a personal lecture to the Emperor and his wife. One can just visualise the perpetually smiling, pleasant little bloke, his runty figure attired like the pox doctor's clerk, listening to the 1998 offering, a lecture by a professor emeritus of Osaka University on 'Cell Fusion and Cell Engineering'.

If you are fortunate enough to be a Tokyo University *sensei*, you've got it made. Bill once told me that he kept his position at Todai secret from his friends and acquaintances in the Kemigawa area for fear of introducing an unwanted element of rank into the relationship, a reflection of the hierarchical nature of Japan's so-called 'vertical society'. I had no such compunction. The maze of Tokyo life was too intimidating for a disoriented, defensive newcomer not to use the one ace he had been dealt. I discovered that doors opened and problems were solved when I casually displayed my Todai *meishi*, or namecard. People swooned, whistled low, or uttered the long rising 'eeeeeeeh' that the Japanese use to register amazement.

The mystique surrounding Japan's premier educational institution is not merely self-created. Soon after I arrived home the Hong Kong-based magazine *Asiaweek* published its second annual ranking of Asian universities, based on criteria such as academic reputation, faculty resources and research output. Again the University of Tokyo topped the list; the University of Melbourne ranked ninth and my home university, Monash, twenty-fourth. I have since scratched my head red raw at this outcome, which must have had a high self-assessment component, but who am I to argue with it?

Foreigners with personal experience of Todai, from the fleeting to the substantial, tend to be less impressed than the Japanese. The famous British reformers Beatrice and Sidney Webb dropped in on the Imperial University to give it the once-over during their tour of Japan in 1911, and did not think much of what they saw. They described it as 'suffering somewhat from government control' and being staffed by professors who with 'some exceptions' were 'not men of distinction', including a few 'very third-rate English and

Americans'.[2] No doubt the Webbs' reaction was harsh; those inhabiting the cultural centre tend to sneer at pretenders from the margins. Some visiting English academics used to adopt a similar attitude toward the Australian universities where they worked, until the cut-backs of the late 1990s enforced an amazing new respect for their employers.

Certainly, Todai's intimate connection with the government bureaucracy, namely Monbusho, the Ministry of Education, ensures a degree of conservatism in the place. An equally negative outcome of Todai's governmental dependence is the paucity of its funding. The air of penury about the Komaba campus contrasts starkly with the splendour of many private universities, something noticed way back in 1911 by the travelling Webbs. My weekly journey across Tokyo to Keio, one of Japan's pre-eminent private universities, to deliver an Australian Studies lecture at the International School, seemed like a holiday. Keio's sumptuous facilities and its ambience of professional competence were temporarily revitalising after stuffy, scruffy old Todai.

Funding aside, it often occurred to me that Todai's general squalor was wilfully imposed. Many of the staff took a perverse pride in the run-down facilities, as if to proclaim that Todai really is about intellectual commitment and scholarly dedication, not just privileged dilettantism. If Todai is Japan's Oxford, then it is the Oxford of several hundred years ago. Staff work in conditions from the Middle Ages. Perhaps this suited my genial office-mate Jun Terasawa, a medievalist; I never heard him complaining. I had to lobby hard for a desk computer upon my arrival, as the Heath Robinson contraption used by my Australian predecessor had finally given up the ghost. I then had to push and push to be connected to the Internet, so as not to be called a liar by colleagues back at Monash, who could not believe that, working in technologically advanced Japan, I did not have an E-mail address. My pushing only bore fruit in the week before my departure.

The office itself was cleaned once annually, around New Year, by one of the shuffling dotards the university employed as a commendable if ill-advised act of goodwill to the aged and unwanted. Apart from Terasawa *sensei*'s impressive collection of Old English and medieval texts, there was little ornamentation in the room to please the eye or to distract one from the exertions of the saxophonists outside the window. I had been bequeathed a video of Peter Weir's *Gallipoli* (taped from Japanese TV, with interminable advertisements), not one but two copies of Anthony Giddens's *The Consequences of Modernity* (as if to reinforce the message of the title), a critical reader of Foucault, a book called *Genghis Khan: His Life and Legacy* and also Humphrey McQueen's *Japan to the Rescue*, the ironic implications of which were not lost on me. In a corner, as if left over from the set of Pinter's *The Caretaker,* stood a pile of written-off electrical equipment alongside a battered metal cupboard containing half-a-dozen bottles of Wolf Blass that had miraculously escaped being drunk at some Oz Studies bash or other. They didn't last long. Other than a plastic pepper bottle and an old jar of Nescafé, no other evidence testified to my predecessor's presence in the Australian job for the previous two years. Luckily I had brought plenty of documentary material with me, although I was soon forced to seek help from the staff of the Australia–Japan Foundation Library at the embassy and the tireless Sachiko Tamai of the embassy's Cultural Relations branch.

The average Tokyo University *sensei* is no more of a 'wanker' than academics elsewhere. He could be worse, given the absurd adulation directed to him. (I am using the male pronoun. From my observation of my fellow staff at faculty meetings—difficult as that was through the thick haze of noxious nicotine—men far outnumbered women, though not in the English Department, in which there were numerous high-ranking females.) He's there just about every time you turn on the TV, offering his compatriots the benefit of his wisdom on 'discussion panels' of one sort or other. In Japan these are often impossible to distinguish from game shows: is there any other country in the world where the line dividing 'high' and 'popular' culture is more blurred? Or you might catch him on programmes with unappetising titles such as 'Interesting Intellectuals'. *The Wind-Up Bird Chronicle* (1997) a gargantuan novel by Haruki Murakami, the most self-consciously 'post-modern' of contemporary Japanese novelists, contains a devastatingly accurate portrayal of the Tokyo University *sensei* as TV intellectual gladiator. After publishing a book in which he coins the sensational expressions 'sexual economics' and 'excretory economics', Noboru Wataya, an economics professor at Todai's Graduate School, is taken up by the mass media, which hail him as a 'hero for a new age'. He finds himself in the papers and on TV commenting on the important political and economic questions of the day, or jousting with his peers in televised debates. 'On the television screen, he looked far more intelligent and reliable than the real Noboru Wataya', the narrator notes.[3]

One of the stars of Todai/Komaba was the flamboyant Hideo Morimoto, a Chaucerian-cum-Shakespearian scholar of some standing in Japan. Professor Morimoto was a man of the world. His interests were broad and scrupulously up-to-date. At my first encounter with him (in early 1997, after he had returned—'with great dejection'—from a stay of some months in Florence) he leant across the table during a faculty meeting and asked in a confidential undertone, 'You don't happen to be interested in postmodernity, do you?' I felt as if I was being offered some kind of illicit drug. Yet Morimoto was a charmingly anachronistic figure. With his magnificent mane of lustrous hair, his superb clothes and Oxbridge mannerisms, he was a spectre from a bygone age, a character from an early Anthony Powell novel. Like Bill, Morimoto seemed not to notice the ugliness of his professional environment; it was almost as if he revelled in the squalor, knowing it made him shine that much more brightly. And he had connections, so necessary to achieve anything in Japan. When we were looking with increasing desperation for some funding to stage the Japan–Australia symposium, it was he who magically produced the goods. He had the Midas touch; he made things happen.

Professor Morimoto was perhaps less constructive in his input into the content of the symposium itself. I had submitted a proposal that the subject of the symposium should be the inter-cultural legacy of World War II, an admittedly delicate topic that had the potential to become another Jap-bashing exercise. We all wanted to avoid that, not least the locals, who understandably get a bit sick of being reminded of their turpitude by moralising foreigners. Morimoto offered a counter-proposal so panoramic in its approach to the theme of 'mutual understanding between Australia and Japan' since World War II as to include (1) comparative national responses to modernity; (2) comparative national responses to the end of modernity; (3) comparative national responses to imperialism; (4) the reception of Hegel and Spencer; (5) the understanding of Nietzsche and Weber and the attitude toward Heidegger; (6) the contemporary state of classical studies in both countries; (7) attitudes to humanism and the reception of 'French anti-humanist thought'; (8) attitudes toward Orientalism; and (9) new cultural visions of the Asia–Pacific. Oh, and the cultural response to the Pacific War.

This was a man with a voracious intellectual appetite. I felt overwhelmed. As I considered Morimoto's proposal and wondered how in the hell we could put it into effect, he confused the issue by asking me if I knew any 'sensible academic feminists' to invite to speak. I replied that I thought I did, declared his proposal to be 'triffic' and fled the room to go and shoot myself.

The point of Professor Morimoto's far-reaching critical vision having been made and mutually understood, it was eventually decided that my modest proposal was the more practical, and it went ahead—very successfully—with two invited guests, Peter Pierce from James Cook University talking about fictional images of Japan, and Peter Fitzpatrick from Monash talking about Australia/Japan theatrical exchanges, both with an eye to cultural outcomes from World War II. They performed with a combination of tact and panache to an interested and thoughtful audience, only some of whom had been shamed into attending in order to spare the hosts the embarrassment of presiding over the emptiest space in Tokyo that day.

Morimoto chaired the symposium with great bonhomie, marred only by introducing Peter Pierce as 'Professor Purse', and also presided over a spectacular Chinese banquet in Shibuya that evening, again confirming the generosity of Japanese hospitality. It is difficult to imagine Morimoto in any university other than Todai; impossible to place him in a contemporary Australian university. The ideologues—the bitter and twisted, the proselytisers and parvenus—would simply devour him. That was one reason among many to like the man.

Power in Japanese academia, as in the political sphere, resides in individuals. Yes, there are deans, heads of department and section heads, but the real influence is wielded by individuals with prestige and status, like Morimoto perhaps, people to whom, in the complex Japanese practice of *giri* (duty, obligation), favours are sought or owed. That, at least, is the case in the ordinary human world. But over and above these academic figures with clout are the bureaucrats, omnipotent deities before whom even revered scholars are powerless.

The deep and thorny way that led to Komaba was marked by several bruising encounters with Japanese university officialdom. Before I left Australia, Todai requested my complete educational history. I was asked to produce all my primary-school records, a tricky enough request in any case, nigh on impossible when one went to eight or nine primary schools, as I did. These documents were needed, I was assured, to calculate my salary. Was I to assume that the mark I received for Nature Study at Amstel State School in 1960 (for the record, eight out of ten) could determine a difference of some thousands of yen? Further requests for various certificates and personal statements followed: they demanded everything bar my inside leg measurement. It was all to no avail, anyway. Deborah and I dropped everything, rented out the house, boarded the cats and flew off to Japan still in the dark about exactly what how much we would have to live on in a city so proverbially pricey that ordinarily one would hesitate to spend a single day there. My salary was not finally calculated until months after my arrival. I belatedly came to understand the meaning of patience, and learnt to trust my betters in the bureaucracy. The buggers always come through in the end: that is how they get away with behaving the way they do.

2 RIDING SANTA'S SURFBOARD

It was not only the Todai bureaucrats who haunted me before my departure for Japan. In order to secure official approval for two years' unpaid leave of absence from Monash, I had to produce a letter from Todai testifying to my Tokyo appointment. This was a simple enough request, but did not take into account the byzantine Japanese selection process. The letter I received from the then head of the English Department, Hiroshi Ogawa, was so vague as to be useless from Monash's point of view. 'Out of the list of candidates presented to us by the Australian Committee', Professor Ogawa wrote, 'you were selected by the Personnel Committee of the English Section and this has been sanctioned at the Section meeting and subsequently by the Department of Foreign Languages. But before this materialises as anything of official nature', he continued, 'it remains to be discussed at three more meetings at the Faculty level . . . I hope to be able to inform you of the results in due course.' And I was supposed to be up and going about three months hence! Eventually the official invitation to become a full-time faculty member of the College of Arts and Sciences, The University of Tokyo, 'treated on an equal footing with the Japanese national personnel and subject to Japan's Laws and Regulations', was faxed through in February, a month or so before our scheduled departure.

Hiroshi Ogawa and myself therefore got off to a bad start, and things did not improve much in the first months of my appointment. A small, perpetually worried-looking man, Ogawa could make one's life difficult when he was department head. When, just before the long summer vacation in 1996, I informed him as a matter of courtesy that I intended to take a trip to Hokkaido, he literally leapt out of the chair he was sitting in. He had heard something shocking. I could see him silently asking himself: 'What could happen to this foreigner wandering around Japan unsupervised? What is my personal culpability if something goes wrong?' Thoughts of potential kidnapping appeared to cross his mind. Would I end up in North Korea, along with several other denizens of Nippon who have mysteriously vanished over the years? I could tell that administrative obstacles were about to be put in the path of my simple holiday.

I was furious: this bloke clearly had it in for me. 'That shit Ogawa made a big fuss about Hokkaido,' I told Deborah that evening. (From that time on, she thought that my boss's name actually was 'Shitagawa'.) It was only after several placatory telephone calls from other Japanese colleagues (for the word had passed around) that I was assured it was all right to go ahead with the trip. Ogawa, who was quite a charming chap when his guard was down, was not motivated by malice. It was just that, like many Japanese, he was a stickler for procedure and found personal responsibility an impossibly heavy burden. I suspect he was a relieved man when he passed the headship over to someone else midway through my time in Japan. At an end-of-year party thrown for the foreign staff, I said to him that it would be a weight off his shoulders to relinquish his post. 'Yes,' he said reflectively. 'I have such slim shoulders.'

Not unlike the typical contemporary Australian university, Todai was preoccupied with administrative rather than intellectual matters. Faculty meetings in particular were devoted to the issue of some filthy old dormitories that the university wanted to demolish and replace with new facilities, a desirable act of campus renewal steadfastly opposed by a motley collection of student residents and 'Bohemian' squatters. Apart from the fact that these individuals were holed up there for virtually nothing, it was unclear why they were so passionately protective of this slum. A rumour had it that graffiti from the 1960s were scrawled on some of the dorms' grimy walls, and so the place had become a revered site for a small bunch of activists who hankered for that celebrated era, when student turbulence at Tokyo University made Monash look like the local kindergarten.

One of the ploys used by the squatters to resist the wrecker's ball was to set up the 'Komaba Kunstraum', a so-called 'gallery of resistance' in which the students and various hangers-on could display their 'underground' artistic endeavours. Another gallery and performance space, called 'Obscure', featured 'live painting' accompanied by music, Butoh dance and other artistic happenings. Being creative is thirsty work, so the Zero Bar was established, in which the dormitory stalwarts could engage (according to a report in the *Asahi Evening News*) in 'all-night Go-Go dancing, frequent spontaneous performances, and wild bang-the-saucepan percussion jams'.[4] Alas, after a drunken brawl involving some Butoh dancers who had a disagreement over who could drink the most, the bar was closed down to safeguard the residents' continuing solidarity.

This ongoing controversy was no joke. My first inkling that something was afoot came on my initial visit to the campus on 1 April 1996, when I could not help noticing that whatever structure had once been adjacent to Building 9, my new workplace, was now a smouldering ruin. In the latter part of 1996 staff were rostered to guard the Administration building. The next year a burnt-out car appeared in the road by the Union supermarket, where it stood for months as a symbol of defiance. The drama was still being played out when I left, though some demolition work had begun. Unwisely some senior academics, reliving their own student days, had taken up the activists' case. Faculty meetings turned into long, acrimonious (for Japan) debates that would go on for hours and make the trip home a late-night epic accompanied by staggering herds of drink-delirious salarymen. In front of a couple of Japanese colleagues, Ohara half-jokingly recommended that Todai take up what he called 'the Chinese Option'—that is, round up the malingerers and troublemakers and simply shoot them. The Japanese laughed uneasily, as people do when they hear a wicked but secretly attractive idea.

⌘⌘⌘

With very few exceptions, the gulf separating the Japanese and Western staff was too big for either party to be willing or able to cross, and inevitably the foreigners tended to stick together. In 1997 Ivan Hall, an American who taught for several years in Japan, published a study of Japanese educational insularity, the intellectual closed shop that prohibits genuine participation by foreign scholars and researchers.[5] But the discrimination was social and cultural at least as much as it was intellectual, and it was practised equally by both parties. Michael Hinds and I— enjoying the luxury of our fixed-term sentences at Todai— called the permanent foreign staff the 'lifers', men and women whom circumstances had contrived to imprison in a place from which they entertained dreams of eventual escape or temporary parole in the form of several overseas trips a year. Arthur Koestler might have been talking about the Todai lifers when he described the Old Hands he met in Japan as living in a state of 'unstable equilibrium'.[6] In some cases their professional status was extremely tenuous, differing little from that of the *gaikokujin kyoshi*, the 'foreign instructors' who were first introduced into the Japanese education system in the Meiji era. Needing to have their contracts constantly renewed, they lived in a permanent state of anxiety that they be allowed to stay on. This explains their excessively deferential demeanour at staff gatherings (where even Ohara behaved himself) and their unwillingness to rock the boat. Meanwhile, they got away from Japan as often as they could.

Entrapment in Japan is financial as well as merely circumstantial. The foreigners at Todai knew they were earning more in Japan than they would at home, wherever that was, even if they managed to secure a job elsewhere. Ohara admitted as much to me one evening, this time in one of the tiny bars in the 'Golden Gai', a collection of watering holes in Shinjuku that has tenaciously survived the local department stores' efforts to crowd out everything else that competes with them for space (except of course the various establishments devoted to the sex industry, as common in urban Japan as milk bars in suburban Australia). Years of living and working in Japan, Ohara conceded, had made him unfit to live, let alone work, anywhere else. What was the alternative? Teaching in a high school in Iowa? He knew he was on a good thing. Whatever the strange insularity of a Tokyo University existence, he was being well paid to live in a Great City, a city populated by millions of available women only too ready to be impressed by a Yank teaching at such a prestigious place. Ohara could never understand my disinclination to stay on in Japan. Being a Todai *sensei* had to be better than living in Melbourne, a place known only to him as located in a land of legendary philistinism populated by intimidatingly assertive women, a place so impossibly remote on his map as to exist on another planet altogether.

Bill was another of the lifers to be content with his lot. He actually *enjoyed* Komaba, though he did not spend any more time there than he absolutely had to. Bill was a talented linguist, fluent in French and German as well as Japanese (he knew a lot of Chinese and Russian as well), and his Tokyo life was a crowded itinerary of seminars, symposiums, concerts. Tracking him through the metropolis would have involved an urban odyssey. Around noon he might be found eating a huge buffet lunch in Chinatown down in Yokohama, or maybe sampling the *prix fixe* in the 'Ile de France' just off Omotesando; in the evening it might be a cocktail party at the French embassy or a film followed by drinks in Ginza. If the Saturday evening hadn't been too bacchanalian, Sunday morning was cups of tea and some gossip at St Alban's Anglican Church in Kamiyacho, with maybe a Russian restaurant in Shibuya in the evening.

Bill comfortably inhabited a world of fellow *déracinés* drawn from Tokyo's large floating international population. Rarely did he mention his native Canada without a sneer of contempt. Yet even Bill had to get out of Japan occasionally, to breathe non-Japanese air. I noticed that he seemed to spend a lot of time planning his next foray to the outside world, usually to France, his great love, or to rarely visited parts of Baltic Eastern Europe. Every Christmas for many years he visited Hong Kong, a practice he swore to abandon after the colony's return to China in mid-1997. An unreconstructed monarchist and British imperialist who was unimpressed by the ideological compulsions of 'post-colonialism', he found the hand-over intolerable. To help him through the trauma, I lent him my copy of Paul Theroux's novel *Kowloon Tong*, in which some long-term British residents of Hong Kong speak not of the 'Hand-over' but of the 'Chinese Take-away'.

2 RIDING SANTA'S SURFBOARD

Bill shared his office with Colin Quirk, a Londoner who had been holed up in Tokyo for years and who dreamed of the day, not too far distant but seemingly for ever out of reach, when he would retire to a cottage in the Home Counties and write books. He had already published a novel, *The Moaning of Makiko,* a Japanese *Madame Bovary* detailing the eponymous heroine's marital travails and tragic end. Colin seemed to be an Englishman of such a classically 'correct', strait-laced kind that reading his novel—presented to me as a gift soon after my arrival at Todai—came as something of a shock. His ability to enter and inhabit the mind of a Japanese woman, especially during times of sexual congress, of which there are an exhausting number in *The Moaning of Makiko,* was truly astonishing.

Belying the steaminess of his fictional imagination, Colin was a fastidious man with a Howard Hughes-like fear of germs and disease. I gathered he found living in Asia a bit of a trial, though he was happily married to a Japanese woman of singular charm and lived the life of the foreign husband. The great gusto with which Bill hurled himself into the cesspool of Tokyo life bothered and irritated Colin. Most of all he disliked his office mate's habit of leaving his swimming trunks draped over his desk chair after his frequent visits to the Komaba public pool. (Bill penitently swam several laps a few times a week to atone for a life otherwise committed to pleasure and the voracious pursuit of his various intellectual interests.) The plagues that damp garment might conceivably have harboured were awful for Colin to contemplate. Colin's diet appeared to consist of cups of tea and dry biscuits: the prodigious lunches Bill sometimes brought along to the office—luscious avocados, ripe cheeses, slices of succulent pink ham—were another bone of contention. Tolerant, compliant, the most equable of men, Bill accepted Colin's prickliness with good grace. By contrast

Ohara, always ready to share his thoughts on anyone or anything, once said to me that what 'Quirky' needed was 'a steak, a bottle of red and some time with Betty Styles'.*

    Colin's intense demeanour could be a bit oppressive, but he was intelligent and possessed an engaging knowledge of what was happening in the world outside Todai, outside Tokyo, outside Japan. This was not always the case with one's other colleagues. Colin suffered, but he also had a sense of humour and self-irony. I was less fond of Hugh Loftus, or should I say *Professor* Hugh Loftus, for to forget the professional title in addressing him would have been regarded as a calculated and inexcusable insult. The foreign Englit hot-shot at Todai, Loftus had landed in Tokyo some years before after a chequered career in provincial universities in Scotland, Canada and (it transpired) Australia. He came from that earlier era before 'theory' complicated criticism and made life miserable for literary scholars, that happier time when books were books, not 'texts' or, even worse, 'discourses', when they were simply 'good' or 'bad' in the eyes of men of superior sensibility: i.e. Englishmen, preferably from Oxford and Cambridge.

    Chatting to him about my teaching and research interests at a party in the rooms of the British Studies section at Komaba—a gathering brilliantly catered for by Professor Kusamitsu, a chap of impeccable taste who was customarily given responsibility for this most important task—I happened to mention Edward Said. (Admittedly this was an indication that the conversation was not going well.) I might just as well have farted, or called Loftus's wife a whore. A look of horror and outrage crossed his face; his shock of red hair stood on

---

*This trifecta had once done the trick for Ohara, apparently: Betty Styles, I gather, was a memorable girl from his drug-store-and-diner late adolescence.

end. 'That man! What *rubbish* he talks!' Like other Westerners who have built their academic careers in the East, Loftus found *Orientalism* offensive, though he had probably never read it. Said's thesis bore too many implications for his own position within the system. Loftus did not want his privileged status challenged—or 'problematised', as one of the new breed of trouble-makers might say—by any nonsense about 'master narratives' and 'hegemonic discourses'. He may even have had trouble spelling the word 'hegemony', let alone 'Yale School' or 'zeugma'. Intimidated, perhaps, by the far reaches of the Roman alphabet, he taught a one-year fiction course consisting entirely of Hawthorne's *The Scarlet Letter*.

Memories of Loftus aside, however, after my eventual return to Australia it was not long before I began to look on Todai more fondly. Back in Melbourne, I felt like the protagonist in *The Masukagami*, a Japanese historical romance written in the fourteenth century, who remarks when he ponders the consequences of moving on: 'If I go from here to some/Yet more hateful place/Perhaps even these lodgings/Will stir nostalgic regret.'[7] Demoralised by lay-offs and cutbacks, by hit lists and bureaucratic hit-men and women, Australian academics looked an unhappy lot next to their more collegiate-minded Japanese counterparts. A lot of envy and back-biting was about. My own university, Monash, seemed to be tortured by internecine warfare. Addicts of 'restructuring' had given research away and contented themselves with building private administrative empires. The power principle was in full play and enemies were detected everywhere: official academic gatherings resembled scenes from *Dr Strangelove*. Meanwhile, once-promising academics, well into middle age, had donned the dress and demeanour of used-car salesmen. Todai at least treated students *as* students and not as business 'clients' to be bled dry and sent on their way. The entire system of Australian tertiary education seemed to be a sorry mess, and I saw what Ohara meant by the parting message he inscribed on the gilded going-away card presented to me by the Todai staff: 'AFTER HELL, PURGATORY'.

I caught a glimpse of what was happening in Australia during my absence when I encountered someone from a tertiary institution Down Under who was visiting Komaba to flog his university's educational software. A harassed Japanese professor summoned me to one of the more commodious offices in Building 9, where he and one of his colleagues had been attempting to entertain this fellow. Appalled by his hard sell but too embarrassed to send him on his way empty-handed, they didn't have a clue what to do with him. For his part, the Australian looked both bewildered and irritated. When I entered the room he greeted me as a long-lost friend, although we'd never met. Now he was going to get somewhere.

The two Japanese quietly left the room, relieved to be rid of this antipodean pedlar. 'Mate,' my countryman immediately began, 'these are tremendous programmes, really tremendous. You could do yourself a favour, do education in *Japan* a favour, to take them on board. Honestly. I just can't get through to these dickheads how really good they really are.' He went on to tell me of his bold plan to hire a luxury boat, in which he would ply the waters of Asia persuading selected senior academics and administrators of the necessity to buy. 'But these blokes here, fair fuckin' dinkum . . . !' I decided that Ogawa *sensei* and his slim shoulders were preferable to an Australian with a chip on his.

⌘⌘⌘

2 RIDING SANTA'S SURFBOARD

Desperate situations demand desperate measures. Confronted by fifty fresh-faced freshers on the first day of my Australian Studies introductory course at Tokyo University, I hit upon the idea of asking them to jot down five things they knew about Australia. It would be instructive, I thought, to discover what perceptions and misconceptions I would have to negotiate over the next two years. And these students, after all, were the chosen ones, the scholastic elite, those who had triumphed over a ruthless selection process and had gained entry to Japan's premier institution. Their responses would provide a mirror of Japanese attitudes toward Australia.

I anticipated droves of kangaroos and koalas, and got them. But there were also several tentatively reproving references to the White Australia Policy and to the fate of the Aborigines. Uluru appeared as often as the Opera House. Many students were impressed by Australia's vast desert landscapes. One student made mention of Australia's 'character of sand and rock', in a manner reminiscent of the terse metaphysic of Patrick White. Another observed that it is 'populated by gay people'; another still that one of the main attractions is the 'Great Barrier Leaf'.

Possibly indicating Australia's insignificance in the Japanese view of the world, two students commented cruelly that 'it is near New Zealand'. That really stung. Who knows, maybe the Japanese saw in the Shaky Isles the untainted geographical sister of their own now polluted, overcrowded archipelago? In any case, the persistent and excessive Japanese admiration for New Zealand, for its economic policies and its unspoilt environment, was enough to rouse the slumbering patriot in me. This just goes to show that people need to feel superior to *somebody*, a notion that is sometimes used to explain the visceral contempt the Japanese reserve for Korea and Koreans.

Most of the students at least knew what was expected of them in this simple exercise. One, however, maddeningly itemised 'It will be fine tomorrow, too?', 'Japan is lacking in good national servants' and 'the train was crowded' (actually spelt 'clouded') in his selection of five Australian things. Of all the responses, the most perplexing comment, the one that most aroused my curiosity, came from a student who suggested that 'at Xmas Santa comes with surfboard'. I pondered this observation for days. The remark of a comic genius with a surrealistic sense of humour? A smart alec taking the piss out of a gormless antipodean visitor? Or the articulation of some observed advertisement, a promotional logo, perhaps?* Whatever, I was going to have my work cut out.

The central pedagogical problem, as I saw it, was not so much a matter of Japanese ignorance (what would Australian students have to say about Japan?), but of deciding what mattered about Australia. What fiction of 'Australia' should I construct? What is important about the place and how it has evolved? What is worth remembering from its history? What should the students know? Where, in short, should 'the facts' end and the interpretation begin? These fundamental questions are rarely asked in Australian Studies courses at home, where a degree of prior knowledge is guaranteed, where the cultural discourses are more or less understood and where both teacher and student know the critical game all too well.

It is one of the myths of Japanese life that its university students don't bother doing a scrap of work, their futures having

---

*In fact the student must have been a stamp collector. A philatelist from New South Wales—thank you, Dave Hatley—has informed me that the 1977 Christmas stamp issue featured an image of Santa 'hanging five'. It was a controversial stamp, as earlier Christmas issues had featured distinctly Christian themes.

already been decided for them by the name of the university they are able to scramble into after at least three years of frantic cramming at high school. In his novel about a Todai graduate living in London, *Brrm Brrm!* (1991), Clive James describes Japanese universities, 'even the greatest one . . . Todai', as 'a beery hiatus between working too hard at school and working too hard at one's career'.[8] James is half right—probably the Japanese do work too hard at school and in their professional lives—but I'm not sure that Japanese students are more 'beery' or otherwise drugged than their counterparts in contemporary Australia. They seemed interested enough, most of them, and moderately industrious.

Nevertheless it was hard to overlook the atmosphere of torpor that often hung over the classroom. I learnt to ascribe a charitable, or at least self-protective, interpretation to the fact that some of my students spent long stretches of class time in a coma. It was not uncommon for them literally to fall asleep, which horrified me at first until colleagues assured me that this routinely happened in their classes as well. I was less inclined to put this down to hangovers or boredom than to the rigours of the train journey into Todai. Or indeed to the punishing schedule of classes, which saw students spending all day, every day, doing one subject or another.

Or to working part-time, away from the campus. Many of my students had jobs—waiting in restaurants, teaching English privately—that either kept them up half the night or severely cut into their recreation time. This may seem somewhat strange. While Todai likes to see itself as a meritocracy, offers a fairly generous scholarship system and charges fees that are modest compared with elite private establishments like Keio, the fact is that most of its students come from families who can afford to prepare their children for the prestigious universities' notorious entrance exams by sending their offspring to a superior *juku* (cram school). An article published in the *Japan Times* in December 1996, mischievously entitled 'UNIVERSITY OF TOKYO PREREQUISITE: YEN', reported that a university survey had found that parents of Todai students had an average annual income of 10.95 million yen in 1995, about double the national average. Just over half the students' parents held managerial positions, and the bulk of the rest were white-collar professionals. Significantly, however, the article also stated that 85.3 per cent of students questioned said they had part-time jobs, up more than 17 per cent from the previous year.[9]

Visiting Japan in the mid-1950s, the Australian travel writer Colin Simpson commented on the poverty of the Todai students with whom he came into contact.[10] In retrospect, it does not seem surprising that this was the case a mere decade after the war, when Japan was striving to rebuild its economy. As Japan endures its current depressed economic cycle, perhaps the post-war pattern is being repeated. Most of the Todai students I came to know personally were hard up, either living with their parents and working to supplement their parental allowance, if they received one, or struggling to get by on their own. Misaki, the postgraduate student whose thesis on Australian poetry I supervised, was so busy hurtling around Tokyo teaching English that she hardly had time for her own study. And she was the daughter of a senior Toshiba executive based in the capital. It must have been tougher still for youngsters from the provinces, surviving by the skin of their teeth in the Big Smoke.

The lethargy was more evident in the English language classes I was asked to take than in the Australian Studies classes. The students did the Australian subjects by choice, but they were compelled to study English, in enormous *Eigo Ichi* (English I) groups and in smaller classes designated 'Listening and Speaking', 'Reading' and 'Writing'. The state of English language teaching in Japan, with its emphasis on book-bound rote learning and its disregard for the spoken language, has long been a source of frustration. The Australian academic and writer Gregory Clark, president of Tama University in western Tokyo, took the radical step of removing foreign languages from the list of compulsory subjects for university entrance, reasoning that students have had their capacity to speak English ruined for life by the way it is taught in Japanese schools. The Ministry shows signs of trying to remedy this through schemes such as the JET (Japanese Exchange and Teaching) programme, which emphasises the spoken English competence of both students and Japanese teachers, and also encourages the employment of native speakers.

If the standard of spoken English at Todai is anything to go by—and its students are supposed to be the best and brightest—new approaches are desperately needed. Ineptitude is exacerbated by resentment: many of the students made it clear that they had no interest in speaking English and made little attempt to use it in class unless confronted. It was not only the students who felt uncomfortable talking English. I often suspected that the reason why some Japanese colleagues appeared to avoid me in the corridor was that they might be forced to speak a language that would make them look inferior. Then again, that is what I *liked* to think: I wasn't able to speak to them in Japanese, was I?

The lack of streaming made the teaching of English even harder. Smart but naive kids from Kyushu who had never left Kagoshima before getting the nod from Todai were lumped in with the precocious sons or daughters of company executives who had spent ten years in Sydney or Los Angeles. This made it hard, if not impossible, to design classes that were not too difficult for some, or else too easy for others. In reality, we instructors could teach the language any way we liked, whatever the class happened to be called. Initially I used short literary texts, supplemented by newspaper articles and pieces taken from 'youth' magazines such as the *Tokyo Journal*, as prompts to discuss cultural and environmental issues I thought might be of interest to the students. I used short stories by the prolific Singaporean Catherine Lim, a Mishima story or two in translation, Helen Garner's collection *Postcards from Surfers*, John Updike's 'Wife-wooing', and Robert Drewe's chilling 'Machete'. On bad days, the resistance to the language extended to the discussion of politics and culture as well. A few of the students up the front got involved, a few down the back went to sleep; one or two stared dolefully into space while others chatted away in Japanese, politely reverting to a brand of English whenever I moved purposefully in their direction.

It was all a bit of a game. Some days I tossed away the class outline and conducted general knowledge quizzes, which always got them going. A particular winner was a quiz, usually conducted in a class scheduled before lunch, in which students in groups had to match various foods with their countries of origin. So now I suppose that there are young people walking around Japan whose foreign culinary vocabulary is excellent ('samosa!' 'pork pie!' 'goulash!'), but who otherwise can speak nothing but Japanese.

It is simply incorrect to stereotype Japanese students as automata responding to every prompt from the master at the controls in front of the class. This image is part of the dehumanisation of the Japanese generally, which is among the

2 RIDING SANTA'S SURFBOARD

most regrettable forms of cultural representation that one can think of. But the students are not exactly livewires either. My guess is that these young people had been trained at school to be passive, an attitude that carried on into university, turning into an outright lack of interest in the case of some students who, for the first time in their lives, had better things to do than study.

In this respect it was enlightening to read the answers to a question in the Todai entrance exam, which all we professors were obliged to mark. In forty or so words candidates were asked to respond to the proposition that young Japanese should be granted the vote when they turn eighteen, not twenty as is presently the case. I calculated that at least 60 per cent of the papers I marked answered in the negative. Common reasons given were that 18-year-olds didn't know enough, were too 'childish', and were too busy studying for entrance exams to think about political issues (a reason given, so far as I could make out, without a hint of irony). A few papers suggested that forty was the proper age to begin voting. This response was fairly typical:

> I am 19 years old now. I have lived in schools but not in society from my birth. I am so ignorant. It is dangerous to give people like me the right to vote now.

In my Australian Studies classes I encouraged the students to speak up, to interrupt me any time they wanted clarification, needed more information or had a comment to contribute. Precious few questions were forthcoming; students preferred to sidle shyly up to me after class. The ones who displayed the most spark tended to be the foreign exchange students—until the financial crashes of 1997, when the demeanour of those from countries such as Thailand and Indonesia became more and more woebegone, marooned as they were in one of the world's most expensive cities while the home currency turned to grains of sand. But nothing at all seemed to worry the Chinese students, whose energy and native love of an argument stood in stark contrast to their passive, ostensibly compliant Japanese peers.

I came to treasure the mischievous interruptions of students such as Zhou Wei Guo, a dynamic spirit from Shanghai with an enviable capacity to energise any human gathering. In a class on the Federation movement, I showed the students some representatively racist cartoons from the *Bulletin* of the 1880s and 1890s, when the arguments against Asian immigration became more heated in the run-up to nationhood in 1901. The bogeyman of Australian nationalism at that time, the evil Chinaman, was depicted in various forms of shocking caricature. Smirking, Zhuo put up his hand and loudly opined that the grotesque, pigtailed figures looked Japanese. This nonplussed the locals, some of whom were showing signs of rather enjoying the visual evidence that another culture shared the Japanese opinion of their mainland neighbours.

For all their frustrating diffidence, however, my Japanese Australian Studies students had a fair bit of charm on their side, possessing a characteristic courtesy and a quiet earnestness that contrasts with the casual cocksureness of their antipodean equivalents. Each day gave evidence of behaviour both touching and quaint. After the final Australian history lecture before the Christmas/New Year break, a young fellow came up to me, the uprooted foreigner, and played a rendition of 'Silent Night' on his harmonica while his friends listened attentively.

2 RIDING SANTA'S SURFBOARD

⌘⌘⌘

Whatever their lack of personal self-confidence, Japanese students are the products of a country with a firm view of the value of its own cultural uniqueness. Accordingly they nurture a sort of intellectual self-containment that simultaneously stimulates a curiosity about the 'outside' and 'outside people' (the literal translation of *gaijin*, foreigner) and a resistance to foreign ideas and attitudes. Unless, of course, those ideas and attitudes happen to hail from America. Most Japanese know Australia as a constellation of visual clichés from a travel brochure, a view reinforced by strictly supervised package tours to tourist sites such as 'the Great Barrier Leaf'. In trying to attract interest in the cultural forces that have impelled Australia's history and that should compel attention to its contemporary character, one has to deal with the undeniable fact that Australia is, well, *not* America. Although the Japanese are a singularly courteous people, many of the individuals I met both casually and professionally looked visibly disappointed when they discovered that I was not from the Land of the Free.

Enjoying a solitary drink one evening in a boisterous beer hall run by Sapporo Breweries in Ginza, I was drawn into conversation by a salaryman at the table next to me. He leant across my table, dropped cigarette ash on to my plate of 'sashimi salad' (not the tragedy it might have been, as the fish had been served up underneath a crunchy layer of what appeared to be Kelloggs cornflakes), blew smoke into my face and asked me what State I was from. When I replied 'Victoria' he looked perplexed, for the Garden State was not on his US itinerary. It transpired that this fellow visited a different American State every year on his all-too-brief annual holiday. Utah last year, Oregon this. Only Florida and Minnesota to go—and now Victoria as well. He'd have to consult his atlas.

Though the Japanese admire Europe and aspire to some of its civilised niceties, the United States is the one country to which Japan defers politically and culturally. Outside Japan (and New Zealand, it seems) that is where everything important happens in the world. Indeed, it *is* the rest of the world. 'The foreign country', one of my students said to me in halting English, 'means America to Japanese.' I discovered this dispiriting truth when I came to teach the exotic topic of multiculturalism. Multiculturalism is the intellectual pornography of Japan, an intriguing and titillating form of foreign life to be peeped at then discarded for the comforting embrace of the great Japanese 'monoculture'. Of course, Japan is a more diverse place than the ideology of uniqueness promulgated by *Nihonjinron* (Japanese culture theory, or literally, 'discussions of the Japanese') customarily allows. But as long as the ideal of uniformity and the emphasis on group identity remain so dominant, the interest in multiculturalism will remain vicarious.

At the same time, there is a degree of genuine fascination with multiculturalism's material impact on the social fabric and how it affects the 'national psyche', an old-fashioned concept that still has currency in Japan. I was given to understand that racial diversity in America is good—stimulating, enriching, invigorating: Al Pacino! Arnold Schwarzenegger! Tiger Woods!— but that elsewhere it is bad, Very Very Bad. Decadent, divisive, debilitating. When I lectured on the subject, I tempered a personal enthusiasm for the benefits of multiculturalism by describing its detractors' scepticism and the complacency of those who glibly celebrate it. Afterwards, a student came up to offer his condolences that Australian multicultural society in the Age of Hanson was such a vicious chaos compared with that pacific, harmonious mixed-race nirvana, the USA.

Irritated by the students' unwillingness to accept any foreign phenomenon unless it bore the American brand name, I strode into the next class determined to impress on them the need for Japan to think more even-handedly and internationally. I began by quoting from Pauline Hanson's moving long poem, 'The Individual, The Species, The Planet', a copy of which Michael Hinds had helpfully deposited in my pigeonhole. (Or I assumed it came from Hinds, as the paper was smudged with errant cigarette ash, marked by several brown circles indicative of overflowing glasses of Guinness, and embellished with the names of a couple of likely racehorses running at Fuchu the following weekend.) By Pauline Hanson I mean the respected American poet Pauline Hanson, not the Queensland politician Pauline Hanson, though I deliberately didn't make that distinction to my students, just to set them wondering. 'Humankind', the poet says, 'must take for itself a global face'. The young men and women before me seemed to take note. Would they be the hoped-for generation to undertake the remaking of Japan? I would like to think so, but somehow I doubted it.

⌘⌘⌘

Yet, for all my students' propensity to believe the worst of Australia, they found antipodean subject matter irresistibly romantic. Coming from a once-beautiful country that has largely been turned into an ugly jungle of ferro-concrete illuminated by gaudy neon, the Japanese are fascinated by the moth-eaten mythology of 'The Bush', no matter how hard one tries to demystify it, and are beguiled by visions splendid— or even, for that matter, moderately picturesque. I had to work hard to convince them that my country was not one large sheep run populated by men wearing hats fringed with corks; that, statistically speaking, Australian society is even more urbanised than Japan. But try selling the idea of urban Australia in Japan when the bald statistics show that Australia's entire population is far fewer than that of greater Tokyo, a conurbation of over 26 millions. And indeed it took just one flying visit back to my homeland during my stay to realise that what we mean by 'urban living' in Australia is something different from urban living in Japan. My home town, Melbourne, looked just that—like one of those once-thriving but now struggling rural townships left to moulder after the main highway had been re-routed. Teenagers were skateboarding at the top of Swanston Street, up near the State Library, in a scene as desolate as any in the film *On the Beach*. The general air after frenetic Tokyo seemed more sluggish than easeful, as if the city had channelled all its energy into following the footy and there was nothing left for anything else.

In my teaching at Todai, it proved problematic to adopt a hard-headed critical attitude toward my homeland without appearing to be treacherous or offending the patriotic sensibilities of my charges. The students were amazed and appalled by both the concept and the implementation of the White Australia Policy, as anybody would be who considers it afresh, or indeed considers it at all. Soon after my arrival in Japan I read the Melbourne historian Greg Dening in *Australian Book Review* arguing that there is 'no temptation stronger than to make the past a grotesque and laughable mimicry of our civilised present'.[11] I took the point: it is too easy to ridicule times past. (Not that the present seemed all that 'civilised', to be honest.) So I sought to place the policy platform of official racism and the wretched rhetoric that supported it within a cultural frame and a historical context.

There are times, however, when simple moral clarity goes perfectly to the heart of history. The students' sense of outrage at the long narrative of Australian racism seemed to me a perfectly valid intellectual response, though I often wondered if their reactions would be as uncompromising in considering their own country's past. (They seemed disinclined, for example, to consider parallels between the treatment of the Australian Aborigines and the active suppression and forced assimilation of the Ainu, the indigenous peoples of the Japanese islands.) But the co-existence of racism *and* multiculturalism throughout Australia's settler history proved too tricky a phenomenon for many of them to grasp. Not having been encouraged to be critical of their own country, the students tended to believe that such insoluble complexity proved the superiority of their own culture, where things are more cut and dried.

Yet the cultural certitude of Japan can be beneficial. Naturally I took colonialism to be one of the main subjects of an introductory course on Australia. The students found it difficult to come to grips with the idea that 'colonialism' can be something other than constitutional, that it is ingrained in the politics of popular culture and in gender relations—both manifestations of coloniality that the Japanese could usefully consider. But the clarity of their response to my discussion of contemporary Australian republicanism was almost liberating. Respectful though they were of their own imperial family, they found it preposterous that a country should still choose to have a foreign monarch as head of state. Understandably, one student in his list of five Australian things asserted that it 'is', not 'was', a 'colony of England'.

Speaking of the Emperor . . . I was determined to broach the touchy subject of what we call World War II, which is known in Japan as *Taiheiyo senso*, the Pacific War (an oxymoron and inaccurate to boot, because it ignores the years of fighting in China). I wondered how to discuss the conflict and its corrosive impact on Australian responses to Japan without trying to make it sound as if I was trying to wring from these innocents an apology for the misdeeds of members of an earlier generation. It is almost axiomatic that Japan remains wilfully blind to its wartime atrocities, and that school students are not provided with the complete picture. Surveys continue to reveal that young Japanese remain ignorant about the war's beginning—effectively 1931, with the 'Manchurian Incident'—but are comprehensively informed about its dreadful denouement, the dropping of the atomic bombs on Hiroshima and Nagasaki. They don't know much about the savage aggression in China in the 1930s, nor about Japan's ill-treatment of its POWs. The war tends to be remembered from the side of the victims: that's *Japan* as victim, not *its* victims.

Several developments have helped bring the issue of Japanese culpability to public light, including the furore over the so-called 'comfort women' and the prolonged controversy over the official sanitisation of Japan's wartime behaviour and the ultimate legal vindication of the war historian Saburo Ienaga, who ran a decades-long campaign against the censorship of his school textbooks. Yet for every historian, gutsy school-teacher or local politician determined to redress the historiographical imbalance, there seem to be several noisy nationalists—prominent among them a Todai professor of

2 RIDING SANTA'S SURFBOARD

education—who cry foul, scream about patriotism and point the bone at disgraceful traitors and white-anting internationalists. The nationalists sadly underestimate the intelligence of young Japanese men and women. I found my students to be remarkably mature in their attitude to the subject of the war, regretful that they hadn't learnt very much about 'what happened', and keen that their nation should collectively acknowledge the past and move on from it. Indeed, they seemed rather less susceptible to chauvinistic sentimentality than their Australian counterparts, who continue to be media-fed the archaic notion that military achievements are a reliable measure of national virtue.

But wars seldom go smoothly, even when all you are doing is discussing them. In the first half of 1996 I taught a course on 'Australia and Asia' to a group of undergraduates, including some Australian exchange students as well as several Japanese. The course surveyed the history of Australian imaginative and political responses to Asia, from the inchoate fear and loathing of the mid-nineteenth century to the tentatively constructive engagements of today, as signified by the image of 'enmeshment' coined by Bob Hawke as prime minister in the 1980s. The central argument of my final lectures was that, since the Vietnam War, Australia had acquired a new sophistication in its dealings with Asians and had belatedly recognised the reality of its regional situation. One could confidently predict that the monstering of Asia was a thing of the past.

I congratulated myself that the course had gone extremely well and decided to treat the students to a movie for the final class. Knowing that one of the visitors was a member of a local video club, I conscripted him to bring along an Australian film with an Asian theme and setting, expecting something relatively benign, maybe *The Year of Living Dangerously*. I would even have been happy with *Turtle Beach*. Instead the student unleashed *Blood Oath*, a 1990 film about the trial of Japanese war criminals in Indonesia just after World War II, with Bryan Brown starring in the role of the disgusted, dedicated prosecutor. To my horror the film degenerated into a series of antipodean references to (I misquote from agonised memory) 'mongrels', 'apes', 'yellow bastards' and 'fuckin slanty-eyes'. The one Japanese character who was humanised just happened to be a Christian. The Australian students, including the unsuspecting donor of *Blood Oath*, shifted uncomfortably in their seats; their Japanese friends stared at the TV screen, apparently transfixed. When the video ended, the class filed out more sombrely than usual. And so the semester ended.

Blood Oath's exploitation of vestigial anti-Japanese feeling in Australian audiences impressed on me the tenuousness of my thesis about contemporary attitudes to Asia. A year later the Hanson phenomenon enforced a drastic rethinking of those final lectures. Like others involved in the broad field of what I like to call 'Austral/Asian Studies', I had presented not so much a 'black armband' view of the past as a rose-tinted view of the present. There is a political and indeed personal investment in boosting the 'Australia-in-Asia' business, in facilely asserting that everything is hunky-dory in the Great South Land. Not that the students themselves harboured any illusions about what has been impelling the nation's effort to forge closer links with its Asian neighbours. Forget the cultural-exchange bullshit. As one student wrote in his final essay, 'Australia's present interest in Asia is a hard-headed response to the relentless pressures of economic logic'.

Communicating an idea of Australia in Japan is like riding Santa's surfboard, an exercise in incongruity with a wipe-out always imminent. But I learnt to go with the flow. Someone at the Australian embassy ticked me off, in a most pleasant fashion, for toying with the idea of showing my students *Crocodile Dundee*. (Desperate situations, desperate measures.) But while I quailed at the thought of again sitting through this once-but-no-longer-amusing flick, a cliché from the mid-1980s and the era of Hawkey and Bondy, the film does illustrate the pervasive influence of American consumerism and cultural values, a phenomenon relevant to Japan as well as Australia. Unconvinced by that 'academic' argument, the embassy person told me that *Crocodile Dundee,* and particularly its 'uncouth' star Paul Hogan, would give 'the wrong impression' to the Japanese. I wondered: was a trade deal at a difficult negotiating stage? And what is the 'right' impression? Is a corrective vision the correct one to teach? Would *Priscilla, Queen of the Desert* be a more diplomatic selection? I ended up showing both, along with *Romper Stomper,* which I chose in a moment of depression at the way things were going back home. I lived to regret that decision, as it took some fast talking—during which I taught my students the meaning of the word 'dystopia'—to convince them that the film's grotesque vision of Asian-hating skinhead mayhem was a gross exaggeration, and that they shouldn't cancel their forthcoming holidays in north Queensland.

Questions about content and interpretation reached a head when I came to read the students' essays at the end of the courses. Relatively unaffected by fashionable Western critical ideologies, many of them produced work of real insight and genuine engagement with the subject. There was an abundance of arresting remarks, both consciously and unconsciously fashioned. One student observed that 'since the Paul Keating era, Australia has tried "depommification", but without success'. Another, in an essay discussing the issue of women and work in Australia since the 1970s, wrote several paragraphs defending something called 'effeminate action'. In answer to a test question asking for a definition of multiculturalism in the Australian context, Yoshitaka Kitamura, one of the keenest of the class of '97, pithily described it as 'a mixture, or coexistence of Western culture, Asian cultures, Aboriginal culture, and Tasmanian culture'. And then there were the eccentric essays, summoned from some unfathomable abyss of cultural misunderstanding. In response to the question on multiculturalism, a student extended his answer by applauding the policy for opening Australia up to the pleasures of international cuisine, including a dish described as 'ostrich steak with green pepper sauce', which he assured me had become so popular in my absence that it was now a staple food. This seemed a fair enough absurdity. I gave a tick and turned the page.

⌘ ⌘ ⌘

3 FAULT LINES

The first time I met Hugh Loftus—it must have been the night I upset him by uttering the two deadly words 'Edward Said'—he had attempted to impress upon me the quality of his private Lafcadio Hearn collection, which he assured me was 'world class'. 'World class'? One may as well boast about owning a world-class Max Walker collection. Hearn is the quintessential minor, provincial writer, of interest only to those interested in Japan. He is admired still by the Japanese because he fell so wholeheartedly in love with his adopted country from the moment of his arrival in Yokohama in 1890 and never fell out of love with it, although he was increasingly dismayed by its headlong rush into modernity. How else would Hearn be internationally known but for his identification with Japan?

Loftus's identification was not with Japan but with Hearn himself, because Hearn had for a time held the chair of English Literature at what was then called the Imperial University of

Tokyo. Loftus therefore belonged to the great tradition of foreign interpreters in Japan. How he revelled in this role! Hearn had remade himself as a Japanese, to the extent of giving himself a Japanese name. He adopted the native practice of squatting on the floor and invited his Tokyo colleagues and pupils (even those habituated to Western chairs—the seating apparatus, not the academic position) to squat beside him. Loftus would have none of that nonsense; he'd have his peers and protégés look up to him as an exemplar of Oxbridge Man. No wonder he was discomfited by mention of Said, whose major critical project (and that of his numerous acolytes) has been to discommode the privileged position of Western analysis of 'the Orient'.

Contemporary Western writers on Japan often seem haunted by Hearn's ghost. He *lived* Japan as well as described it: how can they ever hope to measure up to the standard he set? Pondering their ability—or inability—to objectify and identify the 'real' country, they assume there is some national essence waiting to be extracted and exposed to examination. The British travel writer Jan Morris has recalled that the reason she didn't like Kyoto when she first visited the city in 1957 was because she 'totally failed to understand it'. 'In Japan, of all countries,' she observes, 'it is dangerous to be ignorant'.[1] Morris is probably right, but it seems to me that too many writers take this kind of advice too much to heart. The fear of ignorance and the pressure to produce profound cultural insights lead them into making simplistic and sometimes nonsensical generalisations about Japan. No other nation has been invested with so many debilitating complexes, syndromes, neuroses; no other people have been the subject of such derisive caricature.

For this the Japanese themselves are partly to blame. Like Australia, Japan is obsessed with national self-definition and

3 FAULT LINES

beguiled by illusions of uniqueness, as the booming *Nihonjinron* industry testifies. Again like Australia, Japan loves to know what foreigners think of it and is highly sensitive to criticism. Both societies seem to need the approbation of others to stoke the fires of their self-worth. Foreign cultural commentators in Japan are liable to be divided into two opposing camps: the Jap-bashers, whose criticisms bewilder and offend, and the Japan-lovers, whose sensitive and discerning appreciation of the nation's cultural richness is welcomed and respected. You are locked into one grouping or the other; escape is impossible. Say you like the place, and you're 'in'—well, sort of. Dare say you don't, and—well, you would, wouldn't you? After all, you're just a *gaijin*.

In his novel *General Yamashita's Treasure* (1994), the Australian-based, Japanese-speaking novelist and playwright Roger Pulvers pokes fun at the professional Orientalism of Western commentators who 'explain' Japan. In so doing he implies how ill-advised it is for the Japanese themselves to swallow all the rubbish that is said and written about them. One of the novel's central characters is an Australian academic, Professor William Stick, who first visited Japan when he worked for US intelligence during the Occupation, and has since made a career out of occupying the country intellectually. Described as being 'at the forefront of foreign scholars who have locked horns in battle to demonstrate to the Japanese new ways of explaining how successful they have become in the world', Professor Stick has made his mark with his book *Splittable Chopsticks: Key to Japanese Uniqueness*, which purports to reveal Japan's much-vaunted 'uniqueness' by examining the different ways its people separate their chopsticks. Now chairman of the Department of Oriental Sociology in an Australian university, he has returned to Japan to research a definitive study of regional variations in *bento* box lunches in selected railway stations. Such is the silliness of what passes for informed Western commentary about Japan. At one point in the novel, Stick tells his wife that he will eventually be regarded as 'the second Lafcadio Hearn'. 'Lafcadio *who?*' she replies.[2] The irony is telling. But would Hugh Loftus have appreciated it? I thought of leaving *General Yamashita's Treasure* in his pigeon-hole as a parting gift when I left Todai, but decided against it. Better to leave it empty.

⌘⌘⌘

What *is* it about Japan? Why, more than any other Asian country, has it been subjected to such sustained aesthetic, ethnographic, anthropological, economic, cultural, political and pseudo-scientific analysis by Western scholars and writers? Why the obsessive desire to decode and define it? I suspect that the fascination with the country is the result of a combination of ambivalence and ambiguity. The ambivalence among people from nations such as the United States and Australia has everything to do with the Pacific War, in divided responses to a country that was once a reviled antagonist but with whom its wartime enemies now share an intimate, if occasionally troubled, economic relationship. The contradictory feelings that Japan inspires are compounded by the paradoxes apparently embedded in the country itself. People find it difficult to make up their minds about Japan. The travel writer Pico Iyer has remarked that it is possible to maintain two completely contrary attitudes toward the country without their necessarily being in conflict. All statements about it, he writes in *The Lady and the*

Monk (1992) might be 'applied just as surely in the opposite direction'. Ruth Benedict, the cultural anthropologist hired in mid-1944 to tell the Americans about the strange mob they were about to crush and then colonise, was tormented by Japanese contrariness until, famously, she made a virtue of it. In *The Chrysanthemum and the Sword* (1946), she describes a people 'both aggressive and unaggressive, both militaristic and aesthetic, both insolent and polite, rigid and adaptable, submissive and resentful of being pushed around'.[3]

Bill's eyes would roll at talk of Japan's 'contradictions'. He didn't find it contradictory at all, just a pleasant, civilised and safe country in which to live. All countries, even Canada, he would say, have their contrasts. So what? The more we try to pin places down, the more they evade easy classification. This is especially true of Western representations of the 'unknowable' East. Western writers have always had a penchant for assigning dualisms to Asia—the 'spiritual East', 'the sensual East' and so on. I can personally attest to Japan's ability to inspire—sometimes simultaneously—apparently irreconcilable emotions and attitudes. At an analytical level Japan refuses to fit neatly into the pigeon-holes where Westerners enjoy placing Asian countries. As Marilyn Ivy observes in *Discourses of the Vanishing* (1995), the very word 'Japan' appears 'ubiquitous, nomadic, transnational' by virtue of the nation's global economic presence. Like its tourists, it appears to be everywhere, just around every corner, in every nook and cranny. Yet at the same time, Ivy observes, Japan's 'economic expansiveness' is countered by a 'national inwardness', so that the country often seems to reinscribe old distinctions between 'East' and 'West'.[4] I said *seems* to reinscribe. The country cannot be so conveniently delineated; it evades easy classification, which only makes Western commentators try harder. Japan thus challenges the representational 'hegemony' exercised by the Occidental imagination over the Oriental world, as analysed by Said and others. Its elusive character, by turns brazenly 'Western' and inscrutably 'Eastern', intrigues, perplexes, and finally irritates the hell out of foreign observers.

Australians in particular feel keenly ambivalent about Japan, perhaps because wartime resentment has festered longer here and is exacerbated by the humiliation of economic dependence. That is one reason; another may be that the two old adversaries share a sense of ambiguous national identity. Maybe Australians instinctively understand the equivocal nature of Japan because their country embodies something similar itself. Some of the parallels between the two nations are explored by Asian affairs commentator Ross Terrill in an article entitled 'Australia the Ambiguous', published in the *Japan Times* in November 1996. 'Japan', Terrill says, 'is the most Asian country in the developed Western community. Australia is the most Western country in Asia.'[5]

Geo-cultural parallels linking the two countries abound. Fernand Braudel's description of Japan in his epic work *A History of Civilisations* (1987) could just as well be applied to Australia:

> Japan lies at the far extremity of the human world . . . To the East, where its best ports are found, it faces the vast and wondrous emptiness of the Pacific . . . Japan is . . . isolated, insular and alone. To break out of its solitude, it has had to make frequent and conscious efforts. If not, it would be naturally inward-looking. Yet a Japanese historian has pointed out that 'Everything that seems essentially Japanese in our civilisation is actually derived from abroad'.[6]

3 FAULT LINES

Without labouring the point, Japan and Australia are insular Pacific states located at opposite poles of the culturally diverse Asia–Pacific region. Both, in short, share a location on Asia's margins. They are outsiders, not insiders. They feel isolated from mainland Asia and are unsure as to how best to connect with it, except economically. In both cases, as Richard McGregor observes, the early phases of industrialisation and modernisation during the latter nineteenth century were 'accompanied by racial policies which fenced them off from surrounding Asian countries'.[7] Japan's rallying cry for modernisation in the Meiji era was 'Out of Asia and into Europe'. The same slogan might have been uttered by the founding fathers of Australian Federation, so determined to protect Australia as a bastion of Britishness in the South Seas.

As Australia now tentatively moves toward an Asian future, its own ambivalence mirrors Japan's. While professional Australian Asianists such as the former diplomat and academic Stephen FitzGerald feel thwarted by their own country's lack of regional commitment, they are similarly frustrated by Japan's apparent aloofness and its refusal to adopt the kind of communal identity that they see as the Utopian destiny for the region as a whole.[8] Except for the trade imperative, both nations have confused feelings about their neighbours and their own self-image within the Asian context, and both wonder what regional role they might play in the future.

These questions were thrown into sharp relief in 1997 by the controversy over Asian immigration to Australia, which received such extensive coverage in the Japanese press. It was painful to read. Observing my discomfort at the negative publicity Australia was attracting, Ohara was forever regaling me with Pauline Hanson's rhetorical exploits, while I pretended ignorance of her very existence. Yet the tone of the reportage was rather less condemnatory in Tokyo than in Hong Kong, Kuala Lumpur, Singapore, Jakarta and Bangkok. Japan well understands divided sympathies toward Asia. Why, some Japanese commentators wonder, does Australia want to be 'part of Asia' anyway? Remember that Japan gave an early demonstration of its own regional ambivalence in its response to the implementation of Australia's notorious Immigration Restriction Act in 1901. Japan objected, not so much because it thought that the policy of 'White Australia' was immoral, but because it wanted the 'respect due to a great power and a highly valued ally of Great Britain', and demanded that Australia make a distinction between it and 'the backward and dependent' Asian peoples.[9]

Like many Japanese themselves, Australians find it difficult even to conceive of Japan as 'Asian'. The country confounds all the stereotypical conceptions of 'the Oriental' that Australia inherited from Britain. As Edward Said writes, the 'theses of Oriental backwardness, degeneracy, and inequality with the West' sat easily with the theories of biological determinism that provided the racist rationale for nineteenth-century European imperial control of great chunks of Asian territory.[10] Whatever Japan might represent to contemporary Australians, it is not backwardness and retardation, nor degeneracy and chaos, nor inequality and incompetence. On the contrary, throughout the 1970s and 1980s, if not so much these days, Japan has been sold as a success story, some of the social essentials of which—such as energy and acumen, discipline and determination—Australia could do worse than to copy.

It might be wondered whether Australians actually 'know' much about Japan at all. Regrettably, contact with Japan has largely been confined to the business sector. This cuts both ways. Both countries eye each other through the prism of self-

3 FAULT LINES

interest. Yukichi Fukuzawa, the leader of the Japanese Enlightenment in the early Meiji period (and the founder of Keio University), first popularised Australia in Japan as early as 1869, in his travel book *Sekai kunizukushi* ('A glimpse of countries of the world'), which praised the incomparable riches of the goldfields and talked up 'the busy import/export markets' of Sydney and Melbourne as symbolising 'a new world with a prosperous future'.[11]

Significantly, Fukuzawa's information was second-hand, as he did not personally travel to this exciting 'new world'. Until the explosion of Japanese tourism in the 1970s, Japanese people seldom visited Australia. A few were involved in the pearl industry along the northern coast and in isolated agricultural ventures (notably the establishment of the rice-growing industry), but they did not migrate in numbers, or take root as the Chinese did in the nineteenth century and the Vietnamese have done over the past twenty years. These days, though, short-term Japanese travellers are part of the Australian landscape: in 1997, despite a 7 per cent fall in visitor numbers from Japan, the country contributed nearly 20 per cent of all tourists to Australia.[12] They are everywhere to be seen around the continent—honeymooners cavorting on Queensland beaches, trekkers scaling Uluru as if it were Mount Fuji, koala-cuddlers posing for cameras in nature reserves, nattily dressed golfers hacking their way around Melbourne's sandbelt courses, marvelling at the cheapness of playing the game in Australia compared with home, shoppers by the bus-load unloading their yen in the boutiques and bistros of Sydney, helpfully directed by signs in Japanese and later comfortably ensconced in enclaves like the Hotel Nikko at Darling Harbour.

Conversely, relatively few Australians visit Japan. The much-trumpeted Australian 'discovery' of Asia in the late 1960s and early 1970s was based largely on travel and tourism. Australia's supposed Asian 'destiny' is therefore related to the emergence of Asia as a *destination*. But the fact is you will not find Japan on many Australian tourist itineraries. Japan National Tourist Organization statistics for 1997 suggest Australian tourists to Japan in that year numbered a paltry 41 520, about 5 per cent of the number of Japanese tourists who journey here, quite a discrepancy even given the fact that Japan's population is vastly greater than Australia's. Overall in 1997, according to the Australian Bureau of Statistics, short-term Australian departures to Japan came to 56 400 out of a total of nearly 340 000 for the North-east Asian region, which includes China, Korea, Hong Kong and Taiwan. In the same year, almost 720 000 Australian travellers flocked to the popular destinations of South-east Asia.[13]

Travel between Japan and Australia reverses the basic pattern of East–West tourism. In most parts of Asia, visiting Australians are blessed with the purchasing power to catapult them several rungs up the social scale. At a resort in Bali, for example, you might be called *tuan* ('lord' or 'master') by an eager flunkey in recognition of your elevated status; some Indian bellboys still call Western hotel guests 'sahib' (while sniggering behind their backs, if they have any sense). But travel in Japan can be a humbling experience.

Money is the major reason why Australians, so conspicuous elsewhere in Asia, are relatively thin on the ground in Japan. It is simply too expensive for the average traveller. Some friends from home who paid me a visit when I was in Japan became annoyed when I expressed my belief that Tokyo was not really *that* expensive. They regarded this as a cavalier and even callous assessment. 'Try it on an Australian salary,' they advised. It is hardly surprising that the most obvious Australian presence in Japan is the businessman or the bureaucrat on a trade delegation, subsidised by a healthy expense account.

The word 'embrace' is often used to dignify the 'push' into Asia. But Australia's embrace of Japan has essentially been inspired by mercenary motives. When push comes to shove, the politics of money is more important than the politics of cultural enrichment. As Australia's biggest trading partner by far, Japan is absolutely crucial. You can see the Aussie businessmen on the Qantas Sydney–Tokyo run, scouring graphs and spreadsheets, looking over the ledgers of profit and loss, or diligently studying phrase-books and practising their pronunciation ('dome-oh-harry-garto', 'doomo-arigitoo'), preparing to grapple with the Jap. These are men on a mission, envoys to the national future.

It was an instructive exercise to pick apart the eight-page 'Australia Special' lift-out published in the *Japan Times* marking the occasion of John Howard's prime ministerial visit to Japan in September 1996. Less than one page was devoted to cultural matters. Apart from the usual homilies by diplomatic functionaries and tame journalists about the importance of promoting healthy bilateral relations, the focus of the lift-out was unremittingly economic—a one-page spread for Qantas and a large Ansett advertisement accompanying a feature article entitled 'TOURISM MAJOR SOURCE OF EARNINGS, EMPLOYMENT'; a substantial article exhaustively analysing Australia's healthy performance in its trade with Japan; an arresting advertisement placed by Toyota offering Howard a warm welcome ('OH WHAT A FEELING!'); another half-page salutation by members of the Australia and New Zealand Chamber of Commerce in Japan; and messages of goodwill from various Japanese corporations such as Sumitomo. The lift-out also contained an advertisement displaying an attractive

Japanese housewife extolling the virtues of 'Aussie Beef', an analytical piece on Australia's status as the leading supplier of cheese to the Japanese market, and, last but not least, an advertisement that especially captured my eye, placed by a Tokyo-based purveyor of antipodean wines with the unmistakably Australian name of 'Ken's Wine Club'.[14]

The cynical view is that Australia's relationship with Japan is just a more open and perhaps more honest demonstration of the real reason why the push into Asia is seen as so urgent—it means money. Australia has feared Asia, but has also always known that Asia is an economic mountain waiting to be climbed. After all, it had the example of Britain to follow. 'Banjo' Paterson's visit to China in 1901 to cover the Boxer Rebellion taught him that the British people had a duty to 'walk' into the region and take 'the boss mandarin's seat at the top of the table'.[15] Maintaining a close association with a powerful economy such as Japan guarantees Australia a seat at that table, rickety as it appears these days.

Japan is rarely included in the idealistic platitudes about cultural exchange used by proponents of Australia's 'Asianisation'—themselves becoming increasingly isolated and unpopular in the wake of political, social and financial instability in the region. The country is guilty of too many environmental and social sins for it to be an object of affection to Australian Asiaphiles, a sanctimonious mob given to jejune disparagement of Western 'materialism' and idealisation of Eastern 'spirituality'.

The guidebook produced by the Australian publishing house Lonely Planet confirms the common reservations felt toward Japan. Now enormously successful world-wide, the Lonely Planet 'travel survival kits' for budget travellers first came to prominence in the 1970s as the palpable documentary evidence of the new Australian interest in Asia. They have the reputation of catering for travellers who see themselves as discerning and politically aware, independent-minded, adventurous, and—not to put too fine a point on it—a bit strapped for cash. Most of us, in other words. I don't mind admitting to buying Lonely Planet guides. In fact, I possess a constellation of them. My own battered 1991 edition of the LP *Japan* begins by casually remarking that the country inspires 'a love–hate relationship' in its visitors and that it can be 'horrifically expensive'. It soon goes on to list Japan's environmental failings—its engagement in driftnet fishing and whaling, its wasteful over-packaging, its mangling of its own landscape and its complicity in the destruction of others, through, for example, its prodigal use of throwaway chopsticks. 'Forests fall', the guidebook complains, 'in order to supply these one-use-only utensils'.[16]

Elsewhere there is praise for Japan's cultural offerings (if you can afford to sample them), but the country's failings are relentlessly enumerated—polluted, crowded cities populated by pitiless chain-smokers, rampant consumerism and the crassest of crass commercialism. Lonely Planet likes its countries to be 'unspoilt' so that they can be properly enjoyed by the discriminating, eco-sensitive traveller. (For 'unspoilt', read economically dependent, chronically poor, materially primitive.) Furthermore, Japan cannot be forgiven for evolving beyond its nineteenth-century image as a land of cherry blossoms and pagodas, painted geishas and tea ceremonies. Once again, Japan evades easy Orientalist classification: the East is supposed to be timeless, immutable, incapable of 'getting ahead' unless taken by the hand by its masterful Western benefactor. Japan cannot be forgiven for reshaping itself *by* itself; it cannot be forgiven for becoming so damnably 'Western'.

Foreign observers have tended to invest so much idealised sentiment in the anachronistic image of a picturesque Japan that they have found Japan's industrialisation almost personally insulting. Lafcadio Hearn was bewitched by Japan upon his arrival at Yokohama in 1890, but was level-headed enough to recognise the ephemeral nature of the enchantment, and indeed to imply his own eventual disillusionment as Japan turned itself into something other than the country he first visited. 'The traveler who enters suddenly into a period of social change—especially change from a feudal past to a democratic present', he remarks, 'is likely to regret the decay of things beautiful and the ugliness of things new'.[17] Hearn, of course, never tried to hide his emotional engagement with Japan. His strength as a writer about the place lies in the way he personalises it.

The undertone of resentment in the commentaries of Japan 'experts' is perhaps a surer indication of Japan's characteristic ability to infuriate outsiders. The classic case is the British scholar Basil Hall Chamberlain, another of Hugh Loftus's role models. Chamberlain arrived in Japan in 1873 and stayed for nearly forty years, helping to 'introduce' Japan to the West in his role as professor of Japanese and philology at Tokyo University. Chamberlain is a wistful but fatalistic observer of the country's transformation from 'the nearest earthly approach to Paradise or to lotus-land' into a modern industrialised state. In his *Things Japanese* (1890), he laments the passing of 'Old Japan', with its virtues, arts and graces, for something lesser and meaner, something debased. 'Old Japan is dead', he writes, 'and the only decent thing to do with the corpse is to bury it'. Yet perhaps the reason why Chamberlain

3 FAULT LINES

is so accepting of the destruction of 'Paradise' is that he thinks traditional Japanese civilisation inferior anyway. 'We foreigners', he writes of the Meiji Restoration, 'may no doubt sometimes regret the substitution of common-place European ways for the glitter, the glamour of picturesque Orientalism. But can it be doubtful which of the two civilisations is the higher . . . ?'[18]

Modernisation, to Chamberlain's mind, rendered an inferior civilisation merely absurd. 'All the nations of the West have . . . a common past, a common fund of ideas, from which everything that they have and everything that they are springs naturally, as part of a correlated whole . . . Japan stands beyond this pale.' Try as it might, in other words, Japan will not be allowed to join the club. It was much nicer before it got all uppity.

This was not an uncommon attitude at the time. Chamberlain's disdain for hybrid New Japan is echoed by the Englishwoman Isabella L. Bird, among the most indefatigable of nineteenth-century travel writers. Like Chamberlain, Bird went to Japan for reasons of health, and travelled around the country for about seven months. In *Unbeaten Tracks in Japan* (1880), the reader finds her fleeing the Western-influenced treaty ports in search of 'the real Japan'. A devout Christian with a powerful missionary impulse, Bird admired many things about the country but reacted against what she saw as its careless attitude toward religion and sex, declaring it to be 'sunk in immorality'. Her description of the degradations attendant on Japan's brazen embrace of the West is a bit of a give-away. 'The Japanese of the treaty ports', she remarks, 'are contaminated and vulgarised by intercourse with foreigners'.[19]

The themes of cultural loss and degradation foreshadowed by Chamberlain and company in the late nineteenth century have made a comeback in Western writing about Japan since the 1970s. The tone of *The Inland Sea* (1971), by the doyen of present-day Japanologists, Donald Richie, is profoundly elegiac. The totem of 'New Japan', Richie writes, is the bulldozer; it is the totem, indeed, of the twentieth century, destroying Japan along with everywhere else. Escaping from the factory-littered shoreline of mainland Honshu and Japan's 'sad future', Richie heads for the beautiful islands of the Inland Sea to savour 'the last of old Japan' while he can.[20]

Evanescence, the inevitable passing of all things, is fundamental to the traditional Japanese sensibility: it is most exquisitely rendered in the *haiku*, with its customary focus on the frozen moment, captured at the point of oblivion. So it is no wonder that, at a point in its history when so much really has disappeared and the country has turned transition itself into an art form, contemporary Japan is depressed by a feeling of loss. Significantly, the titles of two of the 'big' books about Japan by foreign residents to have appeared in the past few years—Alex Kerr's *Lost Japan* (1996), the author's own translation (published by Lonely Planet) of his award-winning *Utsukushiki Nippon no Zanzo* (1993), and Alan Booth's final, masterful work, *Looking for the Lost: Journeys Through A Vanishing Japan* (1995)—appear designed to capture that public mood.

In fact both titles are misleadingly suggestive of the barren nostalgia that often marks travel narratives concerned with 'traditional' culture. Both the American Kerr and the Englishman Booth mourn the disappearance of Old Japan (the former trenchantly, the latter more obliquely and suggestively); but they are also alert to its tenacious survival here and there in the provinces and its miraculous transformation in the unlikeliest of urban places. Kerr's celebration of the city of Osaka—that most unlovely symbol of Japanese modernity—is perverse but deliberately confronting, a challenge to those who weep and wail over the disappearance of thatched roofs and the like. With its 'charismatic' geisha madams, colourful *yakuza* (the gangster as latter-day samurai), its street humour and iconoclastic spirit, Kerr's Osaka is true to its former identity as the seaport Naniwa, and embodies the ancient ambience of a country increasingly overtaken by dreary homogeneity. 'When friends ask me to show them the "true Japan of ancient tradition",' Kerr remarks, 'I don't take them to Kyoto: I take them to Osaka'.[21] Yet after twenty years even the phlegmatic Kerr finally had to admit defeat, as I discovered on a visit to Kyoto in late 1997. I picked up a copy of the *Kansai Time Out*, seeking relief from hours spent reverently gazing at gardens consisting solely of stones—some large, some small, some mere gravel—and there was Kerr, announcing his decision to leave Japan (for Thailand) because of the country's heartbreaking environmental self-destruction.[22]

⌘⌘⌘

Where do Australians fit into this gloomy picture? Rather uncomfortably and unevenly, as it happens. Australian literary travellers to Japan in the early Meiji era were entranced by Japan's purity of culture and landscape, which stood in stark contrast with the West. An especially enthusiastic visitor was the journalist James Hingston, who arrived in Japan in the 1870s to have a look at a country then only very recently opened up to the foreign gaze. He later recorded his findings in his two-volume *The Australian Abroad* (1879–80), perhaps the seminal Australian travel book. Hingston's admiration for

Japan is so boundless that he makes Lafcadio Hearn look like a miserable cynic. He writes of a salubrious paradise, a 'land of health' whose inhabitants are truly to be envied. 'Nature's gentlemen are the Japanese,' Hingston enthuses, 'made in the older fashion of the world before money-grubbing had soiled the souls of men'. Struggling to communicate a sense of this 'land of the picturesque', he constructs an analogy with medieval England 'when there were maypoles and morris-dancers, and caps with bells to them; when the theatres were open to the sky, and when there were tiltings and jousts and tournaments'. The analogy is fantastic but revealing: Britain remained the benchmark for travelling colonials in the nineteenth century, and would remain so well into the twentieth. Indeed white Australians abroad had difficulty defining themselves without explicit reference to a 'British' identity and heritage.

On the surface Hingston's version of Japan seems impossibly anachronistic, as though he is oblivious to the irresistible changes taking place in the idyll. In fact he isn't: the changes are observed and noted, but not catastrophised. Hingston is sanguine about Japan's future. 'Imperilled as Japan is now by the financial troubles consequent on her many reforms,' he writes (sounding to this point very much like a contemporary columnist from an Australian newspaper), 'nothing but what is pleasing in prospect seems to lie before her'. In Hingston's book, the process of modernisation could bring 'improvement' as well as 'innovation'; the two were not mutually contradictory.

Another Australian nineteenth-century traveller to Japan, the Scottish-born James Murdoch, later the Professor of Oriental Studies at Sydney University and author of a four-volume *History of Japan* (1903–26), also relished the natural and

3   FAULT LINES

cultural pleasures of traditional Japan without decrying its new receptiveness to the West as some dreadful cultural apocalypse. Murdoch saw the development of 'an Occidento–Oriental civilisation' as an object of wonder, not as a matter for regret. In 1919 he argued that the Japanese 'are not, and never have been, mere servile copyists', that they modify new ideas without compromising their native culture.[23]

I find it touching that these Australians in the Meiji period are so much more sympathetic to a modernising Japan than members of the Old World such as Chamberlain and Bird. Is it fanciful to think that it was because these antipodean travellers were also from an emerging nation that they were less threatened by Japan's independent efforts to remake itself? They were certainly less ready than the English to mock Japanese ambitions to don the borrowed clothes of 'civilisation'. Perhaps this is because these colonial writers had felt the chill of Old World disdain themselves. Thus the despised outsider recognises himself in the face of another.

But I don't want to get too carried away with this thesis. When it comes to sinking the boot into the Japs, Australian writers are no less eager and capable than the English. Take Hal Porter. According to Alison Broinowski, Porter epitomises the so-called 'Hearn Syndrome', the disillusionment and disenchantment of the Japan-lover who loved too much.[24] Porter's interest in Japan was sparked when, as a young child, he was impressed by the Japanese designs on some of the household crockery in the family home. What he called 'successive jabs of the needle'—reading Hearn and listening to *Madame Butterfly*, wearing the kimono—had made him a Japan 'addict' by the time he first went there in 1949, as a teacher to the children of Australian Army officers in the Occupation forces. Actual experience of the country did not break that addiction; after Porter's return to Australia he spent years pining for the place and extolling the virtues of its people, both privately and publicly. In 1958 he published *A Handful of Pennies*, a sympathetic account of Japan during the Occupation, if not of the Occupation itself. Then, in late 1966, the Australia–Japan Foundation arranged for him to make a lecture tour of Japanese universities. Porter jumped at the chance to ascertain whether he was 'clear-sighted' in his enthusiasm for Japan and the Japanese, or had been 'the willing victim of an illusionist's trick'. But the Japan he visited in 1967 was not the humbled loser of 1949. The country in which he enjoyed 'the conqueror's privilege of *carte blanche*' had become a newly self-confident and vigorous nation engaged in the process of transforming itself into an economic powerhouse. Porter was displeased. The Japan of his dreams and memories had become 'a land obsessed with demolition and reconstruction'.[25]

Porter's disillusionment is amply expressed in his travel book *The Actors: An Image of the New Japan* (1968) and the collection of stories *Mr Butterfry and Other Tales of New Japan* (1970). Note the adjective in the subtitles. Like Meiji-era observers such as Basil Hall Chamberlain, Porter prodigally trades on the old/new dichotomy favoured by those who like to plot modern Japanese history as a story of cultural decline. *The Actors*, in particular, is a shocker, combining a racist tirade against the Japanese character with a crude version of the kind of cultural analysis that everywhere crams the bookshelves marked 'Japan'. The old Japan Porter had so admired had become 'an infernal carnival of sideshows' whose capital, Tokyo, is described as 'the marvel and horror of the century'. What had brought Japan undone, in Porter's mind, was the wholesale prostitution of its indigenous culture in the cause of Western, and especially American, modernity. Yet it was not

3 FAULT LINES

so much that Japan had 'paraphrased' the West, but that it had done so uncritically and unoriginally. Not understanding Western civilisation, Japan had become a travesty of it; the more it aped the West, the more essentially Japanese it became. The more the Japanese affect Westernisation, Porter argues after the manner of Chamberlain, 'the wider the split between the Oriental nature and the Occidental nature becomes, and the easier to see'.[26]

Japan's slippery modern hybridity has troubled more generous intellects than Hal Porter's. Arthur Koestler, for instance, describes the Western influence in Japan as a 'skin graft from an alien donor which, though eagerly accepted, never took'.[27] (An ugly metaphor that in itself indicates how Japan confounds even major writers' attempts to portray it.) But Porter trenchantly, if glibly and complacently, identified the problem of Japan's paradoxical image—the image of a country that can never be truly 'Western' because it does not really belong, but that has long ago outgrown the 'Eastern' character once ascribed to it. The country inhabits a geo-cultural void. Is it any wonder that it withdraws into itself?

⌘⌘⌘

Reading the broadsheet *Japan Times* on a Tokyo train in peak hour—or any hour, really—is no easy task. I mean the logistics of it, not the content. It requires a constant, subtle pressure on your neighbour with your thighs, reinforced by the odd assertive jab to the ribs. ('Oh, *gomen nasai!*', feigning innocence.) Even then, the skills of an origami master are required to fold and unfold the paper into manageable configurations. That's if you are lucky enough to be seated: standing, forget it. Most days en route to Komaba, however, I persisted. The economics pages made especially gripping reading, replete with tales of turmoil, dire warnings, resignations, wild swings and rallies on the stock and currency markets. The sports section was obsessed with North American games of no interest to me and took about a minute, though I did take a liking to an occasional column by a hirsute Englishman called Fred Varcoe, who specialised in mocking Japanese sports idols such as the golfer 'Jumbo' Ozaki, a swaggering sports giant at home but a notorious under-achiever everywhere else.

The book-review pages were often interesting, with good reviews syndicated from abroad or produced by one of the large community of foreign littérateurs beached in Japan. On the way into town one day I came across a review of a book of modern Japanese *tanka*, the 31-syllable poetic form that is the bigger, older brother of the more famous *haiku*. The review quoted this meditation on war by the journalist and academic Zenmaro Toki (1885–1980):

> an old soldier
> lodged in our house
> tells a war story
> that says nothing
> about killing an enemy

I was struck by this poem's dry-as-dust irony and its oblique reference to the crude focus of conventional war narrative, with its customary concentration on the simple dynamic of antagonism and murder.

3 FAULT LINES

War itself is a pretty reductive activity, of course. Consider the way Australians regard Japan. Brought up on horror stories of Japanese military turpitude, many Australians do not need prompting to associate Japan with war—*the* war—however hard some of us resist the temptation to blame the entire race, past and present, for what took place. As I pondered the poem, I remembered my own surge of anger on that first demoralising morning in Kemigawa, when I waited in the rain for Bill. Irritation in Japan . . . irritation *with* the Japanese . . . remember the war . . . the murderers! It was a pattern of instinctive response against which I had to be constantly on guard. I have no memory of my father's ever bad-mouthing the Japanese, and he fought them for years in the scrub and jungle of the Solomons and New Guinea, an experience that contributed in no small measure to his early death in 1966. It would be a touch vicarious of me to fulminate on his behalf. For much the same reason I've always been suspicious when Australians call for the Japanese to apologise for their wartime conduct, at least when the calls come from the lips of people who didn't live through the conflict. In many cases I strongly suspect these are the rationalisations of covert racism.

But there is no forgetting the war. Clive James, whose father was a prisoner at Changi and never returned, is known for his coruscating satire of aspects of Japanese society (its antic game shows, for example); less well known is his knowledge of Japanese culture and language, and his fondness for the county in general. 'There are so many things I love about Japan that are just too deep to describe', he once remarked in an interview with an Australian journal. Yet in the same interview he had to confess, 'I can't sit having my cup of coffee in Tokyo without thinking of the fire raids and the bombs. It's over but it's not over.'[28]

For Australians, the horrors of those years are constantly being revisited in a variety of popular discourses; undeniably, they continue to condition reactions to Japan. As Humphrey McQueen has observed, contemporary Australian attitudes to all of Asia are still affected by cultural memories of the Pacific War. The Coral Sea, Changi, the Thai–Burma railway and the Kokoda trail are 'not merely place names but mythic sites'. These sites are 'mythic' not so much in the heroic sense invested in places of Australian military striving such as Gallipoli, but in their ability to ignite outrage beyond the specific body of men and women who actually lived and suffered through the war.

Fanned by angry POW narratives such as Rohan Rivett's *Behind Bamboo* (1946) and Russell Braddon's *The Naked Island* (1952), strong anti-Japanese sentiment lingered well into the 1950s, even as Australian governments sought to restore diplomatic and economic ties. Frank Clune's *Ashes of Hiroshima* (1950) is a lengthy diatribe against a people variously described as 'pariahs', 'robots' and 'insect-like automata'. That the Japanese take offence at being called 'Nips', Clune argues, is evidence of their 'touchiness' and inability to laugh at themselves. Most Australians 'taste bitterness' when they think of Japan, Colin Simpson argued in his Japan travel book *The Country Upstairs* (1956). A decade after the war's end, Simpson was defensive about even setting foot in Japan, and felt it necessary to justify his trip on the grounds that there is a need 'to know and understand' the old enemy.

That bitterness is still around in a muted form. I detected an inherited antagonism among people of my acquaintance who knew I was going to Japan. And these were people of my own age. Virtually all the best-loved Australian figures to

3 FAULT LINES

emerge from World War II, most notably the revered army surgeon Sir Edward ('Weary') Dunlop, suffered grievously as prisoners of the Japanese. Their folk-hero status has helped to exacerbate racial animosity and to keep painful memories of the war alive beyond their 'natural' historical lifespan.[29]

In *The Chrysanthemum and the Sword*, Ruth Benedict characterised the Japanese as 'the most alien enemy' the United States had ever fought. This was an assessment with which many Australians have concurred. The Australian literature of World War II reveals that the Japanese were perceived to be more than a mere military opponent. In *Island Victory* (1955), his novel about air warfare in the South-west Pacific, Norman Bartlett writes of an enemy who was 'enormously more of an opponent than a German or an Italian, fellow products of Western Christendom, could ever be'. Their ill-treatment aside, some Australian POWs found their forced incarceration difficult to accept because it was at the hands of people they considered to be their inferiors. One of them, Norman Carter, registered his frustration at being imprisoned by members of what he calls 'a nation of geishas and houseboys'. Like many people of his era, Carter had been acculturated to the view of the Japanese as a 'simple-minded people, politely bowing their way through life amid a shower of cherry blossoms'.[30] That was Hal Porter's position too. He most liked the Japanese when they were humbled and subservient; dominant, they lost their appeal. It is an attitude improbably still in evidence here and there in present-day Tokyo, in the public behaviour of long-term male expats who would like nothing better than to waltz around in white suits, delicately wiping their brows with silk handkerchiefs *à la* Somerset Maugham, while being waited on hand and foot by some appropriately obsequious oriental manservant.

'Catastrophe and war may make people bestial', Porter argued in *The Actors*, but 'regeneration and peace do not necessarily reverse the process'. Porter was anxious to correlate Japan's peacetime successes with its wartime excesses, and moreover to imply that its breakneck post-war development was an attempt to achieve in peace what it could not do on the battlefield. Both, he suggested, were motivated by Japan's ambivalent attitude to the West, defined as 'an internal warfare between rage and admiration . . . contempt and jealousy'.[31] Many Australians, including those not given to holding personal grudges, find the national reliance on trade with Japan galling, though the growth of trade was eagerly encouraged by successive governments as part of Australia's desperate search for markets to replace an increasingly Europe-enmeshed Britain.

These feelings of historical grievance are dramatised in *The Floating World* (1974), John Romeril's play about an Australian survivor of the Burma railway who takes a post-war tourist trip to Japan. While the psychological seismology of Les Harding's crack-up, carefully graphed through the course of the action, provides the dramatic interest, perhaps the most significant scene in the play is actually the first, in which contemporary Japanese businessmen survey a prize piece of Queensland coastline. Harding's crazed hatred of the Japanese is thus given an explicable social context and (paradoxically in a drama about madness) even rationalised. His racism is explained, not merely by the wounds of the wartime maltreatment itself, but by the outraged sense that post-war Australia has betrayed its wartime defenders by handing over the country to their old enemy on a platter, and for the most meanly mercenary of motives.

To Australians of my mother's generation (her first husband was killed in the Pacific War, leaving her with a newborn son), it makes no sense at all that Japan 'lost' the war but 'won' the peace. The flood of Japanese money into Australia in the 1980s created a new climate of resentment, in which some of the old fears of invasion were again in evidence. In 1984 John Hooker published his revisionary *The Bush Soldiers*, about the *successful* Japanese invasion during World War II. Why not? They may as well have won the bloody war anyway. The Japanese invaders in the 1980s were not soldiers but tourists and businessmen. The octopus emblem famously used in the 1880s by the *Bulletin* cartoonist Phil May to indicate how Chinese migration was throttling the very life out of Australia reappeared a century later, in a cartoon published in the *Australian* showing a Japanese octopus (replete with militaristic Rising Sun headband) extending its tentacles around hotels and condominiums, airlines and various construction projects.[32] In the words of Peter Bowers, a journalist for the *Sydney Morning Herald*, the 1980s saw the 'fanatical' Japanese soldier depicted by scores of war writers transformed into an 'Australian creation'—the 'fiendishly clever' Japanese businessman, succeeding where his military forebears failed.[33] In the federal election campaign of 1990, the Liberal opposition leader, Andrew Peacock, sought to capitalise on widespread public hostility to Japanese investment and invoke the spectre of a Japanese enclave in Australia by attacking plans for a Japanese-financed 'Multi-Function Polis', a hi-tech 'futuristic' city then the subject of a joint Japan–Australia feasibility study. As I recall, the political reckoning was that the issue gained the Opposition some votes, though not enough to win them the election.

Whingeing about Japanese economic control of Australia has been on the wane for some years now. These days the complaints are more likely to be about the decline in Japanese tourism. Places like Cairns, with huge investment from financially troubled Japanese corporations, brace themselves for the sell-off. The Queensland resorts, Uluru and even Sydney wonder about tourist revenues lost as Japanese travellers stay home, or say sayonara to Australia and go elsewhere. At the Australia–Japan Foundation library in Tokyo I read a *Bulletin* cover story on just this subject, suggesting that the Japanese, having enjoyed Australia as a 'fad', are now turning to countries such as Italy and France. Apparently this is akin to an act of treachery. The fickle things, you just can't trust them, can you?

The part-smug, part-amused reaction of the Australian press to Japan's economic troubles has been tempered only by the knowledge that if Japan's economy goes down the tube then surely the regional economy will follow. During this period of gross instability in Asian currencies, which in turn has imperilled Australia's own economic position, the bone has been pointed at Japan for not doing enough to stabilise the situation. In February 1998 the *Sydney Morning Herald* published an article entitled 'Living Dangerously on the Fault Lines', in which the commentator Max Walsh located the Asian and even global economic crisis in a specific Japanese context by invoking the metaphor of the country's notoriously unstable geology. The most threatening 'fault line' in the world economy, he said, was Japan. The 'tectonic plates' under it were shifting alarmingly; it needed to get its own house in order and do its duty to provide an 'anchor' for a floundering region.[34]

Australian journalists have been prominent in promoting a gloomy picture of Japan as it staggers toward the new millennium, beset by the succession of calamities, natural and ecological, economic and social and political, that have hit the country in the past few years. Negative stories come in a never-ending stream; the criticism is unremitting. As Ben Hills admits in *Japan: Behind the Lines*, disasters of one kind or another are 'professional consolations' to the foreign correspondent.[35] Bad news is good news, especially if it comes from Asia. It reminds Australians of how lucky they are that they live in such a safe, secure, 'civilised' place. But there has been a particular edge to the coverage of Japan's trials over the past few years: it is as if the country has finally been given its comeuppance. Cashing in on Japan's diminished status, John Howard in September 1998 felt free to boast that Australia was now the 'economic strong man' of Asia because of his government's canny financial management.[36]

What do Australians, I wonder, make of apocalyptic accounts of today's Japan? The pragmatists among them well appreciate that constructive relations with Japan are very much to the national benefit and that Japan's good health is important to Australia's own well-being. Politically, the relationship between the two countries is close. As Richard McGregor has written, Australia and Japan have gone from being 'worst enemies' to 'best friends', economically interdependent democracies located at either end of the Asia–Pacific with a keen interest in encouraging regional prosperity and stability.[37] For Australia's part, it has too much political capital invested in Japan to be able to hedge its bets about the country's capacity for economic renewal.

Yet, despite mutual economic and political interests and the current popularity of the study of Japanese as a foreign language, and also despite fatuous assertions about the vigour of the cross-cultural connection—I attended several talk-fests on the subject while in Japan—the relationship between the two countries remains curiously low-key. It looks almost less strong now than it was in the late nineteenth century. Alison Broinowski's survey of Australian impressions of Asia, *The Yellow Lady* (1992), reveals some surprising connections from those years. For example, the Adelaide-born Henry Black, whose grave I chanced upon in the Foreigners' Cemetery in Yokohama, emigrated to Japan, where he became a popular orator and famous performer of *rakugo* (traditional comic story-telling) who at the peak of his career led a troupe of more than twenty performers. Also active at around the same time was John Smedley, a teacher of architecture and drawing at Tokyo University in the late 1870s. Smedley designed buildings, pavilions and stage sets in both Tokyo and Yokohama, and organised exhibitions of Japanese art in Australia in the 1870s and 1880s.[38] But the intense cultural marriage envisaged by Rosa Praed in *Madame Izan* (1899), her novel about an Australian traveller's rediscovery of her Japanese husband, has never come to pass. The most obvious contemporary Japanese influence in Australia is in interior design and decoration, in both domestic and theatrical contexts—not much of an advance on the craze for *japonaiserie* that swept Australia as well as Europe from the late nineteenth century.

Japan has not been a conspicuous source of literary inspiration. Certainly, Australian poets have experimented with Japanese forms such as the *haiku* and *senryu*, and at least one major poem, Les Murray's 'Aqualung Shinto' (1973), has used Japanese subject matter as the catalyst for a reappraisal of local cultural identity. (Though Murray's aqualung dive to examine a sunken Japanese warship, described as a 'Dante-style' sightseeing tour looking at 'grotesques of courage/performed by knights of bushido in/tight black jackets', is hardly an unequivocal endorsement of mucked-up, uptight Nihon, 'the ultimate taut ship'.[39]) But few Australian writers have made of Japan a cultural home, let alone a literal one. The notable exception is the poet Harold Stewart, who settled permanently in Japan in 1965 and eventually died there in 1995, having penned the monumental *By the Walls of Kyoto* (1981), a sort of spiritual autobiography shaped by his commitment to Buddhism. Significantly, however, Stewart despaired at Japan's modernity; in his final years he could not bring himself to visit the newer parts of Kyoto, let alone big bad Tokyo.

What *has* happened, though, is that Australian writers have belatedly begun to write about the Japanese as human beings first and as culturally constructed 'Orientals' second. They have also begun to find in Japan a rich source of subject matter to be put to imaginative use rather than subjected to prescriptive, historically predetermined 'analysis'. This is even true of contemporary novelists, such as Steven Carroll in *Momoko* (1994) and Brian Castro in *Stepper* (1997), who have used World War II to frame their representations of Japan. Although *Stepper* is set in Tokyo against the gaudy backdrop of wartime geopolitics, it rarely allows its focus to stray from the individual human level. This is another way of saying that Castro does not attempt to assess the morality of Japanese historical behaviour from any 'national' point of view. His interest, rather, is in Japan as a register of the catastrophes that have punctuated twentieth-century history. Within that universal context, the dreaded Tokyo geological fault line is a signifier of the turbulence that unites the private lives of individuals with the history of our times.

⌘⌘⌘

It is debatable whether Australians can transcend historical grievances and present resentments to arrive at a more creative engagement with Japan, but some such move seems necessary if the relationship is to progress beyond the merely mercenary. The same, it almost goes without saying, is true of Japan. Australia's contradictory mixture of arrogance and self-doubt, ambition and insularity may be characteristic, but it is hardly unique. Some time in 1997 on the train on the way home from Komaba, passing through the riverine land of south-eastern Tokyo towards Chiba, I read a comment in a review by Gore Vidal published in the *New Yorker* that stuck in my brain for the duration of my stay in Japan. 'We all bathe in the same river,' he remarked. There's a message there for Australians, and perhaps even more pressingly for Japanese people as well.

⌘ ⌘ ⌘

4 THE BIG SMOKE

Some years before he killed himself by jumping from a bridge into the Mississippi River (it was half-frozen), the American poet John Berryman paid Tokyo a visit. Exhausted by travel, he checked into his hotel and immediately revived himself by ordering a massage, which was expertly administered by a geisha, after which he employed the services of a prostitute.[1] Ohara passed on this priceless piece of information about his countryman one afternoon in my Komaba office while relating his own introduction to 'Edo', as he liked to call Tokyo. (He reckoned he'd lived in the city so long he was allowed to call it by its pre-Meiji name.) Ohara had originally arrived in Japan overland from Europe on the Trans-Siberian. During the journey he had forced down quantities of disgusting food and drink, only to expel them from his system spectacularly on the tempestuous ferry crossing from Nadhodka ('rhymes with vodka') to Yokohama. He was so sickened by the journey that he spent several days recovering in a friend's dingy one-room flat in Ikebukuro, one of the capital's more enervating districts.

Hearing the grisly gastric details of Ohara's arrival, I thought of Paul Theroux's boat trip to Russia from Japan in the company of two Australians, one named Jeff and the other Bruce (naturally). It had been a rough crossing. Just after dawn Theroux, who was customarily made nauseous by the mere presence of Australians, awoke to hear the following exchange of voices:

'Hey, Bruce.'
'Mm?'
'How's your little Ned Kelly?'
'Mawright.'
'Ya throw ya voice?'
'Naw.'[2]

⌘⌘⌘

My own introduction to Tokyo was less exciting than Berryman's but healthier than Ohara's. After the overnight Qantas flight from Melbourne via Sydney, I was met in the Tokyo airport bus terminal by Yoichi Kibata, who put me in a taxi for a guest house on the fringe of the Hongo campus of Tokyo University, where I was to spend a few days while our permanent accommodation in Kemigawa was sorted out. Too tired to sleep and curious to have a look at a city I'd never set foot in, I went for a walk. It was a sunny Sunday morning at the very end of March, and the season's first cherry blossoms were coming out. I made for Ueno Park, not far from the campus.

4 THE BIG SMOKE

It was downhill all the way. Much later, when I read Edward Seidensticker's indispensable Tokyo history *Low City, High City* (1983), I began to understand the importance of the district's topography. The campus of the haughty old imperial university, created on the estate of the powerful Maeda family in the mid-Meiji period, is located in upland Hongo; more than a hundred years later, its intellectual denizens are still conscious of their elevated status. Down the slope towards Ueno, as I passed through the old pleasure quarters of Yushima and Nezu, I left behind the stolid sobriety that characterises the university. Signs of the previous night's excesses were painfully evident. Outside a thousand bars and clubs young men were at work, scraping and swabbing the footpaths of their so-called 'pavement pizzas', the dried pools of vomit that dot the streets of Tokyo, deposited by millions of off-duty salarymen who have unwound that touch too much. Is there a more depressing sight than a nightclub the morning after? You could almost feel the hangover in the air; I started to feel sick myself, and all I had was jet lag.

At first sight Tokyo might seem nothing but a vast, indivisible urban sprawl, but the city's geography is crucial. Ueno itself is located in the *shitamachi*, Seidensticker's Low City. Literally 'the land below' (the castle), the *shitamachi* is located in the low, flat country around the Tokyo Bay waterfront and the once-marshy mouth of the Sumida River. The pre-Meiji *shitamachi* was a shanty town of waterways that housed the common people of feudal Edo, the merchants, craftsmen and labourers, while the feudal lords and their samurai inhabited the *yamanote*, the hilly 'high' country mostly to the west and north of the shogun's castle, now the emperor's palace. Another of those seductive Japanese dualisms presents itself: it is easy to see this socio-geographical division as evidence of the hierarchical structure of Japanese society, enforced in this instance by the Tokugawa regime, of which Edo was the creation and instrument. But in fact, as Seidensticker points out, the *shitamachi* is as much 'an idea as a geographical entity'. Plebeian enclaves could be found in the High City, while the Low had its 'aristocratic' dwellings, as well as several important temples.[3] And the brilliance of Edo culture, the picturesque vivacity depicted in innumerable *ukiyo-e* woodblocks, derives very much from the sense of the *shitamachi* as providing a 'counter-cultural' but cultivated rebellion against the bureaucratisation of the Tokugawa shogunate and the rigid Confucianism of High City samurai life. The courtesans and kabuki of the *ukiyo*, the 'floating world', were a reaction against rules, however stylised and ritualised their practice, and represented the triumph of popular culture over autocracy. In this context the *Edokko*—the child of Edo, the raffish commoner equally at home in the elegant Yoshiwara pleasure quarter or the plebeian vaudeville of Asakusa, the Low City connoisseur of the High Life—embodied a new kind of culture-hero in Japan.

Like much that is gorgeous about 'traditional' Japan, the world of the *ukiyo-e* is a prettified, though not necessarily fake, version of the reality. The *shitamachi* residents of the nineteenth century lived in squalor, in tiny, fragile wooden buildings on floors of mud, in an area periodically hit by earthquakes (half of the Low City was destroyed in the earthquake of 1855) and repeatedly ravaged by fires. One New Year's night in the 1870s James Hingston had his visit to Tokyo enlivened by a fire in 'distant' Asakusa, the quintessential *shitamachi* district, a little north of the Low City proper and on the way to the enticements of Yoshiwara. He took off from his lodging in Ginza in a rickshaw, only to find himself in a terrifying, bewildering shemozzle of dead bodies, frantic firemen and overworked stretcher-bearers. It was a scene from hell:

> The earth was strewn everywhere with smoking and smouldering wood ashes, reddened now and again into a glow as the wind came their way. The fireproof stores or go-downs stood in bold black relief over the frightful scene, and looked like to giant monsters standing sentry in the fiery, infernal regions. The smoke was unbearable to the eyes, making them smart and water in a way that stopped all progress through the streets of this fire quarter. Away on every hand it looked like a wilderness of flame and smoke and burning logs . . .[4]

That particular conflagration consumed some six thousand houses, not such a great number on the *shitamachi* scale of things. It was an irony not lost on the denizens themselves that the literally low-lying Low City was prone to flood as well as fire. The Sumida was liable to break its banks twice a year. Given the amount of water about, the poor sanitation, insects, the foul odours and the preponderance of filthy fish markets, it is no wonder that there were frequent cholera epidemics. Throw in a few highly destructive typhoons and you have a somewhat ill-favoured city. Visitors who complain about the seediness and ugliness of the present *shitamachi* (what is left of it) miss the point. The Low City always *was* pretty awful: its attraction was its energy, not its aesthetics.

Cynical English-speaking tourists tend to think that 'shitamachi' is an appropriate term for places like Ueno. Hal Porter thought it was the pits, the hang-out of 'unemployed restaurant boys, small-fry gangsters, petty-criminal larrikins, rag-pickers, pimps, panders, failed anarchists, drunken castaways, and superlative degenerates'. He described its food market and shopping precinct, the Ameyoko, as a nightmarish conglomeration of cul-de-sacs harbouring a collection of 'cut-rate abortionists and cosmetic surgeons', 'astrologers, faith-healers, palmists and mind-readers', 'mountebanks, mystics, evangelists, cranks, and vegetable-peeler demonstrators', plus the odd 'perv' or two, on the lookout for 'maso-sado-homo magazines, obscene dolls, aphrodisiacs, and gruesome flagellatory devices'.[5]

Alas, the present reality is rather less exciting than the Hieronymus Bosch picture painted by Porter. Yet the polite tourist cliché 'lively' (to which the anti-tourist Lonely Planet resorts in its *Japan* guidebook) probably does not do Ameyoko justice. The market area reminds the visitor to Tokyo that he or she is in Asia. The drama of buying and selling, the fetid crush and ferment, seem more redolent of a South-east Asian city, Jakarta maybe, than ordered, northern, sophisticated Tokyo. Furtive, mildly sinister Iranian touts, illegally trying to sell recycled telephone cards to passers-by, contribute a touch of the bazaar. Ohara used to say that he enjoyed venturing into Ameyoko on Sundays, when it was at its busiest, to remind himself that he was living in an Eastern country—and to give quiet thanks that he lived out in western Tokyo, in a pleasant, suburban neighbourhood that was about as Asian as, well, Des Moines.

Ueno Park is a good place for the foreigner to begin an acquaintance with Tokyo, for in a sense it is where what we know as modern Japan was born. It was on Ueno Hill in May 1868 that some 2000 or more pro-shogunate samurai put up a last-ditch defence against the imperial army, only to be ruthlessly crushed. A few years later the Meiji government turned the woods around the hill and the lowland by Shinobazu Pond into Tokyo's first public park. In a country habituated to

4 THE BIG SMOKE

small gardens, temples, shrines, cemeteries and markets as communal meeting places, the idea of a public park was itself an imported, Western novelty. Other foreign ideas soon found a place in the park—the country's first art museum, first zoo, first electric trolley. Before long Ueno Park became the venue for expositions held to confirm Japan's progress toward modernisation, and over the past century or so a cluster of museums has been erected as concrete testimony to Japanese uniqueness and worldliness—the Tokyo National Museum, the National Museum of Western Art, the Tokyo Metropolitan Museum of Art, the National Science Museum and even the humble little Shitamachi History Museum, positioned by the pond and located handily near a McDonald's, for the ever-expanding number of Japanese who find that the contemplation of the past induces an acute desire for a burger.

On that first sunny Sunday morning, as on most Sunday mornings, there were a lot of people about, families especially, bravely taking the air. But there didn't seem to be a lot of life. Ueno Park is pretty desolate: scruffy and ill-designed. Like many public parks in Japan, it is strewn with rubbish, owing to a perplexing scarcity of garbage bins. Apparently one is expected to carry one's garbage home, a custom that extends to dog excreta, so that the public spaces of Japan are heavily populated by men and women walking around with plastic bags containing their pets' poo. It is not uncommon to see owners solicitously wiping their dogs' arses, then peering up under the tail just to check that they've got the lot. Consequently there are more embarrassed dogs in Japan than in any other country of the world.

But back to Ueno Park. Its self-consciously 'imposing' modern buildings are undistinguished at best, and a few of the traditional structures, notably the mid-seventeenth-century

Toshugu shrine to the Tokugawa Ieyasu, are in a scandalous state of disrepair. I had arrived in Japan at an opportune time, the beginning of the cherry-blossom viewing season. Admiring the new season's blossom is one of Japan's great spectator sports. *Hanami* parties—drinking and eating under the cherry trees—arouse the same fervour as Australian football finals, and Ueno Park is the MCG of *hanami* locations. Several parties were in full swing that morning. But to my eyes even the *hanami* in Ueno Park seemed a bit muted; they were certainly more inhibited and less joyful than in other parks that I later visited, such as Inokashira Park, way out west near Kichijoji. Perhaps it was the presence of the numerous drunks, down-and-outers and out-and-out weirdos who wander around the area, though they are harmless enough; perhaps it was the community of homeless men flush by the National Museum. Whatever, I found Ueno Park to be an alienating place.

Or perhaps the park's bloody history had put me in mind of war, and thoughts of war are not conducive to an ecstatic participation in the joys of natural rebirth. The first thing one sees on entering Ueno Park from the station is a large bronze statue of the famous samurai Saigo Takamori, one of the leaders of the Meiji Restoration. My guidebook informed me that he was revered as Edo's saviour for negotiating with a vassal of the shogunate to secure the bloodless surrender of the city; it told me also that he later turned against the government he had helped to create and committed *seppuku* in battle. The story behind the statue's subject didn't make much sense to me. Too inscrutably Japanese. That the statue depicts the stocky, neighbourly-looking samurai out walking his dog only made it more difficult to understand.

But it is not only over-sensitive, gormless first-time foreign visitors like me who have found Ueno Park disturbing.

4 THE BIG SMOKE

The Battle of Ueno was the first disturbance of the peace of Edo for three hundred years. A *haiku* by Tosai Torigoe (1803–90) suggests how much that event, then still fresh in the memory, impinges on the serenity of the natural scene:

> I will shut my ears
> And, thinking only of blossoms,
> Enjoy my nap.

'On Fleeing the Battlefield at Ueno', a *haiku* by Eiki Hozumi written around the same time as Torigoe's, evokes the irrepressibility of the war experience, the way it lingers and intrudes even when you think you have transcended it. The *haiku* depends for its power on the nightingale's legendary association with the coughing of blood:

> Rain washes away
> The blood: just at that moment
> A nightingale sings.[6]

I walked out and away from the gloomy trees, the monuments and littered (but faeces-free) pathways, dashed across a horrendously busy thoroughfare, negotiated the seething masses surging in and out of Ueno station and entered the boisterous Ameyoko-cho. I found this pulsating labyrinth enlivening after the depressing park. Ameyoko had begun its life as a black market in the desperate days after the war, when today's prosperous metropolis was a smoking ruin, with thousands upon thousands of its inhabitants starving. War, war, war. Earthquakes, fires, floods. And they reckon they breed them tough in the Australian bush! The people of Tokyo have been through a lot; they have to put up with a lot still. It's not a place for the faint-hearted. Think of them, man, woman and child, not as city folk but as warriors, urban warriors.

⌘⌘⌘

Tokyo is big, appallingly big, spreading unstoppably across the Kanto Plain, the largest level area in Japan. And that is not the whole of it. By turns appalled and delighted by the city's vastness, Clive James observed that 'Tokyo' as a discrete urban entity does not really exist, being 'just a name for one of the more drastically overpopulated districts in a single, enormous city that goes on and on for hundreds of miles'.[7] Think of London and multiply by as many times you like, I wrote to an English friend back in Australia, trying to impress him with my mastery of the most enormous conglomeration of concrete and steel on the planet. How did it get so bloody big?

The economic, political and geographical reasons for the city's immense growth are evident enough, and of less interest anyway than the psychological impact of living and working in a conurbation with a population about one-and-a-half times that of Australia. The fires that have periodically destroyed Tokyo have had much to do with the evolution of its physical and psychological configuration. The combustibility of Edo-era housing is legendary. It is a measure of the Shogun city's quirky perversity that its people were proud of their city's fires, calling them *Edo no hana*, the 'flowers of Edo'. Fires occurred so regularly that it was said no house in the *shitamachi* could expect to last more than two decades, though in fact many did. You can still see them here and there, survivors not only of the nineteenth-century fires but of the 1923 Kanto earthquake and

4 THE BIG SMOKE

the tremendous conflagration that ensued, as well as the ruthless American bombing in 1944 and 1945.

Pragmatic *Eddoko* thought the periodic destruction did the city good, because it compelled a spot of urgently required urban renewal. Just as bushfires reinvigorate the Australian countryside, so the fires of Tokyo have reinvigorated the city. From the fire of 1872 the new Ginza emerged. Seidensticker reports that after World War II some residents of the few untouched pockets of the Low City were heard complaining that they wished they had been bombed (and had lived to tell the tale, presumably) so as to get better, more modern housing.[8]

Complaints about Tokyo's size are more common among visitors than the permanent residents themselves, who have to negotiate its vast, crowded expanses year in and year out. In a short story published in the 1950s, 'House Girl', Hal Porter used the 'flowers of Edo' metaphor to bemoan the ugliness that has attended the city's unstoppable growth. It spreads, he wrote:

> like a weed far and flat on the plain as though the fire-sprung pods had sprayed seeds farther and farther afield, as though earthquake and typhoon had scattered the multiplying tiled huts farther yet, as though cloudburst Allied bombs had splashed seeds to the very limit to infest the millet and sweet-potato fields with ramshackle factories, slums and suburban labyrinths.[9]

And 'House Girl' was written well over forty years ago, when Tokyo was just a dwarf next to the monster of today!

I did not need to go to the top of the Tokyo Tower, the city's answer to the Eiffel Tower (only taller, of course), to appreciate the city's immensity, because I traversed a good deal of it most days of the week. Chiba Prefecture was once known as 'Edo's Kitchen', the capital's food bowl. Large parts of it remain rural. A short bicycle ride along the tidal river behind our apartment block in Kemigawa would take me beyond the subdivisions and supermarkets and into a landscape of rice paddies and market gardens. While I was on the train I would sometimes concentrate on this sylvan scene (relatively sylvan: even the Chiba backblocks were chokingly criss-crossed with power lines) to offset the sight of the tawdry housing interspersed with industrial development that forms a dispiriting umbilicus between Chiba City and Tokyo. From the elevated Chuo line, my main means of transport in and out of the Big Smoke, I had a perfect view of this cancerous suburban horror and of the haze of pollution that hung malignantly over it. It was after I returned to Australia that I read Isabella L. Bird's account of Tokyo in the late 1870s, which is even more relevant today:

> Masses of greenery, lined or patched with grey, and an absence of beginning or end, look suburban rather than metropolitan. Far away in the distance are other grey patches; you are told that they are still Tokiyo [sic] and you ask no more. It is a city of 'magnificent distances' without magnificence.[10]

The ugliness of Tokyo is self-evident. Or is it? I admired the capacity of long-term residents such as Bill and Ohara to see through the ugliness. The Tokyoite tolerates the horrendous cityscape, ignores the grubby concrete, the hideous overhead cables and architectural eyesores too numerous to mention, doesn't hear the cacophony, doesn't smell the smells or seem to mind inhaling smoke sometimes so thick you could roll it into a carpet, and good-humouredly puts up with the human crush. This, of course, is a psychology of survival. But it is more than that. The Tokyoite knows he or she is living in an important place, somewhere formidable, a place for which the very word 'city' might have been invented. There is comfort in the crowd of commuters and shoppers, comfort too in the conviction of participating in such a tremendous communal activity. And it can even be an attractive city, especially at night when all the blemishes are hidden and the seductions of the city's opulent night life dazzle and titillate. Untidy and unattractive at an elevated distance, the city takes on different and more beguiling aspects up close, at street level. The shapes form, the local characteristics of distinctive neighbourhoods can be discerned, the living city reveals itself.

Nevertheless, it is true that Tokyo is a city that frustrates touristic expectations. It is has a long and venerable history by comparison with Australian cities, but so much of it has been destroyed that Sydney and Melbourne—and tiny Hobart, come to think of it—have more of the 'old' public buildings that tourists admire. Apparently so young and impermanent, it seems rootless to some observers, and in a way not even particularly Japanese. Sidney and Beatrice Webb felt they had lost 'all sense of old Japan' in Tokyo—and they were there in 1911, before the earthquake of 1923, the wartime destruction and the excesses of the post-war construction industry. In a similar vein the Australian travel writer C. H. Bertie, visiting in the 1930s, remarked that 'from the viewpoint of the sentimental tourist' Tokyo is 'an uninteresting city . . . it is not "Japanesey"'.[11]

Tokyo is a city of sites rather than sights, of atmospheres rather than aesthetics. This too bothers 'sentimental tourists' more than it does most residents. In an essay on Seidensticker, Ian Buruma comments that the city's 'unhinging pace of change' elicits 'a poignant sense of what has been lost', for it is 'only memories that lend a sense of continuity'.[12] Seidensticker's writing, he argues, is 'steeped in nostalgia'. I think Buruma overestimates the elegiac aspect of Seidensticker's portrait of the city, which is concerned less with physical appearance than with ambience. With the kind of cock-of-the-walk contempt for provincial pleasantness that New Yorkers evince in boasting of the Big Apple, Seidensticker (writing in 1957) offers this celebration of the city:

> Its charm is not on the gray, formless surface. 'Where then is the charm?' asks the newcomer. Well, he must walk the streets until he sees for himself. The roar about him is not just the roar of trains and taxicabs. It is also the roar of sinews and blood. A good Buddhist, in the days when the species survived, might have described Tokyo as smelling of meat; Walt Whitman might have said that it had the fine, clean smell of armpits. Tokyo is a stewing mass of people, and there are no beautiful, dead surfaces to distract one from the vitality once it is known.[13]

The city's 'vitality', in other words, is that of a pulsating organism rather than that of a tourist brochure. This is probably why old Tokyo hands tend to be consistently and unequivocally disdainful of Kyoto. Bill, for instance. His face would become contorted with irritation at the very mention of the place, and he'd let fly a torrent of abuse, the substance of which is that Kyoto is a dull, lifeless dump. 'Never be in Kyoto when the sun goes down', was one of his many memorable pieces of traveller's advice. When in the Kansai region, he preferred to stay in Osaka, a satyr of a city. I suspect that Bill, like many Tokyoites, had an inferiority complex about Kyoto, knowing that the former capital is still the cultural capital of the country, its historical heartland. What he said about Kyoto implied an attitude toward Tokyo similar to Seidensticker's—the 'charm' of Tokyo is revealed not to the passive tourist, but to the urban adventurer. Not to discover it is a kind of personal failure, a failure of the senses and of the imagination.

In thinking this over I am reminded of David Malouf's novel *Johnno*, in which the narrator laments growing up in Brisbane, a place that was 'too mediocre even to be a province of hell'.[14] (Actually the problem lies with the narrator, not Brisbane.) It would be difficult if not impossible to conceive of Tokyo as being 'mediocre'. Nevertheless, while it is all very well for old Tokyo hands to deride the qualms of new-chums, the fact remains that it is a hard city to show visitors, who tend to be overwhelmed by the logistics of getting around it and underwhelmed by what is on offer when they do emerge, battered and hyperventilating, from its transportation system.

I used to worry about how our visitors would respond to the city. One occasion sticks particularly in my mind. A very old and good friend, Rene, a refugee from Sydney who had chosen to live in bucolic splendour in the hinterland of the north coast of New South Wales, paid us a brief visit during August, high summer, when Tokyo turns into a seething cauldron. He arrived tired, like most Australian travellers to Tokyo, on the overnight Qantas flight from Sydney. On his first afternoon I thought we might venture into Ginza, a journey of forty minutes or so (and two trains only), just to ease him into the place.

'There's a great restaurant just near the Ginza Crossing, in the centre of town,' I said encouragingly. Rene survived the subway journey in, though he noted acidly that the air conditioning in the carriages was so effective that he should have brought an overcoat. A dedicated smoker fed up with the disapproval with which his ilk is treated in Australia, he remarked—after we walked out of the subterranean central city into the Ginza glare—that smoking seemed to be mandatory in Tokyo. As we waited at the traffic lights at the crossing, everybody seemed to be puffing away. When I told him that I'd even seen joggers smoking in Japan, he started muttering about migrating.

We arrived at the restaurant, an up-market establishment in a decidedly up-market part of town, helped ourselves to the splendid buffet and took our seats at a table by the window, eight floors up from Chuo Dori, Tokyo's main commercial thoroughfare. We starting eating, and then I noted that Rene, who was sitting opposite me, was staring in amazement at a spot somewhere up over my left shoulder.

'Crikey, that's a rat! A fucking *rat*!' he exclaimed. I quickly turned around, and there it was, a plump, grey-brown rat, abseiling down the window, *inside* the restaurant! I don't think Rene's appetite for Tokyo ever recovered. It was with some mutual relief that after a couple of days we put him on a train to—where else?—Kyoto.

The Edo-era bravado, the cockiness that laughs at vicissitude and mocks misfortune, can still be discerned in the fatalism of the contemporary Tokyo dweller as he or she ponders the earthquake that is long overdue. It probably did not make much sense to build up Tokyo on a great area of loosely consolidated landfill, given the city's proximity to the most violent lines of contact of the region's three tectonic plates. It is reckoned that when the Big One hits much of the terrain on which the city is built will turn into a kind of McDonald's thickshake. Indeed there often seems to be madness in Japanese methods. Myself, I never did manage to get used to the seismic shudders that are as much a constant of life in Tokyo as showers of rain in Melbourne.

I even used to dream about them. One of the more vivid of these dreams caused me to spring bolt upright from my futon, my heart pounding, the sweat rising on my forehead. I related this experience to Ohara the next day. 'That was no dream,' he told me: there *had* been a severe jolt the previous night. Hardened Tokyoites like Ohara regard earthquakes as a part of life, and are somewhat less terrified by the tremors than amused by the foreigner's fear of them. In January 1998 the *New Scientist* published an article entitled 'Any Day Now' about the increase in geological activity along one of Japan's most dangerous fault lines, not that far west of Tokyo. Expert seismologists predicted an impending earthquake in the region with a magnitude of 8.1, much more powerful than the devastating 1995 Kobe quake.[15] I knew about the article because Ohara had photocopied it for me and attached it to the door of my office with the legend: 'GET OUT—WHILE YOU CAN'.

Yet the one serious trembler I experienced in Tokyo had a positive effect on my outlook. It happened one day while I was vacuuming the flat in Kemigawa. Some domestic drama! Over the roar of the appliance I discerned the sounds of things falling. Then I noticed things on the wall swaying and heard a general gnashing and grinding and noticed the thud, thud, thud of my heart pumping, and pumping hard. The noise seemed to continue for some time. I headed for a door frame and noticed it sway left to right, right to left. I heard the sound of a car speeding down the road outside. That made me feel better.

And then the movement stopped. I ventured outside, where little knots of housewives from the apartment block had gathered to discuss the quake, in much the same way that Melbourne work-mates discuss the sports results on Monday mornings. A few of the women laughingly acknowledged my shaken appearance. My next-door neighbour Yuki told me that the TV had already announced that the trembler had registered 4 on the Japanese scale of 0 to 7 (the Japanese rate their earthquakes on their own scale, ignoring the Richter). A pretty decent shake, but nothing startling. Yuki then handed me a bottle of smoked oysters as a gift, as if to apologise for being the cause if my discomposure. It was a lovely gesture, if perhaps unwise, gastrically speaking, in the circumstances. I was hardly going to run inside to wolf down oysters to settle my nerves. Later Deborah telephoned from the city, where she had been attending a symposium at the Hongo campus of Todai. She reported that, when the lecture room started to shake, the professor convening the session had laconically quipped, 'That's an earthquake. We'd better open the windows,' and the paper-giver had then continued uninterrupted.

That trembler had been no big deal. But I thought it was: I had survived my first fair dinkum Tokyo earthquake. I could now smile condescendingly at my visitors from Down Under, who constantly complained that the terrain felt as if it was moving under them. Quite likely it was, though the cause of the trembling was probably the raging subterranean transport system and its vast complex of underground shops and services rather than anything purely seismic. In Tokyo there is always something happening underneath the surface.

⌘⌘⌘

4 THE BIG SMOKE

SCENES FROM THE TOKYO UNDERGROUND
The Ginza line, travelling from Nihombashi to Shibuya Mid-morning, 9 July 1996

I. Middle-aged man holds a disgustingly soiled but beautifully folded handkerchief over his nose for the entire twenty-minute journey, while furtively glancing—his eyes darting above the cloth like a Muslim woman's above her yashmak—at the muscled and tanned legs of the sailor-suited schoolgirl sitting beside me. Apparently oblivious to his attentions, the girl is talking on her mobile telephone.

II. Another middle-aged man with his right wrist and hand mysteriously bandaged giggles over his *manga* magazine while also casting furtive glances in the direction of the schoolgirl.

III. Having abruptly concluded her call, the schoolgirl resumes what looks (I am furtively looking over her shoulder) like her English homework. The task appears to be a meaningless but possibly pertinent question-and-answer exercise, one question of which has the words 'I have: (a) a fever (b) a headache, and (3) a very bad cold', attached to a childish drawing of someone sneezing.

When aficionados of Tokyo talk about how 'infectious' the city is, believe them.

⌘⌘⌘

It is no coincidence that perhaps the most famous sentences in modern Japanese fiction, those that open Yasunari Kawabata's novel *Snow Country* (1956), concern train travel. In the Seidensticker translation, this is how it begins: 'The train came out of the long tunnel. The earth lay white under the night sky. The train pulled up at a signal stop.' Continuing this eccentric but fruitful line of critical inquiry, it must be significant that Tanizaki's *The Makioka Sisters* (1957), the much-loved epic story of a great but declining Osaka family on the eve of World War II, finally ends on a train to Tokyo. This is the marvellously bathetic last sentence, again as translated by Seidensticker: 'Yukiko's diarrhoea persisted through the twenty-sixth, and was a problem on the train to Tokyo'.[16] With what empathy must millions of Japanese readers put down *The Makioka Sisters*! Forget the shrines and temples of Kyoto and Nara, the ikebana, sushi and sumo stuff. Forget even the horribly named SMAP, the multi-media singing-and-dancing-and-selling male ensemble who are the most worshipped idols of an outrageously fecund pop-music scene, the focus of many cultural critics who shoot the rapids of Japanese popular culture to come up with their own version of 'the real Japan'. No, 'the real Japan'—for what writer about the country can resist that phrase?—is to be found in railway stations and on trains. That is the great Japanese common ground, the true communal experience.

    I spent a great deal of my two years in Tokyo on trains. My quickest route to Komaba from Kemigawa took about seventy minutes all up and involved four separate trains, two above ground and a couple in the subway. That was eight trips there and back, plus a few others if I went out somewhere to eat or drink in the evening, as I often did. Tokyoites rarely go home first after work if they have an appointment that evening:

4 THE BIG SMOKE

thus one is liable to see people staggering into movies and concerts bearing several bags of shopping.

To live in Tokyo is to live the life of an urban nomad, a nomad borne on steel wheels. The greatest landmark in Tokyo is not a building. It is certainly not the Imperial Palace, which lies more or less at the geographical centre of the city but which cannot be seen behind its forbidding moated walls and its dense canopy of foliage. Many observers, not least Roland Barthes in *Empire of Signs* (1970), have pondered the cultural implications of this 'central emptiness', around which the traffic of the nation's capital perpetually circles and detours.[17] Nor is the city's major landmark the Tokyo Tower, which is just a vulgar copy of the Eiffel. It is not the stately Meiji Shrine tucked away in Yoyogi Park, nor is it the plebeian Senso-ji Temple in Asakusa, with its tawdry pleasure grounds and teeming approach lined with tourist shops. It is not the department stores in Ginza—Wako with its famous clock tower or, across the street, the imperious Mitsukoshi; and it is not the dramatic shell-like twin structures Tange Kenzo designed for the Yoyogi National Stadium, which are impressive enough but remind you how fantastic the Sydney Opera House is. It isn't the hubristic, Kenzo-designed cluster of skyscrapers in Tokyo's 'Manhattan', Nishi-Shinjuku, nor any of the other post-modern fantasies and nightmares that dot the demented Tokyo cityscape—Love Hotels designed in the style of mad Ludwig's castle or giant mechanical crabs that mince their pincers over the doorways of seafood restaurants. It is not even Philippe Starck's 'La Flamme d'Or', the Asahi Breweries building on the bank of the Sumida across the river from Asakusa, which the locals have irreverently nicknamed the 'Golden Poo Poo' because of the huge, golden turd-like structure propped on its roof.

LEGLESS IN GINZA

No, Tokyo's true emblem is a railway line, the aboveground Yamanote line, which traces a gigantic loop around the central city. Every three minutes a long, green-striped, caterpillar-like train stops at one of the twenty-nine Yamanote stations, the entire trip taking a tick over an hour. Many Tokyoites are so familiar with the loop that they can recite the twenty-nine stations in the correct order. Advertising brochures often include maps of the line in order to direct customers to the correct location. You must know the Yamanote to negotiate the city. As Roman Cybriwsky writes in his fascinating urban study, this is 'a matter of fundamental literacy about Tokyo'.[18]

To live inside the Yamanote circle is to live at the city's epicentre. I did not. So I had plenty of time to become familiar with large parts of the Tokyo transport labyrinth, not merely the Yamanote. Its cartography is imprinted on my memory, the very station names still signifiers of ennui and repulsion, possibility and romance. There were the station stops I particularly hated, either because of the ugliness of the name (Moto-yawata, Gyotoku), or because they seemed like nothing places and I resented the wait as I glanced at them out the train window, impatient to get moving, to reach wherever I was going.

And then there were the names I loved, just for their sound, their romantic resonance—Ginza or Sendagaya or Monzen-nakacho. Knowing the translation could make a difference. For instance, I especially liked Toranomon, by the Imperial Palace. Toranomon: the 'Tiger's Gate'. I also relished the sound of Ochanomizu, a station quite near the Hongo campus of Tokyo University. Deborah, who was studying at that campus, would often spend time propped at the counter of a revolving sushi bar near by, or drinking coffee in one of the snug little cafés once favoured by Mishima and other luminaries. 'Ocha-no-mizu': green tea's water. Apparently it was named after a special spring from which the water for the Shogun's tea was drawn. But it wasn't really that pleasant cultural information that moved me. I just thought that 'Ochanomizu' sounded like a great name for a racehorse: I could hear the hysterical, strangulated voice of an American race-caller announcing it flashing home down the outside . . . 'And it's O-CHAnoMIZOOOOOOOOOO!'

To the non-Japanese speaker some Tokyo place-names contain a hidden pathos. Not far from Ochanomizu is Akihabara, a place to avoid. This is the city's discount electrical and electronic centre, all blinking neon, flashing, buzzing gadgetry, a dirty, scungy precinct daily choked by crowds of bargain-hunters, many of them penurious foreigners, bullocking their way through the crush to buy 'cheap' goods—video players, rice cookers, electronic bidets—they probably do not really need. Even the smog seemed worse in Akihabara than Ochanomizu, though it was just a kilometre or two away in the Tokyo haze. This is contemporary urban Japan at its worst. Such a diabolical place with such a mellifluous name! So redolent is 'Akihabara' of some enticing Middle Eastern *kasbah* that I sometimes felt tempted to hop off the train as it passed through there, until images of the hellish reality of the place slapped me in the face. But in fact the meaning of the word is even more bathetic, and sadly illustrative of what has become of Japan. Akihabara: the 'field of autumn leaves'. . . .

⌘⌘⌘

> The apparition of these faces in the crowd;
> Petals on a wet, black bough.

Could Ezra Pound's famous *haiku* 'In a Station of the Metro' (Paris circa 1916) be written about the Tokyo subway at the end of the twentieth century? Well, no. The delicate 'Japaneseness' of Pound's natural image hardly seems applicable to the subway's muscular push-and-shove, its bump-and-grind, the sheer mechanical rough-and-tumble of it. It is often remarked how the Japanese lose their famous manners and their precious decorousness when they step—or, in Tokyo, barge—into trains. As Arthur Koestler observed on his visit to the city, this daily ritual transforms Madame Butterfly into a hulking sumo wrestler.[19] But I beg to differ. The wonder is that so many millions can cram into a system with so little incident. How would Australians get on in such a situation, I wonder?

The Tokyo transport system is a monument to the Japanese group ethic. People are expected to behave well and to follow the rules for the sake of everybody. Well, not quite everybody. The strength of the Japanese emphasis on the collective mass means that those who deviate from the group are discouraged. Not necessarily behavioural deviation, either. The system's facilities for movement-impaired people or those with other physical disabilities (blindness, for example) are poor, even disgraceful—as in other kinds of public facilities all over Japan. Travelling around the city, if not quite a survival of the fittest, is hard enough for the able-bodied. For the disabled it must be a nightmare.

Visitors often wonder why (and how) so many people go to sleep on Tokyo trains, even on short journeys. Many inventive theories are put forward to explain this phenomenon, but the simplest explanation is that the passengers are tired.

4 THE BIG SMOKE

Trains are places to catch up on some rest. So much time is spent on them, and one is unlikely to get robbed. What is amazing is that many people have perfected the art of falling completely to sleep, only to wake up at precisely the right moment to get off the train at the desired destination: an art as truly Japanese as the tea ceremony.

Along with having survived a decent earthquake, I regarded my ability to nod off on trains as a sign that I had become habituated to life in Tokyo. Yet I never lapsed into unconsciousness for long, because I feared I would not wake up on cue. With good reason. One night I went to sleep on one of the last trains to the Chiba area after dining in the city, only to awake at the end of the line. I was miles from home in a place I didn't know. It was well after midnight, and there was no train back. Furious with myself, I left the station, thinking I'd have to stay in a hotel for the night—most Tokyo stations have hotels near by for just this situation. But no hotel was in sight, not even one of the dubious 'snack bars' that cater to carousing salarymen. There was nothing at all, just a bunch of expectant taxis, vultures feeding on the corpses of crippled commuters. Perhaps this is another reason why people in Tokyo carry a lot of cash around—some urban emergency or other is always lurking just around the corner.

Another explanation for the mass snoozing on Tokyo trains offers itself. Are the passengers sleeping or are they really meditating? It is obvious to me why Zen Buddhism took off in such a big way in Japan: the proselytising monks who introduced it from China in the twelfth and thirteenth centuries knew it would come in handy at the end of the millennium. The deep meditation practised in Zen is a superb antidote to the horrors of the crowded subway, a way of coping, a method of pretending that it isn't happening. The problem with this theory is that Zen emphasises prolonged meditative sitting, called *zazen*, or 'seated Zen', and one is lucky to be able to sit down on most Tokyo trains during peak periods. (These are so numerous as to make up virtually the whole day: little Kemigawa station teemed like Flinders Street at midnight on any weekday.) It felt like winning the lottery if you managed to grab a seat early on your trip. Not practised in the arts and disciplines of Zen, of either the horizontal or vertical kind, I attempted to transcend the ordeal by conjuring up a soothing vision of an Australian beach, a Swiss meadow or a Norwegian fiord, augmenting these images by humming a few lines of 'Easy Living':

> Easy livin' . . .
> That's the way you need to go
> Just take it easy, just take it slow . . .

The spectacle of people being poked and prodded into crammed carriages by station attendants, as if they are going for an entry in the *Guinness Book of Records*, is one of the world's more bizarre urban sights. I witnessed it most workday mornings when I waited on the Ginza line at Nihombashi, a popular transit intersection in the city, for my connection to Shibuya. I could never understand why people rushed to enter a packed compartment when another train was guaranteed to come along in a couple of minutes. I would stand at the head of the queue on the platform and look at these desperadoes with wonder, as their contorted faces—pressed flush against the glass on the carriage doors—moved off into the blackness of the tunnel. And I would think of the horribly evocative colloquial term for these crowded carriages: 'standing coffins'.

4 THE BIG SMOKE

Hal Porter's description of rush-hour train travel in Tokyo bears repeating, not so much because it is typical of the bile-driven exaggeration that characterises his disenchantment with modern Japan, but because it carries enough truth to reopen the wounds of the most hardened veterans of the system:

> Apart from the bruises so often seen on limbs, the most common aftermaths of rush-hour travel are dislocated shoulders, fractured ribs, badly crushed toes, faintings, heart failure and, for babies carried piggy-back, death by suffocation. The more serious accidents occur when, like chessmen toppling over . . . whole welded-together blocks of passengers fall to the floor, and are unable to stand again until the next station is reached. Often people are severely gashed by the jagged remains of windows shattered under pressure. Among the satchels, handbags, umbrellas and parcels littering the carriage after every trip there are also a number of shoes the escapees have been unable to retrieve—straw sandals are provided at stations to be lent to those who limp from the train shoeless, or wearing one shoe only.[20]

The overcrowding was truly horrible some early mornings. A good day was when I could manage to see enough of my *Japan Times* to get through the front page. Often all I could get was a glimpse of the photograph of some disgraced financier or bureaucrat or other being led away to prosecution.

It wasn't only the crush that appalled. The promiscuity of rush-hour life, in which one often found oneself physically entangled with three people at once, brought other challenges. Silently suffering the smells of strangers was one. The stink of last night's grog and this morning's cigarettes, a burped breakfast of fish-and-seaweed and the effluvium of post-breakfast farts made the atmosphere more akin to that of a cloaca than a carriage. People wheezed, coughed, perspired. A zillion germs bred. The nervous tension was almost palpable. No escape, no escape, NO ESCAPE!

Hangovers, that persistent feature of Tokyo living, were a nightmare under such conditions. No doubt my fellow male passengers could attest to this, as a good many of them must have been suffering from the bibulous extravagance of the night before. I experienced the peak-hour hangover hell very early in the piece. Around 10 p.m. on my first night in the Kemigawa flat, as I was contemplating the unappealing prospect of assuming a prone position on the tatami in the 'Japanese room', I heard a knock on the door. It was Bill, who'd given me lunch that first day in Kewigawa but felt unreasonably guilty that I might be lonely. I noticed with alarm that he was bearing a large bottle of vodka. It was not going to be the perfect preparation for the next morning, my initial working day at Todai, when all the newcomers to the faculty were to be formally introduced to the Dean. But I was no piker, and we knocked the bottle off in an hour or two. By the time I emerged from the 'standing coffin' at Komaba next morning—it was lucky that I had been wedged among so much flesh, as otherwise I would have simply sunk to the floor—I was a quivering, gibbering wreck. Wobbly and nauseous, I survived the formal introductions, but only just. And swore 'never again!'

⌘⌘⌘

4 THE BIG SMOKE

The international image of the Tokyo salaryman is not good. I am not out to redeem it here. I have already mentioned the technicolour 'pavement pizzas', which could make negotiating station exits and entrances—favoured places for their deposition—a perilous business. Perhaps Japanese men really cannot hold their drink; they certainly do throw up a lot. Or maybe it is because there are so many drinkers concentrated into one place. I found their habit of spitting equally unsavoury. On hot days I would sometimes take a drink from the drinking fountains located on the railway platforms, but I halted the practice after noticing that male commuters were in the habit of using this facility to perform various gruesome expectoratory rituals. The bolus of phlegm expelled from nicotine-choked lungs is another of those Tokyo sights that are difficult to advertise in the tourist guidebook.

Notoriously, Japanese men also feel free to urinate in the open. This applies more to older men, brought up in an age more tolerant of the public piss, but the contemporary salaryman with a bladder full of Sapporo also sees no reason not to turn the world into a toilet. In Shibuya station one evening peak hour I walked past a well-dressed but pathetically inebriated man happily taking a leak in full view of thousands, the trousers of his expensive suit down around his ankles, fringed by a pair of repulsively stained undershorts. I wondered then and at other times at the arrogance of Japanese men, some of whom think that they can get away with behaving like pigs, and at the compliance of women who put up with it.

A figure of fun in his own country and mocked to the hilt elsewhere, the Tokyo salaryman is indeed easy to despise. But you have to pity him too. Legless in Ginza (or Shimbashi, or Akasaka, or a hundred other night places in the city), he somehow finds his way home somewhere in the mighty Kanto conurbation, only to drag himself on to the train the next day, day after day, year after gruelling year. A contemporary Sisyphus, he is briefcased, hidebound, on the treadmill for the term of his natural life. Virtually his whole existence revolves around the workplace: he fathers children he rarely sees. You'd rather be his missus, wouldn't you? At least she gets to have a life. Maybe that is why she puts up with her husband's excesses. Ian Buruma remarks that marriage for Japanese women is commonly known as 'the graveyard of life', because it spells the end of a career and the beginning of economic dependence.[21] But to me the women, at least those whose children had started school or had grown up, seemed vastly happier and more contented than their male counterparts. They get to control the family purse strings; they have some time on their hands, laughing and lunching together, shopping, going to theatres, exhibitions, pursuing interests. No wonder so many of them confess that they dislike weekends because their husbands are home to cruel their pitch.

But it is curious that a country as resourceful and resource-obsessed as Japan makes so little use of its greatest resource—its women. This is changing slowly. More and more women are entering the workforce, though their access to positions of seniority is pretty pitiful, even by comparison with Australia. In any case, wherever they are, at home or at work, Japanese women have to put up with a fair bit from their men. No wonder they cut loose when they gather together by themselves. At home they do virtually all the housework, regardless of whether or not they are in paid employment. They mother their men when they stagger in from work, running them a hot bath, shoving food down their throats, combing what's left of their hair. In the workplace itself, sexual

4 THE BIG SMOKE

harassment and gender discrimination are rampant. It is on the trains, however, that male indulgences are perhaps most offensively evident. Brazenly the men sit reading their inane *manga*, full of stylised violent sexuality, or insouciantly perusing the soft-porn-riddled popular press, oblivious to the offence caused to the women everywhere around.

A more immediate male threat to women lurks on the trains, especially in crowded, humid compartments, when thigh is wedged against thigh, pelvis against pelvis, and hands are wedged against foreign bodies. Hands and fingers that are liberated tentatively, speculatively, obtrusively . . . It is a measure of the scant inroads made by feminism in Japan that the notorious gropers, or *chikan*, who flourish in the Tokyo transport incubator are a source of titillation in the popular media. After the prince of molesters, Samu Yamamoto, published his *Chikan Nikki* ('Diary of a Chikan'), he became an instant celebrity. The media fawned over him, while feigning disapproval of the compulsion that made him famous. So concerned was the press about the practice that it encouraged him to give public *chikan* demonstrations.

Press reportage of sexual assault in Japan is similarly pusillanimous. Rape—which is more common than generally recognised, however safe women may feel in the nation's capital—tends to be under-reported, or cited by the use of the euphemistic Japanese word *boko*, a general word for assault. Similarly the action that we understand to mean 'sexual molestation' is commonly described by the term *itazura*, meaning 'mischief'. The specific Japanese terms for rape (*gokan*) and gang rape *(rinkan)* are rarely used by the media, even by the salacious tabloids or sex-obsessed sports newspapers. In early 1998, when it was revealed that members of a university rugby team had been arrested for gang-raping a woman at a karaoke club, these publications headlined the story with the English word 'rape', written in the *katakana* characters used to transcribe foreign words.[22]

How could such a dreadful event be described in Japanese terms? Only the foreign concept of 'rape' would do, though that doesn't stop advertisements for so-called 'telephone clubs' from using the word to tease and tempt. The phone clubs are basically fronts for prostitution, often involving teenage schoolgirls who use the money they receive from middle-aged men in return for sex to buy goods such as designer clothes and (unsurprisingly) mobile phones. The Chiba area in particular is a hub of schoolgirl prostitution. In one of the periodic police crackdowns a school principal was arrested for running a 'dating' agency.

It was hard not to know about the presence of the local phone clubs, because our letter-box was constantly full of fliers advertising them, but the Japanese media, including the foreign-language newspapers, seemed loath to canvass the matter. I relied on my mother, concerned for my moral safety, to send me a stack of articles on the issue that appeared in Australian newspapers in the middle of 1996. Paedophilia focused on young girls is everywhere in evidence in the Tokyo streetscape, in large advertising hoardings for bars and peep-shows in shopping precincts, and in and around railway stations, whose vertiginous stairways and escalators appear to have been designed to promote voyeurism, a practice facilitated by the uniforms favoured by many schoolgirls, dinky little miniskirts seductively set off by fluffy white socklets.

Sex with children remains a moral—and, amazingly, in some areas even a legal—conundrum in Japan. Because shame is to be avoided at all costs, little is done about it. The advertisements for the clubs kept appearing in our letter-box long after the scandal involving the Chiba school principal first came to light. They would blow around in the streets and playgrounds near our apartment block, along with discarded pages torn from tossed-out wads of the cheaply produced Japanese pornography readily available from any bookshop or magazine stand in Tokyo. Much of this porn is obsessed with various acts of penetration inflicted on young women, who are usually gagged and bound and clad in school attire. In a preposterous but revealing gesture towards civilised 'good taste', the thrusting male member is customarily blocked out by an elongated strip of silver. I came across one such magazine with the title, in Roman letters, HYPER ABNORMAL FAIRY ANAL FUCK & VIOLATION. Inside was a double-page spread of an anus, photographed close up so that it looked uncannily like the Japanese flag.

It is such a lovely idea, the 'floating world', being derived from Buddhist ideas about worldly impermanence—the 'fleeting' world. During the Edo period it was translated into a fashionable, mannered hedonism, centred on licensed pleasure quarters containing geisha houses, teahouses, bathhouses. But the floating world of today is an unlovely business. It has become the *yakuza*-infested *mizu-shobai*, the 'water trade' of hostess bars, peep shows and live-sex 'pink cabarets', Turkish baths-cum-brothels called 'soaplands', and the *nopan kissa* coffee shop (or *kissaten*), where waitresses clad in skimpy aprons *sans* underwear scurry around on mirrored floors. Most male sexual fantasies are catered to, but for quite a price if the huge sums posted outside the establishments are any guide. In clubs expensively done up as train compartments, for example, aspiring *chikan* can practise on histrionically protesting women. Outside, in the shadows by the Coke machines and accumulated garbage, slot machines dispense the soiled underwear of young women, complete with photographs of the purported wearer so the purchasers can put a face, so to speak, to the bottom. We are a long way from the decorous sensualities of the *ukiyo-e*.

Sordid as they usually are, and flagrantly exploitative of women, Japanese red-light areas are at least safe to enter, as they are often integrated into the general commerce of the district in which they are located. The Kabukicho quarter of eastern Shinjuku, probably the most notorious den of iniquity in Japan, is also an entertainment district where a cross-section of the population, both male and female—friends, families, colleagues, students, tourists—go to eat, drink, see the movies, sing karaoke or play *pachinko* and video games. It was only after some months that I learnt that the Golden Gai area of Kabukicho, where I would often drink with Hinds or Ohara and sometimes take Australian visitors, has a reputation for being hazardous and unwelcoming to interlopers. This surprised me. Frankly, I have felt more threatened in Melbourne's Swanston Street on a Sunday. If a few people look askance at visitors, it is because the bars are so small (often only three or four seats) that locals are unable to take their regular positions if there are newcomers.

Foreigners may drink and dine in Kabukicho, but seem to be forbidden from taking a dip into the water trade. Most of the establishments belonging to the *mizu shobai* are off limits to *gaijin*, and many have the words 'Japanese Only' emblazoned over their entrances. I once saw a doorway where an outraged visitor had responded to this interdiction by scrawling the rejoinder 'RACIST CUNTS'. The huge *gaijin* community in Tokyo must get by as best it can. The city is restless with sex, with the libido and loneliness of great tribes of young, unattached foreigners, particularly male teachers of English who spend every free waking hour in a never-ending quest to lure some comely Japanese girl (or boy) to a love hotel. The 'Personal' columns in publications such as *Tokyo Classifieds* or the *Tokyo Journal* are both an entertainment and an education:

> **CYPRUS MAN**—26, seeks sincere and kink-hearted [sic], fat Japanese woman.
>
> **BE MY VALENTINE!** Good looking American, sinewy-to-muscular, sex-positive, experienced & affectionate, top or ambipositional, seeks love-mate.
>
> **MY WOMAN FROM TOKYO** is still out there. Deep Purple fan seeks his special pretty & sexy girl. If you're 'made in Japan' and want to meet a handsome, white, tall, blond and long-haired European guy, I'm your man.
>
> **BLACK HANDSOME GUY**—27, seeks beautiful, shy ladies. Call Hammer.
>
> **DIVORCED WHITE MALE**, 34, biker seeks scooter trash. Ride with me on my hog! She should be slim, outgoing & sexy. No corn eaters.

Yet the sexual ambience is not exclusively male-created and male-oriented. In Kabukicho there are women-only bars with male hosts (or women dressed as men) to cater for an increasingly independent and moneyed class of urban Japanese women; apparently there is also a large market for erotic *manga* directed at a female audience, but I never saw any women reading it on the train, perhaps for fear of offending the men's delicate sensibilities.[23]

For a few Japanese women a primary aim in life is to snare a foreign husband. Advertisements for introduction agencies and 'marriage clubs' are plentiful in the *Tokyo Journal*, along with 'Personals' such as that of a 'Japanese woman, 30', wanting to live in 'voluntary simplicity' with a 'Caucasian husband' ('not bald, not short, not fat'); and another from a 'Cute Japanese Female' on the lookout for an American partner because she 'would like to live in Los Angeles one day'. But the idea that all unmarried (or even married) Japanese women are looking for a man, foreign or otherwise, is a bit of a myth. This advertisement appeared in the columns of the *Tokyo Journal* one month:

> **JAPANESE MATURE WOMAN** looking for bright, lovely lesbians. Creative, imaginative, expressive sense preferable, to enjoy beautiful relationship. If you like, with taste of schoolbutter and spicy words.

'With taste of schoolbutter and spicy words.' Of all the enigmatic messages, codes and signs I came across in Japan—and there were many that were incomprehensible—those words remain the most mysterious.

⌘⌘⌘

CONVERSATION IN ROPPONGI
Il Quale Restaurant
Evening, 15 March 1998

The major *gaijin* hang-out in Tokyo, the foreign pub and club centre, is Roppongi. Throbbing Roppongi, the

4 THE BIG SMOKE

focus of the substantial American presence in the city since the Occupation. The Hard Rock Café is there, in an area called 'Little Beverly Hills'; so is Tony Roma's for steak or ribs, Spago's for Californian cuisine, Johnny Rocket's for chilli fries and milk shakes and the Lexington Queen for a shot of Jim Beam or a bottle of Bud. I would sometimes drink in the area at an Irish pub called the Celt, knocking back ruinously expensive pints of Guinness with Michael Hinds and his wife Christine, always leaving around 10 p.m. to make sure I reached Kemigawa before dawn. At that hour, the hour when all sensible Tokyoites start wending their way home, the pavements around Roppongi Crossing by the subway entrances would be a welter of Americans—servicemen from the various defence facilities located near the capital, American bankers and brokers and remittance men, American teachers and scholars and ad men, American hustlers, American good-time girls and boys. American men with a Japanese girl on each arm, laughing that generous American laugh and having *a really good time.*

I had time myself to ponder the fatal attraction of America for Japanese women, an attraction that might be applied at a national level. Just before my departure from Japan, I had an evening meal at an Italian restaurant called Il Quale, located flush by the Roppongi subway. I was ushered to a table by the window, with a good view of the various sexual negotiations taking place on the street outside. In the restaurant, a couple of feet away, was a table where an American of about my middle-age was locking eyes with his companion, a pretty young Japanese women of about twenty-two or thereabouts. Naturally, I listened in.

His name turned out to be Dan; she was Setsuko. Dan was talking about himself. He described his home in Phoenix, Arizona, his travel habits (including how many shirts he usually packed), his 9-year-old son and his painful but inevitable divorce. His wife hadn't understood him, the poor bloke.

The conversation started warming up after they had ordered their meal, a process that involved Dan's making fun of the Japanese waiter's pronunciation of the Italian dishes and ridiculing the menu itself. Emboldened by his companion's admiration for his wit, Dan broached the pleasure of massage, then made mention of something called 'thumb wrestling', apparently an erotic practice that is hot in Phoenix. I was dismayed by Setsuko's willingness to engage in this pastime. They were entwining thumbs when their bruscetta arrived.

Later on, after the pasta, I heard her express a desire to marry him and settle down. I was outraged. I felt like leaning over and telling her not to be stupid, that he wasn't worth it, that he's only spinning you a line, you stupid girl! I was happy to observe that Dan looked slightly taken aback at the mention of marriage—his thoughts hadn't extended beyond the next few hours. Undeterred, however, he regrouped, describing the pleasures that awaited Setsuko in the States. Dan had a penchant for 'road trips'. He just loved taking off in the car, out into the 'wide blue yonder'. This was an avenue of escape, Dan reminded Setsuko, not open to the Japanese.

'Where do you go?' she asked.

'Oh, everywhere—I have friends in Knoxville, in Denver, other places. I go to whatever place interests me at the time, that's the point.'

'But where would *we* go?' Setsuko persisted.

'Sets,' Dan began, 'I've always wanted to go to Los Alamos. Los Alamos? You know, the place where we made the Bomb.'

⌘⌘⌘

'The streets of this city have no names.' Roland Barthes' description of mapless Tokyo is not quite accurate. There are some major named roads, like Chuo Dori and Meiji Dori and Omotesando, but even the broad streets and avenues are much less well known than the districts they traverse. One might speak of Ginza Crossing without thinking, or even knowing, the routes that form the intersection. If one attempted to design a Monopoly board based on Tokyo, it would be based on districts, not streets. The very names of Tokyo districts, though often denoted by the anonymous public spaces of railway stations, carry a resonance, what Barthes called a 'strongly signifying identity'.[24]

Perhaps a Tokyo version of Monopoly does already exist, but in any case it would be not be the first board game based on the city. A game called *Meisho Sugoroku* was popular in the Edo period. Each spot on the board represented a famous place (*meisho*) in old Edo, so that when they travelled around the board the players could feel that they were travelling around the city. Places were represented in a simplified and symbolic form—Nihombashi Bridge in the heart of the old *shitamachi*, for example, with a stylised Mount Fuji in the distance—to capture their singular charm and essence. Edo was thus comprehended as a sequence of strongly identifiable, distinctive sectors, each virtually autonomous, not subordinated to the whole.[25] Along with the *Meisho Sugoroku*, the sense of old Tokyo as a cluster of villages was reinforced by Hiroshige's celebrated series of woodblocks, *One Hundred Famous Spots in Edo*, completed in 1859, with their highly stylised emphasis on various picturesque locales in the *shitamachi*.

When in 1880 Isabella Bird complained of a 'monotony of meanness' characterising Japanese towns,[26] she gave voice to a traveller's lament that is still familiar today, especially about Tokyo. But the city is far from a nondescript labyrinth, far from uniform. Once you enter the labyrinth, it becomes possible to understand it as an agglomeration of distinctive neighbourhoods, all with their own *sakariba*, festive spaces focused on shrines and temples, shopping and entertainment precincts, parks and markets. Travelling around address-less Tokyo, as I found out when I went searching for the Uluru Bar, is like journeying without maps. The city can only be 'known', as Barthes argued, 'by an activity of an ethnographic kind'. Orientation is achieved 'by walking, by sight, by habit, by experience'.[27] The visitor does not 'find' places; he or she makes discoveries, discoveries of an ultimately personal and intimate kind.

That's the theory, anyway. Not seeing myself in this heroic mould and not wishing to hack my way through the thickets of this formidable urban jungle unaccompanied, I took along Sumiko Enbutsu's sure-footed *Old Tokyo: Walks in the*

City of the Shogun (1993). I returned to Ueno often after my first unsettling visit, as it offers a side of the capital that many visitors never see, drawn as they are to the glamour of Ginza or the big commercial centres of Shibuya and Shinjuku in the glitzy, affluent 'high' country to the west of the city. By contrast Ueno may be pretty squalid, but the human landscape is intriguing, a living reflection of the city's history and an index of the social diversity underlying the supposed Japanese 'monoculture'.

On a few occasions I ventured into the notorious San'ya district to the near north-east of Ueno. Straddling Taito and Arakawa Wards not far from the old Meiji pleasure quarter of Yoshiwara, San'ya is Tokyo's greatest slum, its Skid Row, home to the homeless, to dossers and drop-outs, marginalia of the great Japanese success story. It is also one of the city's major *yoseba*, places where day-labourers gather in the early morning in the hope of scrounging some temporary work, usually on construction sites. In *San'ya Blues* (1996), a kind of Tokyo version of George Orwell's *Down and Out in Paris and London*, Edward Fowler describes his experiences living and working with the men of the San'ya during the summer of 1991. It was tough enough then, but during the economic slump of 1997 and 1998 it got much worse, as the job market shrank and employers starting to refuse to hire anyone over the age of fifty. I remember seeing a photograph in the *Japan Times* of a Christian missionary conducting a service to a massed crowd of jobless and homeless on a sidewalk along the stretch of the Sumida that borders the area. Fowler describes San'ya as 'a filthy repository for men whose personal world has gone awry, the result of individual excess or error'. But if the area is a dumping ground for social cast-offs, it is also a ghetto for minorities. Fowler notes that it is home to 'a disproportionate number' of Koreans, Chinese, other Asians, Okinawans, Ainu and other groups 'with long histories of discrimination because of their national, ethnic, or social origins'.[28]

The casual San'ya tourist like me, 'living dangerously' to kill time for an hour or two, would be struggling to take all of this in. But you know you are not in Ginza. True, you see as many helpless pisspots in Ginza, but that is late at night, after work; in the San'ya the drunks are daytime drunks, sick with sake and sadness, with shame and obvious despair. I felt appropriately guilty during my walks through the San'ya, checking out the squalor—especially one time when I noticed that my plastic carry-bag (left over from a trip back to Australia) bore the legend, 'Downtown Duty Free: Where Everything's Waiting For You'.

No guidebook would bother to mention the attractions of San'ya and its environs—the vast, desolate Sumidagawa Freight Station at Minami-Senju, for example, or the huge crematorium away to the north-west at Machiya (where there is a large sewage disposal plant for good measure). It is a region long associated with death. The Tokugawa Shogunate used it as an execution site. By 1868 more than 200 000 criminals and political opponents had been beheaded, crucified or burnt, giving rise to a constellation of crematoria and settlements of *burakumin* or *eta*, the outcast social group that assisted with executions and disposed of the bodies.

Local place-names tell the story. For example the Namidabashi, or 'Bridge of Tears', just to the south of the rail yards, an intersection where it is said that doomed men farewelled their families before being taken to the execution grounds near by. Or the so-called 'Street of Bones' (Kotsu-dori) to the north of the intersection, one long criminals' graveyard. To the east of the San'ya is Jokan-ji, the 'disposal temple', where lie the unmarked graves of some thousands of young prostitutes of the Yoshiwara, now itself a squalid locale of 'soaplands' no different from any other. To complete the picture, the area also housed an abattoir in the Meiji era, and today hosts a thriving leather-working industry, a traditional vocation of the *eta*, whose descendants still populate the area. Just as to utter the word *eta* (signifying 'filth') is akin to breaching a taboo, so many Tokyo people refuse to acknowledge the existence of the San'ya. Even Bill referred to it in hushed tones. It is there all right; but just don't bother to look for it in your Lonely Planet guide. It is not 'cultural' enough for that.

There are obvious differences between a *shitamachi* town like Asakusa and a *yamanote* district like Akasaka, with its elite restaurants and hotels and exclusive geishas (here we are close to the Diet, and politicians have to unwind somehow). But individual areas in the mighty conurbation are themselves full of variation. I am not merely talking of the hybrid port city of Yokohama, with its vivid Chinatown, old foreigners' quarter and shopping districts like the fashionable Motomachi, the setting for some of the action in Mishima's devastating novella *The Sailor Who Fell from Grace with the Sea* (1963). Another example is the transit and commercial centre of Shibuya, from which I would often walk to work. Shibuya is broken into many sub-districts—of retailing, of eating and socialising and carousing—and is much more diversified than the featureless monolith it initially appears to be.

A lot always seemed to be happening in Shibuya, more than one could ever hope, or maybe want, to discover. Uphill from one of the area's major intersections is Dogenzaka, a slope (*zaka*) named after the notorious Dogen, a bandit from the Edo era, when Shibuya was just one of the verdant western approaches to the city. In those days, Dogen would locate his potential victims from a vantage point at the top of a pine tree. What would Dogen see from his eyrie today? Just by the slope is a maze of sleazy alleyways leading up to Love Hotel Hill, a concentration of love hotels built in all manner of architectural styles. Downhill is the cultural and shopping complex of Bunkamura; across the way from Bunkamura is Spain-dori, a pedestrian alleyway with some fake Castilian architecture, one of several laneways in a teeming bazaar where one is liable to be bowled over by noisome gusts of sewer-stink as much as by the swarming shoppers. (On the Tokyo register of bad smells, a long list, I rate the small shopping streets of Shibuya just below Piss Alley, the pungently malodorous laneway that connects eastern with western Shinjuku.) At the bottom of the slope Dogen would be able to make out the tall, cylindrical 109 building, one of several multi-level shopping malls in the area, and more McDonald's than he could poke a stick at.

And he would be able to witness the most enormous concentration of high-school and college students it is possible to imagine, thronging through the streets and alleyways, up and down the escalators of the department stores, in and out of the cinemas and travel agencies and fast-food joints and restaurants and bars and Internet cafés and fashion shops and jewellery markets and electronic emporia and 'music stations'. Insatiable consumers, the affluent progeny of the generation who survived the war and rebuilt the city, these ravening hordes of teenagers are palpable evidence of the importance of the youth market in Japan. Shibuya is their Mecca. Many of them are on pilgrimages from dormitory suburbs and un-distinguished small cities in despised Saitama Prefecture just to the north of Tokyo, though few of them would admit it.

4 THE BIG SMOKE

The young girls—maniacally fashion-conscious, barbecued testimonies to the power of the tanning lamp, teetering devotees of the padded bra and the Himalayan heel—are there to see and be seen, living in hope that they will be spotted by one of the TV crews who haunt the area or maybe selected from the crowd by an astute ad man, a music producer or film-maker.

More likely they will be propositioned by one of the louche hustlers hanging around Hachiko Square, the public plaza by Shibuya station. Tokyo's most famous rendezvous, Hachiko Square is named after an Akita dog who ventured to the station every day for years and years, waiting in vain for a master who had died at work. There's a statue of Hachiko in the square, a Japanese 'dog on the tuckerbox', a few kilometres from the Golden Gai, not Gundagai. They stuffed the real animal and put it into the National Science Museum, just as the Australians did to Phar Lap. The story of Hachiko is a touching story indeed, proof of the premium placed on loyalty and hierarchy in Japan, like the legendary story of the forty-seven *ronin*, masterless samurai, who in 1702 gave their lives to avenge the death of their lord. But the doom-sayers must be right: Japan *has* changed. Today the statue of Hachiko the dog looks out over loyalties and obligations more carnal than canine.

Negotiating the maelstrom of Shibuya twice a day most days could take its toll. One can only take so much excitement, only so many hyper-urban frissons. Shibuya made an invigorating change after Clayton, the humdrum suburb in which my home university is located. But invigoration leads easily to enervation. Not cut out for the role of academic-as-thrill-seeker, I usually felt relieved to begin the first leg of my homeward journey at Shibuya station on the Ginza line bound—eventually—for Kemigawa. Living in Tokyo instils an appreciation of the value of the domestic environment, the comforts of home. The words 'Shin-Kemigawa', broadcast in the railway carriage, sounded good at the end of a long, long day. An English translation of Shibuya's *kanji* characters is 'valley of bitterness'. It doesn't sound as attractive in English, does it? 'Coming up, The Valley of Bitterness!' Some days the translation seemed singularly appropriate, and the sound of home all that much sweeter.

⌘ ⌘ ⌘

5 OUT OF EDO I

We had been waiting for God knows how long, pacing up and down the platform, our eyes squinting in the blinding midday sun as we searched the tracks for signs of life: i.e. the belated appearance of our train. We exchanged rueful looks and terse pleasantries with aspiring fellow-passengers; we perused the local newspapers, cast in a language I could barely comprehend. The drinks machine worked overtime dispensing relief as the vehement sun beat down and the day got hotter and hotter. Intermittent blasts of an infernal wind shook the dead leaves of the stunted trees across the way. A small lizard scurried over the burning stones between the lines and a few birds cruised lazily overhead, while in the cool dark of their office a group of surly male railway staff smoked and lounged about, answering our increasingly pressing enquiries with a grunt or a dismissive shrug.

Obviously we were not in Japan. This desolate scene was at Albury railway station in March 1997. After visiting family in northern Victoria during a brief between-semesters break, Deborah and I were waiting to pick up the daylight Melbourne to Sydney 'express', the solitary daytime train, and it was late, extremely late. It did come eventually, and on the long trip north I had ample time to contemplate the shining glory of Japan: the national rail network. If Japan can run scores of utterly punctual trips covering the distance from, say, Tokyo to Hiroshima (roughly 900 kilometres, the same distance as Melbourne to Sydney) in well under five hours, can't we at least organise one reliable slow coach a day? The rail system in Greater Tokyo, serving its many millions of indefatigably mobile citizens, is remarkable; but the national network is a veritable work of art, especially the bullet trains, the *shinkansen*, which bear as much resemblance to our XPT as the Batmobile does to a penny-farthing.

In *The Great Railway Bazaar* (1975) Paul Theroux remarks that riding the trains in Japan reminded him of sitting in an aeroplane—silence, leg room and a reading light. All that comfort had the paradoxical effect of unnerving him, producing 'a sweaty tension' he associated with air travel. He hankered for the homely lounge cars and rackety wheels of 'real' trains and bemoaned the 'uncongenial transitions from city to city' he experienced in Japan. *Shinkansen* travel does indeed feel like being in a jet, though I found it infinitely more relaxing, offering the sensation of swift movement without the damp palms and the nagging fears. Travelling at such speed (though the *shinkansen* seems to float rather than flash), one is hardly able to savour the passing countryside. On some routes, this is no great disappointment. As Theroux observes, the Hikari Express, the limited-stop bullet train that skips the five hundred or so kilometres from the capital to Kyoto in less than three hours, 'never really leaves the pure horror of the megalopolis' joining the two cities.¹ If the pollution is not too bad, the sight of Mount Fuji's lovely cone serves as the only distraction from an industrial landscape so hideous it makes even flying seem like an attractive prospect.

We took in enough of what is left of rural Japan—walking through the fragrant woodlands and ancient villages of the Kiso Valley in Honshu, or travelling past wasabi farms and rice paddies up and over the staggering peaks of the Japan Alps down to the beautiful festival town of Takayama—to appreciate what the country must once have been like. The rape of Japan's once voluptuous countryside is the subject of general despair. No amount of prior warning from guidebooks like the Lonely Planet prepares one for the shock of encountering so many eyesores and so much desecration, so frightful a level of environmental debauchery.

Japan's rivers have been concreted and corralled, the mountains denuded and skewered by highways, coastlines turned into garbage dumps, natural forests obliterated. Local and regional ecosystems have been systematically destroyed. Scores of species of plant and animal life have become extinct—most lamentably the *Nipponia nippon* or 'toki', the Japanese crested ibis, one of the most celebrated traditional motifs. (By the end of 1997 one—*one!*—individual toki survived in its native country, a male called Kin, who could be seen waddling around on his small red legs in the grandiloquently named 'Toki Center' on Sado Island.) Urban planning seems non-existent. New roads go nowhere, commercial complexes stand deserted, power lines proliferate. The air is a noxious mixture of chemicals and gases, including deadly pollutants like dioxin. The ugliness festers, spreading out over the land.

This has not stopped Japanese governments preaching the virtues of 'sustainable development' in various international environmental forums, with the same sort of barefaced hypocrisy shown by the United States when it berates other countries for their nuclear testing. Still, at this critical juncture in the national life, Japanese policy-makers, in collusion with the powerful construction industry, advocate more convention centres, more *shinkansen* lines, more shopping centres, more dams, even, for heaven's sake, entire new cities—including a plan to replace Tokyo as the national capital some time early in the new century.

The men who have 'made' Japan in the past half-century have created affluence but left a tragically diminished quality of life to succeeding generations. Is it any wonder that so many young Japanese people (my Todai students, for example) are bitter at the legacy of environmental ruination they have been left? Bitter, but fatalistic. Alex Kerr has argued that the 'salvation' for Japan, in terms of actually doing something remedial about its environmental self-destruction, will be the emergence of 'a sense of crisis'.[2] One would have thought a sense of crisis must have already hit home by now, yet the nation seems paralysed to do anything constructive (perhaps the wrong word) about itself. Or perhaps it is simply that, as David Suzuki and Keibo Oiwa have argued, contemporary urbanised Japanese have become so profoundly distanced and disconnected from nature that they easily tolerate the degradation their ways of life wreak on the environment.[3]

Pockets of grass-roots environmentalism exist here and there all over Japan, in cities and towns and rural regions, fighting the good fight. But there is a prevailing sense of passive helplessness. Those exquisite feelings of loss in which the Japanese sensibility is all too ready to wallow do not encourage mass ameliorative action. The full-colour 'Flora and Fauna' section regularly run on the front page of the *Japan Times* usually had an elegiac air, as for example in the list of 'characteristics' accompanying a picture of the *kounotori*, the white stork: 'White storks once lived throughout Japan, but the destruction of wetlands gradually pushed them into decline, with no local breeding pairs observed since 1959'.

The tourist pamphlets put out by local authorities are characterised by a similar plaintiveness. Thus the guide to the Hida Folk Village outside Takayama, an open-air museum of representative traditional farmhouses that have been dismantled and removed from their original sites in the Hida district, begins:

> Japan has recently made very rapid progress in economics, but our material success has caused us to think too little about the more important spiritual side of life. We now realise we should pay more attention to the cultural heritage our ancestors have built up for centuries. We must return to some of our traditional modes of living.

But for Japan there is no turning back. Obsessive cataloguers and makers of lists, the Japanese are now, at the end of the millennium, going about the business of recording for posterity what is left of the country before it too passes into oblivion. On television some time in late 1996 a news item indicated that Japan's Environment Agency—which contains as much dead wood as any branch of the bloated Japanese bureaucracy—had registered one hundred quintessentially 'Japanese' sounds that it felt needed to be preserved, so that at least the sound of Japan would remain when the substance had disappeared. Among those to be preserved were the rumble of ice floes on the Sea of Okhotsk north of Hokkaido, the tolling of the bronze bell in the famous Edo-style tower at Kawagoe near

Tokyo, the gurgle of a mountain stream somewhere near Aomori in northern Honshu, and the flapping of a flock of cranes taking flight in Kagoshima in southern Kyushu. Perhaps the rustling of paper being shuffled or the sound of yen changing hands are also in their own way typically Japanese, though I fear that recent newspaper reports suggesting that Japan's rampaging public officials are an 'endangered species' are sadly premature.

In *Discourses of the Vanishing* Marilyn Ivy provides a detailed analysis of the creation of 'a politics of nostalgia' pressed into the service of big-business capitalism. She cites in particular the fabulously successful if inherently self-defeating 'Discover Japan' campaign, launched in 1970 on behalf of the Japan National Railway by Dentsu, the powerful advertising agency. The most successful advertising campaign to that point in Japanese history, 'Discover Japan', Ivy writes, 'condensed the longings of upwardly and outwardly mobile Japanese' seeking to rediscover what remained of Japan's pre-modern past in 'the midst of its loss'. Instead of highlighting the usual famous sites and sights—Mount Fuji, or the fifty-three way stations of the Tokaido, the old road from Edo to Kyoto immortalised by Hiroshige—the campaign focused on obscure places, forests, mountain temples and so on, unindividuated images of a posited 'authentic' Japan.

Not surprisingly, environmental groups opposed the artificial transformation of the country into a consumable itinerary. In 1984, after what Ivy calls the 'official nostalgia' of the 'Discover Japan' campaigns, came the logical outcome of a process that seeks to transform environments into objects of desire: 'Exotic Japan', which highlighted aspects of non-native Japan such as the Mount Koya complex south of Osaka, the seat of the esoteric Shingon Buddhism. Japan, for the purposes

5 OUT OF EDO I

of local tourism, was turned into a paradox—the homeland that is a foreign country.[4] This was a canny strategy when so many Japanese find foreign travel more congenial, and indeed considerably cheaper, than tourism at home.

In the 1990s, according to Ivy, the tourism industry still cultivates a form of neo-nostalgia, perpetuating and promoting a commodified 'Japan' that is kept 'on the verge of vanishing, stable yet endangered'.[5] I will have to take her word for it. Apart from the excellent tourist offices in Tokyo and Kyoto and one or two other places I visited, the tourist literature and official assistance one is likely to be offered in the provinces is impenetrable to travellers who do not read or understand Japanese. To arrive at a town 'on spec' and visit the local tourist office to enquire about available accommodation, at least in the broken Japanese at my disposal, was to risk inciting a nervous breakdown in the person behind the desk, quivering and flushing at the sight of a customer who happens to be a *gaijin*. Japanese courtesies do not necessarily translate to the local tourist industry. Visitors to Nagano for the Winter Olympics in early 1998 complained that there were no maps of the city available in languages other than Japanese. The organisers, who had had years to prepare for the contingency, must have been surprised that there would be foreigners among the spectators and competitors at this great international event.

⌘⌘⌘

Paul Theroux reckoned that he always knew he had 'touched bottom' in his often uncomfortable rail journeys around Asia when he found himself in the company of Australians.[6] Some travellers think the same way when they find themselves ensconced with Japanese, or indeed Americans like Theroux. I worry less about my fellow-travellers than the places I find myself in, and in my case the nadir of my travels out of Tokyo oddly came in my first trans-Japan journey, to Wakkanai, the northernmost town of Japan's most northern main island, Hokkaido. Most travellers to Japan head for Kyoto and its celebrated shrines, temples and gardens: I made for Hokkaido and ended up in a remote fishing port, the major advertised attraction of which is a Herring Museum.

Why Wakkanai? Deborah and I were there because it was the August summer holidays, and our first chance to see a bit of Japan. After finally securing permission for the trip from my traumatised Head of Department, Ogawa *sensei*, we looked forward to escaping Tokyo, which had become a furnace. Hokkaido would be cool, and anyway I had always wanted to go there. The place-name 'Hokkaido' had stuck in my mind, as place-names do, since I was a child. Some time towards the end of primary school in suburban Melbourne (this would have been in the mid-1960s), I had done a project on Japan, carefully mapping the four main islands in my exercise book, becoming fascinated by the words 'Honshu', 'Shikoku', 'Kyushu' and especially 'Hokkaido', the wild island way up north, home to a strange, hairy, blue-eyed people called the Ainu, the aboriginal people of Japan. To a young kid excited by the possibility of a New Year visit to the Mornington Peninsula—I was easy to please—the very sound of 'Hokkaido' on the lips made it seem incredibly, almost unimaginably exotic. (But then again so did Charters Towers, a long journey north of another kind.)

We asked Bill along for the ride, but he had already been there and had hated it. The cold and the conifers, he said,

5 OUT OF EDO I

reminded him of Canada. As a persuader I suggested the islands of Rebun and Rishiri, a national park off the northern tip of Hokkaido, the untarnished beauty of which had been described to me by some of my Todai students. On the map the islands looked remote and romantic enough to excite Bill's interest; besides, they were close to the Russian territory of Sakhalin, and hence he could pretend he was visiting Europe, which is where he always really wanted to go. So it was Rebun and Rishiri—and Wakkanai, which was the terminus of the ferry to the off-shore islands. That is why we came to be in Wakkanai.

With the kind of back-to-front, upside-down Japanese logic that perplexes foreigners, Wakkanai holds a South Pole festival every year. Apparently this is because Japan's first Antarctic expedition trained there, and because regional Japan is compulsively festival-happy: if a place doesn't hold some kind of defining festival then it doesn't exist. Nevertheless, a South Pole festival way up in northern Hokkaido is conspicuously absurd. Latitudinally north of Vladivostok, Wakkanai perches at the very tip of Japan, battered by Siberian blizzards and fringed by those rumbling ice floes drifting southward in the Sea of Okhotsk during its long, long winter. Forty-odd kilometres away is freezing, foggy Sakhalin, a notorious place of exile for Tsarist prisoners. Wakkanai is much like frontier ports everywhere, only more dismal. It is ugly even by Japanese urban standards, which is saying something. Its dingy streetscapes are dominated by establishments catering to the starved carnal appetites of seamen, places so sleazy as to make the sex parlours of Kabukicho look like children's day-care centres.

I overcame what was to prove a recurring impulse in my travels around Japan—the urgent desire to head home to Tokyo—and decided to give the town a go. We had a day to spend before catching the ferry to Rebun. Scratching beneath an unappealing surface had unearthed gems in Tokyo: you never know, Wakkanai might contain something of interest. The disconsolate looks on the faces of the staff who greeted us at the local tourist office were not encouraging. In the tourist industry, being assigned to Wakkanai must be akin to diplomats being sent to Phnom Penh. But no expense had been spared in producing a brace of glossy brochures, some even in English. The staff presented these to us with alacrity, like bank tellers handing over cash to robbers. No doubt they wanted us out of the office, and didn't want to be held accountable for the large claims the brochures made about Wakkanai. With good reason. A quick perusal revealed that, if they were to be believed, Wakkanai was a jewel of the north, not to be missed for its mind-boggling array of cultural and natural attractions.

In fact this dowdy, nondescript town does reveal a bit about Japan, especially in the local authorities' efforts to spruce the place up. Near the airport just out of town there are boardwalks and camping grounds, along with a large pond to attract the migratory bird life that seasonally passes through the area. Naturally this ecological imperative has been supplemented by the cultural bulwark of a golf course. The whole area has been dubbed the 'Airport Park', one of those sad Japanese oxymorons that seem habitually to denote the nation's ill-conceived efforts to preserve its diminishing natural resources. No doubt the swans, storks and the sea eagles occasionally seen in the vicinity find aircraft congenial company.

A few kilometres further west of Airport Park is Cape Soya, geographically the northernmost point of Japan and directly facing long, slender Sakhalin across the Sea of Okhotsk. Called Karufuto by the Japanese, who claimed its southern part

5 OUT OF EDO I

after the Russo–Japanese War in 1905, Sakhalin has long been the focus of tensions with the Russians, particularly since the end of World War II when it was ceded to the Soviet Union along with the Kuriles, a chain of smaller islands to the southeast. The repossession of the Kurile Islands, Japan's so-called 'Northern Territories', is one of the great obsessions of Japan's rabid right-wing nationalists, who regularly hold raucous demonstrations as close as they can get to the Russian embassy near Roppongi in Tokyo. So we had unwittingly come to one of Japan's genuine 'hot spots', most of the time wishing that we were back in cool, urbane Roppongi.

One of the irritating habits of Japanese official tourist literature is its tendency to peddle an aggressive nationalism. Thus in the brochure produced by the Hokkaido Tourist Association, a coloured box beside the Kuriles on its fold-out map of the region asserts that 'at present the Kurile Islands are occupied by the former Soviet Union', but that 'in actuality these four islands were recognised as Japanese territory by the 1855 Russo–Japanese Commerce and Amity Treaty'. At Cape Soya Japan's historical argument is tacitly embodied in the statue of a samurai, armed to the hilt, looking sternly out to sea. (A samurai garrison was stationed here in the closing years of the Tokugawa Shogunate to guard against Tsarist expansion.) These days the Japanese like to be seen as a peaceable people. At Cape Soya is a 'Bell for World Peace', a replica of the bell in front of the United Nations building in New York, indicating that the Japanese peace culture centred in Hiroshima in south-western Honshu extends its tentacles all over the country. But the Russians are not let off the hook that easily. Near by stands a Tower of Prayer built as a memorial to those killed in the Korean Air 747 shot down by the Soviet Union just to the north in 1983. It needs something that drastic to get anything Korean the slightest recognition in Japan. An arresting, unsettling monument, designed in the shape of a broken wing vertically implanted in the ground, the Tower of Prayer did not reawaken my initial impulse to rush back to Wakkanai airport for a quick exit back to civilisation.

Back in town, we decided after minimal hesitation to forgo the Herring Museum and to visit the municipal park, a short cable-car ride above the port. The park provides further evidence of the Japanese passion for monuments, as well as an indication of the kinds of activity and behaviour that are deemed to warrant commemoration. There is a 'Monument to the Nine Ladies', commemorating the sacrifice of nine young telephone operators who committed suicide at a Sakhalin transmitter post at the end of World War II. Engraved on a rock are the words of their last message, transmitted as the Red Army approached: 'This is the end, good-bye everyone, good-bye . . .' Taro and Jiro, two sled dogs (they go in for statues of canine paradigms of dumb loyalty in Japan) are memorialised for their service in the expedition to Antarctica. And, looking out to sea towards Sakhalin, the hideous Hyohsetsu No Mon, variously translated as 'the Gate to Ice and Snow' and 'the Frozen Gate', signifies Japan's intransigence on the question of Soviet Russia's wartime annexation of its territories to the north.

⌘⌘⌘

We may as well as have had a good look at Wakkanai, because it had been a hell of a journey to get there. Well, not that bad really, but a fair hike by contemporary Japanese standards. In

5 OUT OF EDO I

mid-May 1689 it took the poet Basho several weeks to walk from Edo as far north as Hiraizumi in the Tohoku region of northern Honshu, from where he diverted to the Japan Sea coast. This was the journey he famously recorded in his *haiku* epic, if there can be such a thing, *The Narrow Road to the Deep North*. Depressed at the thought of the immense distances lying ahead of him and sad at leaving 'the flowering treetops' of Ueno (it was 1689, as I said), Basho was moved to write: 'Departing spring: birds cry and, in the eyes of fish, tears'.[7]

Travel in Japan at the end of the millennium, alas, does not readily inspire poetic feelings. On my journey to the Deep North, I too could have melancholically taken my leave of Edo by departing from Ueno on the Hokutosei Express, the overnight train that takes sixteen hours from the national capital to Hokkaido's capital, Sapporo. But Bill, who had lived in Tokyo so long that the frenetic pace of the city seemed to have entered his metabolism, insisted that the journey be executed as quickly as possible, and who were we to argue with someone whose ability to speak Japanese would be no small help on our trip to one of the archipelago's remote places? So we journeyed into Tokyo Central from Kemigawa, hopped on to the Tohoku *shinkansen*, and in exactly two hours and thirty-six minutes (as stipulated in the timetable) found ourself in the city of Morioka, a long way north of where Basho reached.

In Morioka we had enough time to read in the tourist brochure that the city was on the same latitude as Beijing and Lisbon—a fact that the peoples of those cities would doubtless be gratified to know—before picking up a regular express train to Sapporo via Hakodate. The trip took eleven hours all up. We stayed in Sapporo for a couple of days and went on to Wakkanai, another five and a half hours due north, no messing about. It is tempting to blame Bill for our precipitous, prosaic movement north, but to be honest I have little sympathy for the idea that the journey is more important than the destination, the belief in the trip for the trip's sake that gained so much currency during the late 1960s and early 1970s. Robert Louis Stevenson's famous traveller's maxim, 'I travel not to go anywhere, but to go', has always seemed asinine to me. No wonder it first appeared in a book called *Travels with a Donkey*.

Naturally Paul Theroux, who had a reputation as a traveller to protect and a book about rail journeys to write, had opted for the 'slow' train north from Ueno. His account of the trip in *The Great Railway Bazaar* suggests that his fellow passengers consisted largely of the farming people I used to see around the Ameyoko market in Tokyo. Among the vacationers heading for Hokkaido's ski resorts, he noticed some 'smaller, darker, Eskimo-faced people', up-country folk from the rural provinces north of the capital returning home after a visit to town to sell their produce or merely to sample the wonders of the metropolis. Theroux cites the pejorative Japanese idiom *nobori-san* to describe these rustics—literally, 'the downers', those who take the *nobori*, or down-train to Tokyo.[8] But looked at another way, these are literally people from up above. 'Nobori' has the connotation of ascent, of rising, of climbing, as in *yama-nobori*, mountain-climbing.

Yet perhaps Theroux is right to look at the Hokkaido 'yokels' from the point of view of the Tokyoites. Their disdain for the northern people is merely the contemporary expression of the historical incursion of the invading Yamato people into the deep north of Honshu, the pushing back of the indigenous population into pockets of Hokkaido and the subsumption of the Ainu into the greater Japanese culture. A policy of forced assimilation was systematically imposed during the Meiji era, when Ezochi (as Hokkaido was once called) was settled as

Japan's new frontier by large numbers of people from the mainland, eager to develop the island's vast natural resources. Colonisation north of Edo in the late nineteenth century was mirrored in the south in 1879 by the annexation of the old Ryuku Kingdom of islands, now Okinawa, whose people were treated then, as to some degree today, as second-class citizens, or, as Suzuki and Oiwa put it, 'country cousins'.[9]

I had quoted Theroux to Bill as part of my campaign to convince him to come with us to Hokkaido. Diversity in the racial and social make-up of Japan was a special interest of his, and when Japanese boasted of their country's racial uniformity he was fond of puncturing their pride by stating the uncomfortable truth that the great Japanese 'monoculture' is actually a big lie. (The idea of a 'multicultural nation', however, was never one he could come at—he thought the concept a nonsense even in the Australian context.) Bill was therefore disappointed to observe that few if any *nobori-san* were on our train. Instead we were accompanied mainly by a selection of apparently middle-class men and women journeying north to visit friends and family, or perhaps to do a spot of business, plus a contingent of hikers, many of them vacationing students off to sample Hokkaido's national parks, which are huge and reputedly spectacular, if in some cases defiled by the presence of highly industrialised towns.

Exaggeratedly though not unjustifiably fearful of the fare offered outside the cosmopolitan capital, Bill had brought along a splendid repast of ham, cheese, bread, tomatoes and olives, victuals to be washed down with a couple of bottles of Beaujolais, a choice of beverage noted with approbation and amusement by our fellow passengers. We happily shared our humble rations with them, and they reciprocated. Cold cans of Asahi Super Dry were snapped open. Peaches were passed around, along with other comestibles from the stock of delicacies that Japanese rail travellers invariably bring with them. I still find Theroux's remarks about the 'silence' in which rail travel is passed in Japan a complete mystery. That trip north was as ribald and as jolly as any jaunt in the *Canterbury Tales*. The only reservation one finds on a trans-Japan train is the one marked on your ticket.

The train sped north while we drunkenly watched the summer landscape of Tohoku pass by, spectacular craggy peaks soaring above cultivated valleys of terraced paddies and orchards groaning with fruit. The only moment of sobriety came on the fifty-plus-kilometre undersea Seikan Tunnel linking Hokkaido with Honshu by rail—presumably knocked up one weekend while the English and the French were boasting about plans for their 'chunnel'. It is in places like the Seikan Tunnel that thoughts of catastrophic earthquakes impose themselves most pressingly. But I need not have worried; the subterranean passage was negotiated in a flash, and we emerged into a landscape of lakes and conifers and A-framed houses that for one glorious moment made me think I was in Norway.

⌘⌘⌘

Topographically the two little islands to which we were headed could scarcely be more different. Rebun is long, slender and undulating: Rishiri, a short hop on the ferry to the south, is a single, perfectly formed volcanic peak rising from the blue of the ocean, a Fuji of the Japan Sea. Menaced by that beautiful but formidable volcano, we opted for the more genteelly configured Rebun for our stay. We checked into a humble

5 OUT OF EDO I

minshuku, the Japanese version of the B&B, but with dinner usually thrown in as well. It was comfortable enough, but it soon became apparent that it was run along the lines of a boot camp staffed by intimidatingly earnest young men and women. Soon after we had settled into our rooms our names were broadcast in succession over a public-address system; apparently this indicated that we were individually to make our way to the bathrooms to have our baths. Later, after a dinner consisting of various unidentifiable *fruits de la mer*, we were treated to a lecture and pep talk about our agenda for the next day: an eight-hour trek around the island. We hadn't been asked if we wanted to join this expedition, so we were surprised to find that our participation was assumed to be a *fait accompli*. But the Japanese can be a smilingly insistent people, and we surrendered to our fate without even a whimper. Depressed by the way our holiday had been progressing thus far, I prepared for the next day's exertions by guiltily smoking several cigarettes with some of our fellow lodgers. It felt like the night before an execution.

The 'eight-hour walk' proved predictably euphemistic, being more a test of character and physical endurance than a nature walk. This being Japan, we set off in a group at what seemed like the crack of dawn, Bill, Deborah and myself accompanied by Japanese travellers who had eschewed their usual vacations in Queensland or California or Tuscany to rough it in Rebun. It did not take us long to start whingeing about how hard the going was, but the splendour of the scenery shut us up as the sun rose and we concentrated on the task at hand. We skirted the rocky coastline and pebble beaches, clung (delirious with fear) to slimy rock faces while the waves roared below, exchanged greetings with fishermen and seaweed farmers, clambered up winding mossy ways into a glorious landscape of cypress and dwarf bamboo, loped across hillsides sporting a profusion of alpine wildflowers and finally descended to a sunny harbour, having savoured a world utterly remote from Tokyo. What Rebun must be like in the long winter, lashed by those vicious Siberian winds, is hard to imagine: in midsummer it was stunning.

But one can take only so much beauty. We three *gaijin*, tempted by the thought of the cold beers and bottles of chablis back at the *minshuku* (Bill always came prepared), opted out of the final leg of the trek and headed back, much to the derision of our Japanese cohort.

There wasn't much else to do on Rebun but walk. The water was much too cold for swimming, the beaches were bad and the museum was full of moth-eaten stuffed seals and bits of broken pottery. After a couple of days, even Wakkanai started to look good. Our hosts looked surprised and disappointed when we announced we were leaving earlier than scheduled, but they were a forgiving lot. When we left Rebun on the ferry, there they were on the dock, strumming guitars and singing a valediction that sounded like some kind of cross between the 'Maori Farewell' and the Village People's 'In the Navy'.

Hokkaido itself, what we saw of it on our more leisurely return trip south, is a disorienting place. Nineteenth-century port towns like Otaru, north of Sapporo, and Hakodate, with their many Western buildings from the Meiji and Taisho periods, seem more European than Asian. Unusually in a country where urban renewal is taken as seriously as women's rights, an attempt has been made to restore Otaru's nineteenth-century canals and cobbled sidewalks and maritime warehouses. You'd almost call the place pretty. When we were there the local museum was hosting an exhibition on loan from the Hermitage in St Petersburg. On display was a model of

5 OUT OF EDO I

Dostoyevsky's study; atop his writing desk was a selection of private papers, which revealed that even the great Dostoyevsky doodled.

Further south, Hakodate had also undergone a facelift. The renovated port area reminded me of Darling Harbour, an effect increased by the fact that a yacht called the *Crocodile Dundee* was moored there. This was closer to home than I wanted to be. But in their endeavour to present hick Hakodate as up-market as well as up-country, some of the local merchandisers confirmed what Tokyoites reckon to be self-evident—that Hokkaido really is impossibly uncouth. The face of one tourist complex is covered by an enormous, lurid painting of two gormless 'Jack and Betty' figures, all pearly white teeth, red lips and shiny blond hair. Betty is saying to Jack:

THIS SHOP SEEMS ENJOYABLE. GO INTO IT.

Actually Hakodate's cultural credentials are impressive. In 1854, when Japan started emerging from its long isolation, the city became one of the first treaty ports. In 1868, in a Japanese version of the Eureka Stockade, forces loyal to the Shogunate took refuge in the famous star-shaped fort at nearby Goryokaku and proclaimed an independent republic before being crushed by the imperial troops of the Meiji Restoration. There were traces of the city's links with the West in its crumbling consular buildings (one of them, the British consulate, had been revamped as a teahouse called the 'Queen's Memory'), a Byzantine-styled Russian Orthodox Church and a Foreigners' Cemetery. Just outside the modest city limits, there was a Trappistine convent famous for the biscuits made by its nuns. A café called the 'California Baby' back in town near the wharf offered a more typically Japanese urban sight. Downtown Hakodate retained a pleasantly faded, picturesque air. Trams rumbled past on ill-paved roads, gardens were overgrown—an unusual sight in Japan, legendary for its horticultural fastidiousness. Overall, with its trendy tourist quarter, fish markets, ocean views and run-down nineteenth-century streets, Hakodate presented an oddly hybrid urban spectacle, a sort of mixture of Sydney's Balmain and the late unlamented East Berlin.

Apart from their tourist potential, the influence of the old Hokkaido ports has long waned. Sapporo is where the Hokkaido action is. Self-confident, gregarious, the city is dedicated to pleasure: Susikino, its pulsating entertainment district, is one of Japan's more buoyant floating worlds. Beer halls and beer gardens abound, many hideously 'German' in character. They take their Sapporo seriously in Sapporo. I wondered what the city must be like in the winter. The large underground shopping centres in central Sapporo, plus the fact that the city is most famous for its ice festival and populated by an abundance of pet huskies, all seemed to indicate something. To Theroux, who visited the place in winter, Sapporo had the look of a Wisconsin city. I was less put off by its provinciality than by the thought of how cold it must be for much of the year. It was chilly enough in August.

I noted this with some self-justification, as I had recently knocked back a job offer at a brand new university to the south of the city, the sister university of a major institution in Tokyo. I had received a visit from one of the university heavies, a senior law professor sporting a pointy goatee beard, which he probably thought looked Confucian but actually made him resemble a dodgy astrologer. He had sought—through an 'education agent', not unusual in Japan, where academic jobs are networked rather than advertised—to recruit me to teach 'Postcolonial Studies'. It was not me he was impressed by, but the fact that I was a University of Tokyo *sensei*. Academic snobbery in Japan makes the English appear egalitarian. After emphasising his Samurai heritage and showing me photographs of the large family estate just outside Kyoto (hinting that one day I might be honoured by being invited for a visit), the professor tried to lure me to the frigid north by promising that I would have a big house up in Hokkaido with a swimming pool. I inwardly scoffed at this nonsensical suggestion. What was I going to do—go skating in my own back yard for most of the year?

⌘⌘⌘

Hakodate's Museum of Northern Peoples is by Japanese standards a professional, scholarly and well-presented exhibition of artifacts and documentation relating to the Ainu and related races, but otherwise much of what remains of Ainu culture in Hokkaido is packaged for tourist consumption in novelty 'Ainu villages' here and there around the island. On the way back down to Sapporo from Wakkanai we stopped at one of these, Kawamura Ainu Village, on the outskirts of Asahikawa, Hokkaido's second-largest city. Apart from a cruelly chained, violently barking dog, my memory is of a cheerless place consisting of a few shacks containing Ainu paraphernalia—tools, implements and so on, plus some damaged and discoloured photographs of Ainu worthies of decades past. A few stalls sold handicrafts and other souvenirs. A charming woman with whom Bill struck up a conversation convinced him that both he and I should don Ainu garb and have our photograph taken for a small consideration. Actually Bill didn't need convincing; he thought it was a fabulous idea. I had reservations but soon submitted, thinking that no one would ever know of this demeaning and politically dubious performance. I did not count on Bill's complete contempt for ideological correctness, which led him to show the photographs proudly to all and sundry at Todai upon our return to work—Bill there in his colourful warrior's garb and most fierce expression, me looking bloody silly.

The Japanese treatment of the Ainu inevitably leads to comparisons with the Australian treatment of Aborigines. In the nineteenth century the Meiji state declared the Ainu's ancestral fishing and hunting grounds *terra nullius*, prohibited their customs and made them take Japanese names. Under the Family Registration Law of 1871 the Ainu were incorporated as 'commoners' (*heimin*) with the additional entry of 'former aborigine' (*kyu dojin*).[10] In order to consummate the island's settlement by migratory mainlanders, the 1899 Hokkaido Former Aborigines Protection Act sought the forced assimilation of the Ainu through farming and Japanese education.

Systematic discrimination ensued for several decades. Since the 1970s the assertion of Ainu ethnicity has led to demands for formal legislative recognition of prior Ainu claims to tracts of Hokkaido territory. In response, the Japanese government identified the remaining Ainu people (who number around 50 000, according to the Ainu Association of Hokkaido) as an ethnic minority, an advance of sorts. But, significantly, they were not stated to be an indigenous people. A further Ainu Protection Law guaranteeing the preservation of Ainu culture and human rights passed through the Diet during my stay in Japan, though again the resolution stopped short of defining the Ainu as indigenes, apparently because of government concern that such a description could raise

5 OUT OF EDO I

questions over aboriginal rights, including rights to land and natural resources.[11] The parallels with Australia are pretty obvious, though my attempt to make the connection at Todai met with a stony response from my students, the cause of which I could only guess.

Hokkaido advertises itself as 'New World Japan', a frontier populated by warm, friendly, 'pioneering' people. They were much more 'open', I was assured by a well-disposed Japanese colleague before my departure, than the more reserved, snooty societies of places like Kyoto. I was told that, as an Australian, I would really enjoy it. And indeed the people of Hokkaido are warm, they are friendly. But in some things Hokkaido was a bit too much like home. After posing for the camera at the Ainu village, we decided to take our leave from the place. That chained dog was really getting to me, and it was starting to rain. We hailed a passing taxi and sped back toward the station. It soon transpired that the driver had often visited members of his family living in the United States and wanted to practise his English, which indeed was superior to the conversational English of some of my Todai students. He made the mistake of assuming that Bill was an American, occasioning a rebuff so unequivocal that he turned his attention—and, disconcertingly, his body—to me. I had a vision of violent death in Asahikawa as he momentarily swerved in front of the oncoming traffic.

'Did you like that Ainu town?' he asked.

I replied, dishonestly, that I had. 'Very interesting,' I said. 'But it is a pity that the Ainu life seems just to be put on show for tourists like us.'

'Listen, mister,' he said, drawing deeply on his cigarette, 'don't you feel too sorry for the Ainu.'

'Why not?'

'They complain all of the time. Complain too much. We don't have a problem with *them*. They have a problem with *we* Japanese. They won't fit in with us. Stupid!'

Hokkaido made a bracing change from Tokyo, but I shuddered at the thought of living there. Bill, desperate to get back home to his Kemigawa garden, his cats and his hectic social calendar, hurried us toward home. At the railway station in Sapporo we were briefly held up by summer storms—apparently a tsunami had washed up over the tracks somewhere to the south of island. Once again I was gripped by the urgent need to get back to the relative security of Tokyo. Eventually the trains started moving and there we were, three foreign *nobori-san*, on the down-train to Tokyo, heading back to the Big Smoke. On the way home, I ruefully reflected that it was on this trip to salubrious Hokkaido that I had resumed my cigarette habit.

6 OUT OF EDO II

> Well, I wish I was on some
> Australian mountain range.
> Oh, I wish I was on some
> Australian mountain range.
> I got no reason to be there, but I
> Imagine it would be some kind of change.[1]

A Bob Dylan fan from way back, Ohara would sometimes annoy me by whining these whimsical lines from the song 'Outlaw Blues', on the assumption that they would send me into a spin of homesickness. He was mistaken. It wasn't the mountains of Australia that I missed—piddling little things anyway by comparison with the vaulting peaks of Japan. Coming from Iowa, a landscape so flat and featureless that its one relatively hilly region is known locally as 'Little Switzerland', Ohara loved mountains. He reckoned it was they that first attracted him to Japan.

The Japanese like mountains too. They climb them, sketch them, photograph them. They even venerate them. Since prehistoric times, mountains have provided the locus of native belief. The plethora of archaic myths constituting Shinto, with their focus on the *kami* or spirit gods governing natural forces and occupying natural places, favoured mountain peaks above all other sites. (Though occasionally islands, caves, waterfalls and so on got a look in.) Mountains are closest to the sky from where the *kami* descend, aren't they? I was able to extract a smirk from my Todai English language students by explaining the multiple meanings of the word 'summit' when Clinton met Hashimoto in Tokyo in mid-1996. Esoteric Buddhism, which was imported from China in the ninth century and became the major source of the various sects and strands of Japanese Buddhism (absorbing some of the various native beliefs constituting Shinto along the way), also stressed the holiness of mountains. Enlightenment became a personal quest achieved through an intense spiritual 'climb', so mountains were the obvious places to build the first Buddhist monasteries, like the celebrated Kongobu-ji on Mount Koya, where aspiring monks could perfect their rituals of obeisance.

Even a cursory attempt to take in some of the shrines and temples of Japan offers ironic reminders of tourism's roots in the religious quest. One of my guidebooks makes mention of the ancient practice of *Shugendo*, whose practitioners are called *yamabushi*, 'those who prostrate themselves toward the mountain'. With memories of heaving lungs and aching calf muscles, anyone who has done any serious religious (or pseudo-religious) tourism in Japan will appreciate the grim irony of that definition. Mountain-top shrines lose their appeal after a while. Some of them have improved their accessibility to the poor staggering public by installing cable cars, which the

6 OUT OF EDO II

Japanese like to call 'ropeways', for the final agonising ascent. Just one of those vertiginous 'ropeway' journeys was enough for me. This was a harrowing experience in bad weather undertaken in a wildly rocking, overcrowded cable car from Mount Soun-zan near Hakone, across a landscape of bubbling mud and stinking fumaroles, the vile effluvium wafting heavenward. Bad enough in transit, the stomach-turning trip was made worse at its merciful conclusion when we were offered a couple of boiled eggs cooked in the diabolical earth of the near vicinity.

I had undertaken that perilous journey not for purposes of religious or cultural betterment, but for that most mundane impulse of tourism in Japan: I wanted to get a better view of Mount Fuji. As Roland Barthes famously said of the Eiffel Tower, Fujisan 'belongs to the universal language of travel'. There is no journey to France, Barthes wrote, 'which isn't made, somehow, in the Tower's name, no schoolbook, poster, or film about France which fails to propose it as the major sign of a people and a place'. Something similar could be said of the sacred mountain's relationship with Japan.[2]

In these days of anti-tourism tourism, it is considered cool to make mock of Mount Fuji and its ubiquitous iconography. Waxing lyrical about it is something mere tourists to Japan do; the real travellers aspire to off-the-beaten-track places like Shiretoko, the rarely visited wild peninsula of eastern Hokkaido (while probably pining for a secret round of golf at Wakkanai's Airport Park). But out of a determined reverse reverse-snobbery, I simply *had* to see the mountain—what would a trip to Paris be without a look at the Eiffel Tower?—and the ropeway journey from Mount Soun-zan is reputedly a famous vantage point. But because of the vapours and the dirty weather, I did not see the famous peak that day, just as I had not seen it on my original flight into Japan. When the Qantas pilot announced its visible presence to the left of the slowly descending and circling aircraft, he occasioned such a terrifying stampede of passengers to one side of the plane that I stayed rooted in my seat, swearing I'd never do wrong again. That was my first moment of panic-stricken contrition in Japan.

I did get to view Fujisan, however, especially on trips to Kyoto on the *shinkansen* as it snaked around the industrial landscape near its foot. The image of the speeding *shinkansen* with the mountain towering in the background: the ultimate visual cliché of Japan's two faces, the old and the new, the natural and the technological, the traditional and the modern, the spiritual and the functional. On a few memorable cold, clear winter days the mountain could be seen from Kemigawa station, a perfect frosted half-cone collared by a wisp of almost transparent horizontal cloud. Way out west of the Big Smoke, it must be well over a hundred kilometres from Kemigawa, down the eastern shore of Tokyo Bay. It was a miraculous sight in a landscape where some days you could barely even see the high-rise offices and hotels of the multi-function polis at Makuhari, the next suburb along from where we lived, fifteen minutes bicycle ride away. The first time I discerned Mount Fuji's distant but distinctive outline, I raced back to our apartment from Kemigawa station to get my camera. But you can make out nothing of it in the photographs I took—just power lines and tawdry buildings and a pale blue sky. Mysterious, mystical Mount Fuji, the conical conundrum. It is there when it isn't, and vice versa.

Fujisan's multitudinous legends and traditions, like the story that it rose out of the earth in a single night, have attracted such a large literature that even the normally voluble Lafcadio Hearn shuts up about it and decides instead to relate the story of his experience of climbing it.[3] He should have known better, as his description of the climb is as tedious as the climb itself must be. (My authority on this is Bill, who found himself sharing digs in a rest hut halfway up the mountain with a group of *'unspeakable'* American servicemen on R&R.) Maybe James Kirkup had Hearn in mind when he wrote his sequence 'Poems on Mount Fuji Written in Pentel Sign Pen Ink on the Second Day of the New Year':

> To climb Mount Fuji
> Is indescribably vulgar. It
> Can only be climbed from a distance.

Writers and commentators as well as anti-tourist tourists have sought to demystify Mount Fuji, including, it so happens, James Kirkup, though the above observation may suggest otherwise when taken out of context. 'Having left Mount Fuji behind', he writes, 'We wonder why/We ever hoped to see it.' But the damn thing gets you in every time. In poem after poem (there are thirty-two in the sequence) Kirkup plays at voiding the mountain of its significance, but the conclusion ironically reinstates its magnetism:

> There is nothing to be said
> About Mount Fuji, so
> I have said it.[4]

In December 1997 Deborah and I returned to the Hakone National Park and its horrid fumaroles in the hope of getting a good close last look. The area was teeming with tourists, great, marauding packs of bustling, diminutive women wearing the funny little sunhats favoured by older Japanese, filling the mountain railways of this scenic region, taking in the sights, the proverbial plague of locusts. Pushed aside once too often by these nuggety female pushers and shovers, I started lamenting the passing of the Edo-era tradition by which women were only allowed on the mountain once every sixty years. (The mountain's deity is female and it was felt she wanted all the attention.) The natural and cultural wonders of the park were supplemented by a host of recently built ersatz 'attractions', such as a 'French style' rock garden and the 'Hakone Open-Air Museum', a sculpture garden sprouting Picassos, Rodins, Giacomettis, Henry Moores. As always in Japan, more was felt to be needed: the site/sight of Fuji was not enough. Cynics might argue that the Japanese don't feel that their national symbol should be able to speak for itself.

Never mind; the sun shone, the day was clear. The late-autumnal maples were revelations of the colour crimson. Down by the clear blue waters of Lake Ashi, we took a long final look at the snow-capped cone. The tourist brochure proclaimed that 'the magnificent view of Mt. Fuji from Lake Ashi is renowned as the "Best In Japan."' This seemed like a reasonable enough boast. I took several photographs from our vantage point in the 'Hakone Detached Palace Garden', which included a villa and grounds intended to look as if they should be adjacent to Lake Geneva. I'd captured that damned mountain at last.

Satisfied that Mount Fuji had been well and truly 'done', we repaired full of self-satisfaction to our hotel, the famous old Fujiya, in the nearby town of Miyanoshita. Built in 1878, the hotel likes to trade on its Victorian atmosphere as well as its reputation as the place where the international jet-set has historically chosen to say on their Fuji-viewing excursions from Tokyo. The Fujiya, the hotel brochure comments,

6 OUT OF EDO II

'enjoys the highest percentage of foreign guests among hotels in Japan'. Photographs of minor European royalty and stars like Charlie Chaplin and John Lennon and Yoko Ono adorn its dank passageways, Lennon incongruously sporting an atrocious pair of thongs, looking like an Australian lager lout in Bali. The hotel certainly housed foreign 'guests' after World War II, when it was acquired as a rest hotel for Allied Occupation personnel and their dependants.

It was a comfortable place. Hot spring water was pumped into the spacious bathrooms of its equally spacious guest suites; the dining room served up the sort of menu that would not have been out of place in 'French' restaurants in Melbourne during the 1970s, including dishes such as 'Kingfish à la Montmorency' and 'Crepes à la Normandie'. Actually I cannot remember exactly what was on the menu (traumatised by the bill, I have suppressed all memory of Fujiya dining), but what I've listed looks pretty right. In any case, that was what was served to Colin Simpson when he visited the hotel in the mid-1950s, and as far as I can tell things have not changed much.

Despite its self-conscious 'Western' sophistication, the Fujiya is actually a pretty docile, even dowdy establishment—Japan's answer to Victoria's Mount Buffalo Chalet. One wing of the building contains two lodges called 'Restful Cottage' and 'Comfy Cottage'. What did John and Yoko make of those? The Fujiya also has an annex, the 'Chrysanthemum Villa', a former imperial residence purchased by the hotel after the war for people desirous of a more native accommodation experience. Simpson records that in his day the annex was advertised as offering 'lodging facilities for those who want to have experiences on Japanese bedding'.[5] An interesting thought, but Deborah and I had opted for the Western decor of the main hotel, and the novelty of sleeping in a real bed for a change. That night I sank deep into my musty old mattress, contented I'd finally 'taken' Mount Fuji.

⌘⌘⌘

Travellers in provincial Japan spend much of their time sitting in baths, a fact not unrelated to all that uphill climbing to mountain shrines. Actually the Japanese fanaticism about bathing has a predictably religious basis, as Shinto in its most basic form is all about purification and is big on ritual bathing. My Kodansha guidebook, *Gateway to Japan* (the Japanese *Michelin*, this is a guidebook for the cultural purist and the politically impure, the traveller who enjoys the creature comforts) talks about the bathroom being 'the spiritual center' of the *ryokan*, or inn.[6] There are plenty of baths to choose from. Japan's combustible geology means that hot springs gush from the earth all over the archipelago. Hence the plethora of spa towns, called *onsen*. In reality many *onsen* are simply places where company men go in groups to get drunk, piss in each other's pockets and get off with fake 'geishas', if they're up to it after drinking vats of beer and sake. Among the bubbling *jigoku*, or 'hells', at Beppu in Kyushu, one of Japan's biggest and tackiest *onsen*, a 'sex museum' testifies to the invigorating properties of all those malodorous minerals in the water.

Himself an *onsen* enthusiast, Ohara remarked approvingly to me of the especially galvanising qualities of the *rotemburo*, outdoor spa baths usually situated in natural surroundings, the more 'idyllic' the better. Apparently he had enjoyed a *rotemburo* on a winter's holiday in Hokkaido not long after separating from his wife. Perhaps he was seeking absolution, though

6 OUT OF EDO II

Ohara was not the guilty type. I can picture him there, grinning/grimacing away in his cloud of steam, while all around the snow mounted higher and higher. Though deeply impressed by Ohara's commitment to local cultural practice, I myself was not inclined to jump into a *rotemburo*. The nice big 'comfy' bath at the Fujiya, fed by a local spring, did me fine, and in it I spent many pleasant minutes contemplating Fuji.

The famous Kyushu spa town of Unzen is located on the Shimabara Peninsula in a mountainous parkland a couple of hours by road from Nagasaki. We went there during a summer visit to Kyushu. Hounded by a typhoon that seemed to follow us wherever we went, we had aborted a planned visit to the small island of Iki in the Korean Strait off the north-west coast of the main island, where the rotten weather looked likely to be headed. In blinding rain, we got as far as the ferry terminal at Fukuoka for the four-hour crossing, but we changed our plans at the sight of all those woebegone would-be Jumbo Ozakis, glumly chain-smoking as they clutched their golf clubs, contemplated the forecast and waited for the ferry's surprising and in my view foolhardy departure. I did not want us to go down to a watery grave with scores of Slazengers. An *onsen*—where the water is piped in rather than tipped by the bucket-load from high above—seemed a happy alternative.

Unzen has a salutary history. Developed in the late nineteenth century as a sort of hill station for wealthy European and American vacationers based in Asian cities such as Hong Kong, Shanghai and Harbin, it was designated a national park in 1934—Japan's first. (On the bus trip to the peninsula from Fukuoka I read with some consternation that it also had a famous golf course, 'the oldest public course in Japan'. Would those blokes at the ferry terminal follow us there?) But Unzen was not always so welcoming to foreigners. During the persecutions of the seventeenth century, recalcitrant Christians were tossed to be cooked alive like lobsters in the boiling, gassy *jigoku* whose sulphur-stench hangs over the picturesque township. It was at Hara-jo Castle on the southern tip of the peninsula that the Shogunate had crushed a rebellion of Christian peasantry in 1637, leading to the expulsion of the missionaries and, in effect, the closing off of Japan from all contact with the West for the next 220-odd years. After a magnificent dinner served in the room of our Unzen *ryokan* I repaired to its spa room ('GUESTS ONLY, FOREIGNERS PLEASE OBEY JAPANESE RULES OF HYGIENE') and considered—not for the first or last time in Japan—how lucky I was to be born when I was.

The waters of Unzen are famous for their therapeutic qualities in the treatment of rheumatism, diabetes and a host of other ailments. They did nothing, however, for my aching tooth, the result of a recent visit to the premises of a certain Dr Kobayashi of Roppongi, whose handiwork in the practice of root canal treatment would torment me for months to come. My molar throbbed while my muscles relaxed.

The staff at our *ryokan* were models of solicitude, but I had doubts about some of our fellow guests, especially a group of four middle-aged men who checked in about the same time as we did. I learnt from one of them, who had been on a golfing tour of Australia, that they were the senior management team of a Tokyo firm that specialised in elevators. ('Try not to be in one when an earthquake strikes,' he told me; I replied that I'd see what I could do.) These blokes were not there to play golf, but they were not there for their health either. Refreshments other than squatting in scalding mineral waters were on offer in Unzen. I became especially suspicious about their commitment to personal fitness when they cracked open a few bottles of Kirin to go with their fags and their 'morning rice' in the breakfast room at 8 a.m.

Frankly, I hated the fumaroles of Unzen as much as those near Hakone, but the surrounding countryside, teeming with bird life, more than compensated. The avian population included Grey Wagtails, something called the Siberian Meadow Bunting and the Great Tit. 'Great Tits can be seen everywhere in Unzen', boasted the brochure. Was it this sight, rare in Japan, that brought the Kirin drinkers to Unzen? I hoped that, on their obligatory tour of the *jigoku*, they had observed that one of the hells is called the 'Hachiman', or the '80 000', supposedly a site similar to that in Buddhist mythology, where people are made to suffer eternally in a hell of agony after death for any or indeed all of the 80 000-odd lusts.

There is something of the religious quest in the enthusiasm with which the Japanese travel around their islands in search of the supremely satisfying bath. Not wishing to appear sacrilegious, I did not take too long to decide upon my own particular *onsen* obsession. It was in Nikko, a couple of hours north of Tokyo by rail, in a little hotel called the Turtle Inn Annex, an establishment to which I loyally returned time after time, on a couple of occasions dragging visitors from Australia along with me. In the beautiful bath at the Turtle Inn you could look out through big windows over a gushing mountain stream toward a Buddhist graveyard by the far river bank, a reminder that bathing is supposed to be a serious business.

'He who has not seen Nikko', wrote Isabella Bird, quoting a well-known Japanese proverb, 'must not use the word kekko' (meaning beautiful, fine, nice, splendid and so on).[7] Well, I have just used it—Nikko *is* beautiful, fine, nice and splendid; its spectacular shrines, set in dense, dark cryptomeria forests, and the volcanic mountains, lakes, waterfalls and marshes of the surrounding national park provide a tonic to the day-tripping Big Smoker.

As is usual in Japan, however, the natural beauty is pockmarked by post-war constructions of singular ugliness. High above Nikko township, the magnificent Chuzenji, a caldera lake located at the foot of the sacred mountain Nantai-san (where every summer pilgrims gather to make a nocturnal ascent), is fringed by brutish concrete buildings. The nearby Kegon Falls are known as one of the country's most favoured suicide spots, a kind of Japanese version of Sydney's The Gap. I can see why. Having travelled up all those terrifying hairpin bends to look at the celebrated lake under the divine mountain, the visitor is confronted by an architectural hell. With all those high hopes dashed, it is no wonder some people want to go jump.

Nikko has been a centre for mountain worship for more than a millennium, feared and famous as a home of the gods and associated supernatural hangers-on. Apart from occasional pilgrimages like the one to the summit of Mount Nantai, these days most people visit Nikko to look at Japan's most expensive buildings, the ornate seventeenth-century mausolea to the Tokugawa Ieyasu and his grandson Iemitsu, the Tosho-gu and the Taiyuin-byo. These lavish shrine-temples either seduce observers with their lurid beauty or repel them with their gaudiness. I well remember Hugh Loftus sneering at their 'vulgarity'. They were too colourful for his liking—'so Chinese, don't you think?' Like many other foreigners living in the capital, Loftus preferred the more austere, more 'Japanese' Zen temples of Kamakura, the other great magnet for day visitors out of Tokyo.

The Japanese themselves seem to disagree with this assessment. By the train, car and bus-load they arrive in Nikko to enjoy the blue lakes and the green forests, the water cascading down the slopes and those 'vulgar', riotously coloured shrines, all vermilion and purple and emerald and gold. *En masse* they admire the pagoda and the lanterns of stone, the bell towers and drum towers; they pore over the carved gates decorated with dragons and lions, tigers and elephants and mythical beasts of one form or another, and gape at the huge carved shrine dogs by the entrance, which is guarded also by the ferocious, semi-human Nio, Deva kings of Indian origin, there to ward off evil spirits. (These shrines are Noah's Arks of worship.) Man, woman and child, the day-trippers tramp up the long, long flight of steps to the tomb of the shogun Ieyasu, brilliant politician and general, the first of the omnipotent Tokugawas, the man who made Edo the new capital of Japan. Revealing all the ego of the modern autocrat, Ieyasu stated in his will that after his death he would become a god and watch over his nation's fortunes, enshrined in his eyrie on Mount Nikko. Famous for his canny caution, his ability to make the right move at the right time, Ieyasu died in 1616, apparently after overindulging in tempura, one of those great moments of Japanese bathos. Now he gives his historical subjects a stitch just to go and have a look at his tomb. But no worries, a nice hot bath is waiting back home . . .

Before visitors to the Tosho-gu arrive at the steps to Ieyasu's tomb they pass a sutra library, the Rinzo, a revolving octagonal structure containing a complete set of Buddhist scriptures, numbering several thousand volumes. One spin and they reckon you've read them all. This pragmatic approach to the business of devotion supports the old argument that at heart the Japanese are a superstitious rather than a pious people. At important times of the year—the beginning of the summer season or New Year—they engage in an orgy of 'religious' ceremonies and festivals, many of which seem risible to the outside observer. At Shimonoseki in western Japan every New Year, for example, women apply an inky mixture of kitchen soot and sake to their faces. The more they manage to smear on their faces, the happier and healthier they will be the next year.

Shinto is a remarkably promiscuous faith, with its roots in folk religion and its various borrowings from Buddhism, Hinduism and Taoism. There are gods and rites of all kinds: gods to find love, protect the hearth and stimulate fertility, gods to make money (like Ebisu, one of the 'Seven Lucky Gods', who was worshipped with particular fervour during the economic decline of 1997–98); rites of safety, rites to protect one's new car from a traffic accident. Shrines purvey 'lucky' amulets the way McDonald's churn out Big Macs, amulets to help conception, to guarantee easy delivery, to study successfully, to pass examinations, to get into Tokyo University (if one is especially blessed). I purchased a sizeable collection of these colourful little objects over my two years in Japan, trying to cover all possible contingencies.

Religion is one thing, photography another. Evidently the Japanese do not believe that being photographed takes away a little of one's soul. So most tourists tend to glide blithely past the Rinzo and its sacred scriptures, intent instead on being snapped in front of the Tosho-gu's famous carving of the three wise monkeys representing the dictum: 'See no Evil, Hear no Evil, and Speak no Evil'. When I visited Nikko I always felt that this was a sensible motto to take back to Todai with me. Maybe I was being Japanised, for it was precisely this attitude that is intransigently taken by men of high public office in Japan toward pressing issues, those of the present, and those— still important to many people—of the past.

6 OUT OF EDO II

⌘⌘⌘

HOLIDAY READING
Hiroshima
6 August 1997

It was a fine morning, windless and sultry, typical for the area around Hiroshima . . . The midsummer morning sunlight filled the sky to the point of overflowing. The brilliance of the light glinting off the mist in the blue sky was almost painful. The air-raid alert had been lifted about thirty minutes or an hour before and I was walking absentmindedly along the dusty paved road. I came to the east side of Shin'ozu Bridge. I stopped there for a minute, and just as I looked toward the sea and noticed the way the waves were sparkling, I saw, or rather felt, an enormous bluish white flash of light, as when a photographer lights a dish of magnesium. Off to my right, the sky split open over the city of Hiroshima.

From Toyofumi Ogura, *Letters from the End of the World* (1948), the first eyewitness account of the atomic bombing of Hiroshima ever published.[8]

⌘⌘⌘

Tourism is one of the victims of war. Places become temporarily or even permanently off limits, unvisitable. They are marred, destroyed, or simply earn a bad name. Yet tourism also benefits from war: battlefield sites are irresistible sources of vicarious experience. They become famously—or infamously—'tragic', attracting the curious and the ghoulish in the same way as people gather to gawk at the aftermath of road accidents. War, in short, has put some places on the map. Organised military tourism can be traced back to 1865 (at least), when Cook's tourists were shipped from Britain across the Atlantic to look over the smouldering battlefields of the American Civil War. Much more recently, macabre tourist itineraries to Indochina have cashed in on the notoriety of the 'killing fields' of Cambodia, Asian equivalents of European tourist mausolea such as the former Nazi death camps at Dachau and Auschwitz. The especially inquisitive can enjoy an enticing side-trip to a notorious Khmer Rouge interrogation centre. A tourist brochure issued in 1991 by an Australian company specialising in these tours for the more 'intrepid' traveller contained the caution: 'WARNING: Many people may find these [visits] intensely disturbing'. Visiting Cambodia thus becomes a dare, an Adults Only Asian Horror Show—NOT TO BE MISSED. George Johnston memorably called the Diggers of the two world wars the 'soldiers of far fortune'. It was the impulse to travel, he wrote in his novel *My Brother Jack* (1964), that propelled Australians across the globe to fight in foreign wars, as much as any patriotic or other ideological commitment.[9] Something similar can be said of Australian military tourists. In recent years the *Australian* newspaper has run tours to the battlefields of Gallipoli, with academic guidance so that the poor ignorant common folk are properly apprised of the sites' import.

Though I have never been to Gallipoli, I too have done my share of war tourism, visiting the World War I battlefields of northern France in the early 1980s to research a book. So many sites of mass death, 'created' over so many years and covering so little terrain, located in a flat landscape looking as if it had been designed for a battlefield—a testimony to the criminal absurdity of Western Front warfare. And I have been to Hiroshima.

It is a quirk of twentieth-century history that some of its cataclysmic events occurred in otherwise relatively insignificant places. The Bosnian capital of Sarajevo, for example, where the Archduke's assassination triggered World War I, or Dallas in Texas, where JFK was murdered, or the Ukrainian town of Chernobyl, which provided the scene of perhaps the century's greatest environmental calamity, or even that most banal-sounding place of all, 'Jonestown' in Guyana, where the ritual self-destruction of the People's Temple community in 1978 seemed to signify the death of the great counter-cultural experiment of the late 1960s and early 1970s. And Hiroshima, a provincial port city on the Inland Sea in western Honshu. 'Hiroshima'—of all place-names, does any other more potently encapsulate the life-and-death struggle of the twentieth century, its dreadful, electrifying human/political/technological drama?

Did my desire to visit Hiroshima partake of the ghoulish vicariousness I have been describing? Perhaps, in a way. I *could* say that I went there to sample the famous Hiroshima oysters (which do not glow in the dark, contrary to popular opinion); or to explore the islands of the Inland Sea, islands so exceptionally beautiful, according to Donald Richie, because 'a part of their beauty is that it is passing' (which again goes to show the head-turning power of Japanese nostalgia).[10] Or merely to visit the nearby island of Miyajima and the famous shrine of Itsukushima, with its massive vermilion *torii* 'floating' out of the silvery water. But these were peripheral attractions.

It was the Atom Bomb Dome that I wanted to see—the old industry promotion hall located near the epicentre of the tremendous explosion that occurred on that 'fine morning, windless and sultry' in early August 1945. Visualised in childhood, read about at school and seen on TV, that skeletal, skull-like steel frame exposed to the sky, that monstrous mushroom cloud, that awful image of the victim's irradiated shadow indelibly imprinted on the stone steps, were part of the imaginative baggage that many people of my post-war generation have carried through their lives. The name, 'Hiroshima', has such a historic resonance that it seemed it seemed a natural inclusion in my Japanese itinerary.

It was the summer holidays of 1997. The previous year was pure pleasure, walking in the Japan Alps around Kamikochi and swimming in the Japan Sea at Wajima near the tip of the Noto Hanto Peninsula, north of the splendid old city of Kanazawa. It was time to get serious. So we went on our own Atom Bomb tour, lobbing in Hiroshima for the 6 August commemoration, then travelling on to Nagasaki for its anniversary three days later.

As I suppose must be the case for many foreigners, especially those from the countries allied against Japan in the Pacific War, I visited Hiroshima with a confusion of feelings. None of them, I confess, was guilt. Why should contemporary Australians feel any more guilty about Hiroshima than young Japanese do about the deeds of their forefathers? The same could even be said of the Americans, who were the ones who dropped the damn thing after all, although when I was there the city was full of contrite-looking Yanks (all earnest warmth and good wishes, moist eyes and clammy hands) who had evidently assumed personal responsibility for the tragedy. But, like a stranger at a funeral, the foreign visitor is liable to feel a fraction uncomfortable in Hiroshima, especially on the occasion of 6 August, when what Ian Buruma calls the 'peace industry' is in full swing.[11]

That industry has turned Hiroshima from a pleasantly prosperous provincial city—with its rattling trams, rivers and bay, it reminded me a bit of a Japanese version of Melbourne—into a self-styled 'City of International Peace and Culture'. (I quote from the Hiroshima City Tourist Association's official brochure.) 'Peace' hits the visitor from all sides in Hiroshima, especially in and around the 'Peace Park', which is located on a delta island across the river from the Atom Bomb Dome. As well as its large and occasionally contentious Peace Museum and commemorative architecture such as Kenzo's cenotaph to the A-bomb victims and Flame of Peace, there is a Peace Memorial Post, a Peace Tower, a Stone Lantern of Peace, a Peace Bell, a Peace Fountain, a Statue of Prayer for Peace, a Pond of Peace, a Prayer Monument for Peace, a Peace Cairn, even a Prayer Haiku Monument for Peace, along with various monuments and emotive statuary dedicated to those who were killed by the explosion or suffered from its after-effects, particularly children and students.

It was hard not to be sympathetic. I am unconvinced by the argument that the dropping of the bomb was a Good Thing because it ultimately saved more lives than it cost, because it was the only military endgame open to the Americans and because it brought about an end that justified the means. Equally, I have no time for the 'serves them right' school of Australian war historiography, a few Jap-hating members of which still teach in Australian universities, bovver-boy historians who compensate for never having personally fought their way out of a paper bag by writing tough about war. But I do not deny that their criticism of the Hiroshima myth—the universal symbol of peace, disarmament and international brotherhood—is understandable.

Before Hiroshima the City of Peace, there was Hiroshima the City of War. Its *raison d'etre*, at least from 1894, when Japan's Supreme Imperial Headquarters was moved to the Hiroshima Castle compound, was to provide a vital strategic staging base, sending soldiers and supplies off to the various military ventures upon which Japan embarked over the ensuing decades. Hiroshima grew rich out of the war boom. Ian Buruma has observed that, as the Second General HQ of the Imperial Army, it was 'swarming with soldiers' at the time of the bombing. But it was also 'swarming' with civilians, especially first thing in the morning and mid-city. That is the point. To talk about Hiroshima's commemorative insistence on 'the point of view of the victims', as Buruma does, is a bit irrelevant.[12] That 6 August 1945 was an atrocious event is beyond dispute. Who else's point of view *should* be preserved but that of the thousands of innocent individuals who perished, suffered, had their lives suddenly and shockingly destroyed?

Nevertheless, the aesthetic of Peace Park is overdone and ultimately cloying, and the ideology underlying it is disaffecting to say the least. Even the casual observer cannot help noting that the memorial to the Korean victims of the Bomb—some 20 000 of them, including many forced labourers—is located outside the park itself. This is an irritating pointer to the criminal self-absorption of the local authorities, who, like many others in Japanese intellectual and political circles, would have Japan take out a patent on nuclear martyrdom. If it is any consolation, the Korean memorial (erected by the Japanese South Korean residents association) is all the more moving for not being so surrounded by the plethora of peace paraphernalia that makes Peace Park a theme park much like countless others all over Japan.

Of course, modern Hiroshima, an industrial and commercial city with excellent public facilities and cultural amenities, has a life outside 6 August 1945. It is we tourists who gravitate toward the park and museum to make our aesthetic assessments and moral judgements. But by comparison with Nagasaki, Hiroshima has made 'the Bomb' exclusively its own, even though the 'Fat Man' that wiped out a third of Nagasaki had more explosive power than Hiroshima's 'Little Boy'. (Has there ever been a sicker name for *anything*?) Perhaps this is because the thing exploded above the middle of town; in Nagasaki the bomb fell well short of its target, detonating instead over Urakami, probably the centre of Christianity in Japan, with its large, grotesque Catholic cathedral and decent-sized congregation. Perhaps it is because Hiroshima came first, and so registered the biggest impact. Or perhaps it is merely that Nagasaki, with its rich Chinese and European heritage and lively, 'exotic' ambience, its lovely harbour and long list of tourist sights, simply has other things to think about, another image of itself to sell. In the Peace Park kiosk it was the T-shirt of the Atom Dome that the consumers were clamouring to buy.

The view of Japan as victim is much more problematic than seeing individual human beings, randomly slaughtered, as victims. As Buruma argues in *The Wages of Guilt* (1994), 'Hiroshima' has clouded Japan's wartime culpability by allowing it to take the high moral ground over the war.[13] All shades of the Japanese political spectrum—from rightists who believe that war guilt has ruinously sapped the national will to leftists who exploit the tragedy to assert an egregiously idealised 'Hiroshima spirit'—are susceptible to what Saburo

Ienaga has called a 'collective amnesia' about the war and its 'costly lessons'.[14]

The common Japanese equation of Hiroshima with Auschwitz as 'absolute evils', Buruma notes, has made it easy for the Japanese to construct themselves as victims of racism, like the Jews. Apparently in the late 1980s there was even a plan to build an Auschwitz memorial in a small town near by. It did not eventuate, though a Hiroshima Auschwitz Committee exists in the city. Interestingly, at the International Peace Center in Osaka, a museum that addresses Japanese atrocities in Asia during the 1930s more unequivocally than either of the museums at Hiroshima and Nagasaki, a fair amount of wall space in the section devoted to the Pacific War is assigned to Auschwitz, and those dreadful images of its inmates. I found this curious, given that the exhibition allocated just a photograph or two to Allied POWs of the Japanese.

Historical astigmatism afflicts even some astute Japanese commentators on the war. So a professor of Peace Studies at Hiroshima University, Mitsuo Okamoto, in writing about the placing of the Atom Bomb Dome on the UNESCO World Heritage list in 1996 (joining, indeed, the death camp at Auschwitz), mars his argument about Japanese historical responsibility by asserting that the atomic bombing was special not merely because it ushered in the nuclear age and the 'civilisation of death', but also because it was 'a violation of international law'. Thus it 'belongs to a different category' of war crimes from Japan's military medical experimentation on Chinese civilians, its research into germ warfare and its sex slavery of Korean women.[15] Strangely, Japan's flagrant contempt for the Geneva Convention in its treatment of its prisoners of war does not rate a mention in this list of 'lesser' offences.

⌘⌘⌘

I was not in Japan for the fiftieth anniversary of the end of the war, but I saw enough personally and in the Japanese media to know that these commemorations are regarded as major events. In August 1997, on the same day as Japan's abject surrender fifty-two years earlier, a diehard nationalist screamed praise for the Emperor on the steps of the Tokyo Metropolitan Police office and then promptly shot himself in the head. That day I had taken myself off to the Yasukini Jinja in Tokyo, the shrine for 'the Peace of the Nation', where the spirits of those who have died in the emperor's name since the Meiji Restoration are venerated. Among these 'spirits' are those of prosecuted war criminals like Tojo and members of the vicious Kempeitai, the Japanese secret police. This would be akin to the Germans worshipping Goering and the SS. Not surprisingly, the Yasukini is a constant source of controversy in Japan. Cabinet ministers continually pay their respects there; prime ministers Nakasone and Hashimoto also dropped in, prompting official complaints from the Chinese and Koreans and disquiet among the many Japanese who abhor the shrine as concrete evidence that their country refuses to face up to its military past.

In the shrine grounds stands a war museum, the Yushukan, which houses assorted war relics, such as blood-stained, bullet-holed uniforms from the Russo–Japanese War and kamikaze memorabilia from the Great East Asian War. The theme of sacrifice is emphasised. But there is no reference of any kind to war atrocities, or even misdeeds, apart from an evasive reference to the suffering of those who built the Thai–Burma railway, and this in front of a shining, restored steam locomotive—the first to traverse the completed railway—which takes pride of place outside the museum's entrance.

Inside, a cabinet showcased a copy of Charles Lindbergh's journals, opened to a page where the famous aviator complains about American mistreatment of Japanese POWs somewhere or other in the Pacific theatre. The relevant passage was crudely underlined in red biro; but nowhere among the displays was there any mention of Japan's treatment of *its* prisoners. When I made a return visit to the museum, around the time when there was public unease at the number of knife attacks taking place in schools, the room containing the Lindbergh text had been taken over by an extensive exhibition of samurai swords. I left the Yasukini feeling as angry as I ever became in Japan.

In contrast to the hype that surrounded them, the actual peace ceremonies I attended at Hiroshima and Nagasaki were low-key, decorous affairs, although the typhonic weather in which the latter commemoration was held seemed suitably apocalyptic. The emphasis oscillated between sombre memories of the fatalities and concerns for the welfare of the survivors, the ageing and afflicted *hibakusha*, and an insistent plea for disarmament (with mayoral raps over the knuckles for America's hypocritical nuclear weapons policies), combined with a renewed commitment to a peaceful future. In both ceremonies pacific aspirations were scripted to representatives of the cities' children, their shrill, eager, amplified voices testimony to the irresistible power of clichés. At Nagasaki a group of kids made the following oath:

> We will make efforts to realise the aspiration for peace,
> understanding the feelings of others and helping each other,
> treasuring nature and living creatures,
> thanking the many people who support and encourage us.

6 OUT OF EDO II

In the powerful film of Ibuse's novel *Black Rain*—which I saw on daytime television after my return to Australia, thinking it would be less harrowing than the alternative programmes, which included something called *Midday With Kerri-Anne*—a Hiroshima survivor complains that the 'hell' he had lived through had been 'turned into a festival'. He was right. Peace Park the day before the ceremony had a festive if quasi-religious atmosphere. Buddhist monks were out in force, chanting long and hard enough to give one a headache just by looking at them. Penitent Americans wandered around depositing wreaths and practising their Japanese. Meanwhile earnest members of the New York-based Society of Prayer for World Peace mingled in the crowd, distributing an expensively produced brochure containing photographs of various people holding 'peace poles' emblazoned with the society's motto, 'May Peace Prevail on Earth'. Disconcertingly, one of those photographed was the American pop singer John Denver, who was to die in a plane crash while I was in Japan. The society also formed prayer and meditation groups and conducted a lengthy celebration of 'the oneness of humanity' by raising the national flags of every country on earth, one by one, each greeted with a chorus of the same motto. Coming from Australia has its advantages. Had Deborah and I hailed from Zimbabwe, we might never have made it to Nagasaki in time for the commemoration three days later.

But the highlight of the Hiroshima commemoration occurs at dusk on the evening of 6 August, when crowds gather along the bank of the Motoyasugawa River near the Atom Bomb Dome to watch thousands of paper lanterns being released on the water, each containing a candle for the spirit of an individual casualty of the explosion. Downriver to the sea they float, thousands upon thousands of lanterns glowing in the Hiroshima dark. It is quite a sight. There are times when cultural analysis of the kind Buruma offers in his condemnation of the Hiroshima myth—however well-motivated, sensitive, informed and intellectually persuasive—is simply beside the point. At least that is what I thought as we walked back to our hotel that night. On the way we passed by a 'country music saloon' called the El Paso—a reminder, in case the Atom Bomb Dome did not suffice, of who really did win the war.

⌘⌘⌘

I have photographs of places in Japan that mean nothing to me. I mean the photographs themselves. What are they of? I took so many that I would have had to employ somebody full-time to write up all the captions. One, a close-up taken with my Canon Autoboy, reveals a low circular stone pedestal surrounded by small pebbles, like a kind of terrestrial ulcer. It was obviously snapped at a Zen rock garden; just as obviously it was taken in Kyoto. Taking intimate shots of the ground is the kind of thing one does in Kyoto.

In fact a search through my mound of Japan tourist brochures reveals the image to be of the Stone Garden of A-un, one of the five gardens of Ryugen-in, a small sub-temple in the grounds of the great Zen monastery of Daitoku-ji, in north-west Kyoto. The stone garden, the brochure helpfully explains:

> represents the truth of the universe. 'A-un' means inhale and exhale, heaven and earth, positive and negative or male and female, and those are inseparable from each other. A-un shows the truth of the universe and the essence of Zen.

6 OUT OF EDO II

It may perhaps indicate something of the consciousness-clearing capabilities of Zen (which is sometimes mystified as the achievement of understanding without the attempt to understand) that I can barely remember visiting the Ryugen-in temple. I even have limited recollection of the famous garden at Ryoan-ji near by, the abstract garden *par excellence*, which according to my diaries I visited on three occasions just in case there was something I missed. All that concentrated contemplation, staring hard at those stones, has left me with little memory of actually being there at all. What I can recall is guiltily sneaking out the back of a meditation hall, from whose veranda I had sat gazing at one of those Zen gardens, to check the amount of yen in my wallet, counting the cost of looking at a few rocks placed here and there in a sea of gravel. Call this the price of Kyoto.

It is easy, too easy, to be cynical about Kyoto. Its mystique as the epitome of 'Japaneseness' can be extremely annoying to the Tokyo resident, irritated that the capital city takes second place culturally to a provincial, insular has-been like Kyoto, now a mere suburb of gregarious, boisterous Osaka. Seeing only ugliness in Tokyo, travellers see only loveliness in Kyoto, even though much of it is at least as unlovely and ramshackle. The ancient imperial capital's celebrated temples and shrines and monasteries and gardens, the things with which the city is synonymous, are but a sprinkling of diamonds in a steaming pile of urban shit. But the diamonds are so numerous and dazzle so blindingly that visitors tend to be oblivious to the fact that essentially Kyoto is another big, sprawling Japanese city, its elegant Chinese grid of streets choked by traffic, strangled by power lines, despoiled by the anarchic urban development that one sees all over Japan. Ian Buruma has noted that in 1983 Japanese atom bomb literature was published in fifteen volumes; so great is the Japanese interest in its nuclear martyrdom.[16] One wonders how large a compendium of foreign writing about Kyoto—most of it of the swooning, salivating, 'golly, geishas' kind—would be. There is plenty of it, anyway; more than enough for me to want to add to it.

Bill loathed the place and refused to go there. Ohara claimed not to like it either, though it amused him greatly that one of the city's major attractions is actually called Ohara. This small village in the hills to the north of Kyoto, considered since ancient times to be the holy place of those who believe in Jodo, the Buddhist Pure Land, is the home of the Sanzen-in, a temple whose structures and grounds are so upliftingly beautiful that people actually look upon them and *smile*. Ohara reckoned he'd made it in Japan because he had such a captivating place named after him. As if teaching at Todai wasn't enough.

Personally, though, I find it hard to be too dismissive of Kyoto. I liked the place. I liked it on my first visit, at Christmas time in weather so breathtakingly clear and cold it appeared that nature had conspired to preserve its ancient structures by having them snap-frozen. I liked it on return trips, too, working my way through its astonishing list of sights methodically and relentlessly, still making discoveries after many days of exploration. I surprised myself by my discipline in this enterprise. Throw in the even older temples at Nara, an hour away by local train, and it is no wonder that even the most determined cultural tourists to the Kyoto area find themselves seeking out the alternative pleasures of the *pachinko* parlour or department store. (A group of turn-of-the-century travellers touring the city in Rosa Praed's novel *Madame Izan* suffers an acute case of 'temple indigestion'.[17])

Yet today's Kyoto is a working city, not merely a living museum. Pico Iyer, who may have spent even more time looking at the A-un garden than I did, saw the historical glories and 'ugly' contemporary life of Kyoto not as contradictions but as happily co-existent, even symbiotic, forming a whole, indivisible and magnificent, where it was possible 'to partake of the gleaming splendors of the *depato* [department store] and to sip green-tea floats in teahouses; to find moonlit prints in convenience stores and damascene earrings in coffee shops'. Iyer could hardly believe the 'flawless' world on which he had stumbled.[18] He is exaggerating, of course, and he knows it. But Kyoto is not the total travesty lamented by Alex Kerr, whose elegy for the city lies at the heart of *Lost Japan*. The 'degradation' of Kyoto that Kerr reviles is associated in his mind with its becoming a kind of historical theme park that has no real connection with the lives of modern Japanese—a theme park, moreover, much less pleasing than fake constructions like the artificial Dutch town of Huis ten Bosch, north of Nagasaki. Somewhere between Iyer's enthusiasm (the passion of the newly converted) and Kerr's outrage (the bitterness of one whose faith has precipitously lapsed) lies the truth of modern Kyoto.

The Kyoto of the common tourist itinerary—the Kyoto of the Kiyomizu temple, the Katsura imperial villa and the mesmerising Kinkaku-ji, the Golden Pavilion—is precious in every sense of the word, self-consciously and classically 'Japanese'. But *that* Kyoto is representative of only one Japan. Another 'real Japan' might involve an alternative itinerary like this, beginning in Nagoya and ending up in Tokyo:

MONDAY: Toyota Motor Corporation, Motomachi Plant: 1 Motomachi, Toyota-shi, Aichi Prefecture. (English guided tour available.)

TUESDAY: Kirin Brewery, Yokohama Plant: 1-17-1, Namamugi, Tsurami-ku, Yokohama, 126. (Photography and smoking prohibited.)

WEDNESDAY: NEC Showroom: Hibiya Kokusai Bldg., B1, 2-2-3 Uchisaiwaicho, Chiyoda-ku, Tokyo, 100. (No need for advanced booking.)

And so on.

The Japan National Tourist Organisation puts out a very helpful pamphlet on 'Industrial Japan', listing the above among its riveting sights. But in fact there is no need to go beyond Kyoto for a look at this version of Japan. After all, Kirin has one of its big plants there: open 9.00–16.30 (closed on Monday); tour duration 1 hr. 30 min. (including beer sampling). As rough as guts and as refined as all-get-out, Kyoto is both incongruous and typical of whichever 'Japan' takes your fancy. I have the photographs to prove it.

⌘ ⌘ ⌘

7 BOOMERANG JAPAN

If the Tokugawa administration was in power today, current-affairs commentators (not that they'd be allowed) would probably talk about its 'obsessive' interest in centralised control. During the early years of their long subjugation of Japan, the Tokugawa shoguns introduced a system called *sankin kotai*, or 'alternate attendance', under which the vassal lords from all over the country were expected—no, *ordered*— to spend one year out of every two in Edo.[1] It was a good way of keeping an unruly and endemically treacherous lot under control. My two-year appointment to Tokyo University had something of the *sankin kotai* about it, excepting of course that it was hardly 'alternate'—two years and I was out, and out of Japan altogether.

My contract expired on 1 April 1998. I will resist embellishing the ironic connotations of the date, if for no other reason than that I remain unsure as to whether they apply to my departure or my initial arrival in Tokyo. In any case, after days of gorgeous early spring weather that late March, the moment was fast approaching when I would finally take heed of the advice emblazoned across the T-shirted chest of the girl on the train from Kemigawa, and 'fuck off'. In Japan, that is what the vast majority of foreigners eventually do.

Six months pregnant, Deborah returned home at the end of February, after devouring vast quantities of sushi at several farewell parties laid on by various friends and colleagues. Back in Melbourne, she had to attend to the cleaning up of our house, which appeared to have been let to the local chapter of the Hell's Angels in our absence. Meanwhile I attended to the business of vacating the Kemigawa apartment. I sold the furniture and electrical appliances and cleared and cleaned the flat to make it ready for inspection by the university housing authorities and associated estate agents and builders. The Japanese believe in strength in numbers. Never mind; the flat looked spotless to me, so at the appointed hour I cockily invited the inspectors in to do their worst, expecting nothing more than a small impost for a tiny tear in one of the screen doors in the main bedroom.

I was wrong about that. The inspection was a nightmare. Several non-English-speaking, gimlet-eyed fellows in company with a young female photographer went over the place with a fine-tooth comb, examining every nook and cranny, pointing, conferring, shaking their heads at the slightest scuff mark, appearing to blame me for the fact that the front rooms of the flat were blighted with rising damp, and writing down numbers with several noughts attached to them on an invoice. These blokes were doing me like a dinner, and there was nothing I could do about it. They made me feel like a criminal. Irritated, then angered and finally rattled, I would gladly have ended the

7 BOOMERANG JAPAN

ordeal by offering my wrists to be handcuffed and allowing myself to be led away to be fingerprinted, photographed for a mug shot and charged with being a what I patently was—a dirty, negligent foreigner. Eventually they presented me with a bill for necessary repairs, including repainting, amounting to 80 000-odd yen (about $1000 Australian). They appeared to suggest that they had been extremely generous: I had got off lightly, indeed I had come out in front! Now I know why foreign businessmen complain about how hard it can be to do business in Japan, where cutting a deal often means getting utterly *fleeced*.

I spent the last couple of weeks at the house of Michael and Christine Hinds, out in western Tokyo, near Kichijoji. They had fled Tokyo for their homeland at the beginning of the between-semesters break, fled back to what Michael bleakly called 'the verdant bomb-sites of Ireland'. (And this was before his home town, Omagh, had its guts ripped out by that horrendous explosion in August 1998.)

It was time for me to do and see last things. I made a quick final trip to Kyoto to deliver my stock lecture on Australian multiculturalism to a group of unprecedentedly conscious students at Doshisha University. As usual in Kyoto I stayed at a *ryokan* called the Three Sisters Inn, a studiedly traditional establishment that seemed to cater exclusively to foreigners. The proprietors were three sisters indeed, very attractive still in their (I guess) late fifties or early sixties and great beauties in their day, whom I nicknamed the 'Makiokas' after the famous fictional sisters from the Kansai. They were models of solicitude. When I announced my intention to take a bath before bed, one of them asked me if I had been drinking sake. 'Very, very dangerous', she said, 'to drink the sake before the hot bath.' Truthfully I replied that I had not, though I omitted mentioning the couple of glasses of Australian rotgut I had very recently scoffed at an Italian restaurant significantly called Café Fiasco. I survived the bath, though there would be worse places to perish in Japan than the Three Sisters Inn.

It was hard, on that final visit to Kyoto, not to be struck by its residents' determined if probably doomed efforts to preserve what remains of its architectural heritage. As an urban paradigm of developmental vandalism, the city has become the focus of international environmentalism, playing host to several conferences on the issue. The activist language of contemporary environmental awareness was everywhere, on signs stuck on lamp-posts and temple walls, in newspapers and tourist literature. It had even invaded the cocoon of the Three Sisters Inn. In my room a large handwritten notice spreading the gospel was affixed to the wall above the futon. Not unusually in Japan, however, the message was confusing to say the least:

WE NEED TO WORK TOGETHER FOR GLOBAL WARMING.
PLEASE KEEP THE ROOM TEMPERATURE
LESS THAN 20 degrees (HEATING)
MORE THAN 28 degrees (AIRCON)

Back in Tokyo, I spent much of the time walking, leg-wearily recommitting to personal memory the city's two faces, filthy-rich Ginza and dirt-poor San'ya. I don't mind admitting that, whatever the latter's vicarious anthropological interest, I ended up much preferring the former. An area of reclaimed land not far from the mouth of the Sumida where the Shogunate minted its coin in the seventeenth and eighteenth centuries, Ginza was the first Westernised quarter of Tokyo and for decades the urban epitome of Japanese success, savvy and style. In these days of national straitening, it is still a place of swagger. The name simply resonates. Ginza may be where the tourists go, but it is also where contemporary *Eddoko* themselves naturally gravitate on their day off, for the big day out. Towards the end I would insouciantly stroll into Ginza cafés where the coffee was notoriously expensive, just to show how much I fitted into the scene. What good was the yen going to be to me?

But traditional Japanese culture was never far from my mind. So one afternoon I walked down Harumi-dori from Ginza Crossing to the Kabuki-za, the striking but strange baroque building—a fusion of Vienna and Vientiane—that has been the national home of kabuki theatre since the end of the nineteenth century. People were beginning to queue for tickets, well in advance of the scheduled performance. I was struck by how old and dowdy they were, dotards from the provinces, in Tokyo for one last chance to see the great Japanese dramatic form, these days a show put on just for tourists. Young Japanese do not seem to be much interested. While their grandparents were lining up for the kabuki, the blithe young philistines were cramming into cinemas in Ginza, in Shibuya and Shinjuku and Ikebukuro, to see Hollywood movies like *Titanic*. I didn't really want to go to the kabuki either; I'd performed enough cultural duties already. So I turned away from the Kabuki-za and sped toward one of the local cinemas, hoping I'd catch the 1.30 showing of Harvey Keitel in *Copland*. I'd become Japanese enough to do that.

And I took my leave from Komaba. I'd long since made my peace with Tokyo University and even felt a pang of regret as I cleaned out my office, preparing it for my successor, who was not, it so happened, to show up for another six months. With Ohara I toured the campus, photographing some of its more picturesque sights—a gutted computer screen here, a discarded bicycle there, fields of empty bottles, cardboard boxes, cigarette butts, used contraceptives. Some of the cigarette ends, at least, had probably been deposited by Ohara himself.

Todai was alive with incongruity to the very end. On my final day at Komaba, all farewells made and genuine good wishes exchanged with my Japanese colleagues, I went, as I had done hundreds of times before, to the room that housed the fax machine, my link with the world. Beside the machine was a CD called 'Burt Bacharach and his Friends'. What the hell was this strange object doing there? I picked it up, hefting it in my hand and examining it as one might examine something from Mars, and took a closer look. It was a Japanese pressing of Bacharach's best. One of the songs on the disk was incorrectly but not illogically titled 'What's A New Pussycat?'

Like Hinds, Ohara was getting out of Tokyo for the semester break, heading for Toyama in western Japan 'to do the business' (his words) with one of his lady friends ('a Norwegian!', he told me archly) who was teaching in some university or other over there. Never one for mawkish sentiment, Ohara brusquely shook my hand in Hachiko Square in Shibuya after our last drink together, congratulated me on surviving my Dantesque adventure and wished me well back in Australia. Portentously, he then reiterated the epic poem's narrative movement, which he had brought to my attention a couple of weeks earlier at the farewell party at Tokyo Opera City. 'After hell, purgatory,' he smirked, flourishing his fag and singeing the bizarre, red-ochred coiffure of one of the young fashion plates who haunt Hachiko day and night. And then he was gone, merging into the mass of commuters channelling into one of the entrances to Shibuya station. My urban tracker to the well of the Uluru Bar, my Virgil guiding me through the chthonic depths of the Tokyo underground, Ohara disappeared from my life forever, simply ceasing to exist, like a fragment of some broken dream.

⌘⌘⌘

> Get out of my road
> and allow me to plant these
> bamboos, Mr Toad.

It is hard to come up with a more inane Japanese poem than this horrible *haiku*, a Tokugawa-period offering by a chap called Miurachura, who in fairness has almost certainly been ill-served by his translator. Yet there are many foreigners who have lived, or still live, in Japan who think they know something sillier. It is a *tanka* by no less a personage than the Emperor Meiji himself, the towering historical figure in whose name Japan put an end to its Tokugawan isolationism and embraced the West:

> In my garden
> Side by side
> Native plants, foreign plants,
> Growing together.[2]

Exotics living in Japan, even those who have put down roots in the country over a period of years, might very well consider the Emperor Meiji's dream of harmony an illusion, a deception, maybe even a downright lie. Westerners constantly complain that the Japanese garden is as enclosed as ever. As for the members of despised Oriental or Third World racial groups such as the Iranians and Bangladeshis, who in recent years have formed into sizeable working communities in Japan, they complain of unremitting prejudice, of being, socially at least, cast into the wilderness. Meanwhile long-term residents of Korean origin still encounter manifest discrimination, including being disqualified from the right to take national university entrance examinations if they happened to attend a Korean school.

It is often said that Japan is changing and is becoming more willing to relate to the rest of the world. There is some truth in this, but the change is marginal, and the rate of real cultural exchange (and I'm not just talking about learning English or playing baseball) still astonishingly small. In May 1996 the *Hiragana Times*, which promotes itself as a 'Cross Culture Communication Magazine', triumphantly reported that 1993 figures disclosed that 3 per cent of marriages within Japan were between Japanese and foreign nationals. Hardly a stupendous statistic, though a rise from a measly 1 per cent in 1985. Yet this self-consciously 'cross-cultural' journal—so uncertain of its stance on the topic that it called the article 'International marriage is a gamble?'—felt it important to note that 'international couples that split are also cropping up one after another'. As its contribution to global relations, the magazine announced its plans to establish an 'international marital disputes' corner, in which bi-cultural couples were invited to air their differences.[3] Ever alert to horse-racing's ability to act as a metaphor for life, Michael Hinds saw great significance in the fact that the Japanese racing authorities barred foreign-bred horses from running in their classic races. They might win, mightn't they?

Japan's depressing propensity to blame others when things go wrong remains intact. In private conversation or in the

7 BOOMERANG JAPAN

media, the apparent rise in serious crime is often attributed to some insidious outside influence; isolated instances of foreign misdemeanours within Japan often encourage the blanket criticism of all *gaijin*. After an unpleasant incident involving the 'touching' of a young girl by a foreigner in a swimming pool in Gunma Prefecture in 1998, for example, the local authorities barred *all* foreigners from using the pool. Underlying the pervasive fear of earthquakes that exists among so many foreign residents of Tokyo are the horror stories of irrational retribution against Koreans after the 1923 cataclysm.

Japan's xenophobia, like xenophobia everywhere, lies in the assertion of its own national difference. Absurd assumptions of racial uniqueness still abound. In 1997 the old men who constitute the Japanese medical establishment yet again postponed a decision on whether the contraceptive pill should be made available to the nation's women. They claimed concern for women's well-being and worries over a decline in sexual mores (a stupefying hypocrisy, that), but they were almost certainly more interested in protecting the health of the abortion and condom industries: up to 25 per cent of Japanese pregnancies are terminated by abortions, while the condom is the preferred method of contraception for some 77 per cent of sexually active Japanese.[4] Deborah informed me that some of the male Japanese doctors with whom she came into contact while engaged in research at Todai's School of International Health were suspicious of the Pill because they seriously believed that the biology of Japanese women is 'different'. On the same basis, they blissfully consumed cigarette after cigarette because lung cancer would never claim *them*.

In *Lost Japan* Alex Kerr talks of his adopted country as being like an oyster that, finding the 'invasion' of foreign objects 'intolerable', secretes layer upon layer over the surface of the 'offending' particles, eventually producing a 'beautiful pearl'. 'In like manner', Kerr continues, 'Japan coats all culture from abroad, transforming it into a Japanese-style pearl'.[5] The problem with this analogy is that it implies that the incorporation of the foreign into Japan has produced something superb. In fact, *gaijin* themselves tend to argue that Japanised foreign phenomena tend toward the ersatz—like a brand of olive oil that Kerr mentions, which bears the label 'Specially Reconstituted for Japanese Taste'. Plastic, in other words, rather than pearl.

Most human 'foreign objects' in Japan, however, are well aware that they have been accepted inside the oyster's protective shell unwillingly. Those who are offended by this live their lives in a state of perpetual resentment. An Australian tourist in Japan in the 1930s, Florence Taylor, observed in her travel book *A Pot-Pourri of Eastern Asia* (1935) that the British residents she encountered did not wear the 'amiable smile' universally encountered on the faces of the Japanese themselves, but on the contrary looked 'hunted and haunted'.[6] On bad days I detected the same look on the faces of Todai's *gaijin* instructors, fellows like Colin Quirk, the unmistakable look of captives hankering for their freedom.

Many foreigners become bitter at the way the warm Japanese embrace can so quickly become the cold shoulder. How can it be that a people so friendly and kind, hospitable and generous, always regard you as irretrievably 'Other' merely because you are not of the Japanese race? But if you accept the fact you are always going to be seen as an outsider, if you live in Japan on your own terms while knowing deep down that you are there on its say-so, if you don't give a damn about 'fitting in' anyway, then Japan is a relatively easy and pleasant country in which to live. Bill, as he often told me, loved living

7 BOOMERANG JAPAN

in Japan. He spoke its language and had educated himself in the ways of its culture, but he harboured no illusions about actually 'turning Japanese'. The thought would have appalled him. Bill enjoyed living on the fringes of the great Japanese family, enjoyed being something of a misfit. Better to be a misfit in a foreign land than in your own country—which is perhaps why so many foreigners living permanently in Japan are there in the first place, because they never felt at home in their countries of birth.

Expatriates in Japan exist in 'a kind of social vacuum', argued the poet Harold Stewart. This worries those who want to integrate into the society. But it did not worry Stewart himself, because all he wanted was to 'float free'. As an artist, being considered an outsider (even after two decades residence in Kyoto) had its advantages. 'I'm an onlooker from the sidelines', Stewart said, 'but "the observer sees most of the game"'.[7] This was a view with which Bill, an artist of life, would doubtless have concurred. Living both within and outside Japan, he had the best of both worlds. He would sometimes argue this case a touch too forcefully, as if trying to convince himself of its veracity. But it is a rare person who feels undividedly at home, anywhere.

⌘⌘⌘

As a foreigner in Japan, it is often difficult not to take things personally. Anxious that late March to tick off the remaining unvisited places on my Japanese itinerary before my final departure, I took a three-hour train journey south to Shimoda, the old port on the Izu Peninsula where Commodore Perry returned to Japan in 1854 with his Black Ships, bringing about an end to 220 years of national seclusion and heralding—so the historical line runs—a new era of openness to the West. Shimoda is a pleasant enough town, its lovely natural situation only mildly debased by development. 'Black Ships' memorabilia abound, and there is a pretty area of canals and old houses featuring the distinctive thick *namako-kabe* walls, diamond-patterned with grey and white tiles, that are characteristic of the Izu Peninsula, notoriously prone to battering typhoons. I wandered around the town for an hour or two. Since there were a few more things I wanted to see, I thought I might check in to a hotel for the night. But so pointed was the lack of assistance at the local tourist office, where a blank-faced woman dismissively pushed an accommodation guide in Japanese towards me across the counter, that I strode straight back to the station and caught the first train back to the capital. On the way I passed a brand-spanking-new establishment called the Hotel Marseille, located not far from the old port. That rubbed salt in my wounded traveller's pride.

My abortive trip to Shimoda also revealed to me how Japan's historical suspicion of the West has been exacerbated by the abrupt conclusion to World War II and how deep the victim mentality runs in the country, at least among older people. Before my encounter with the brick wall in the Shimoda tourist office I had visited the well-known temple dedicated to Okichi, the local geisha whom the Shogunate had ordered to keep house for Townsend Harris, America's first consul to Japan, after he arrived in the country in 1856. Complaining that poor Okichi had a skin infection of worrying provenance, Harris sent her packing after just a few days. Alcoholic and stigmatised for her fleeting contact with the foreigner, she eventually drowned herself in 1890. But around the figure of Okichi grew a legend that established her as the embodiment of Japanese self-sacrifice.

A small museum adjacent to the Chorakuji Temple, where the Japan–US Peace Treaty was ratified in 1854, cashes in on speculation about the precise nature of Okichi's relationship with the American consul. The museum is filled with a tawdry collection of erotica and 'suggestive' objects, most notably an exceptionally elongated radish. Its prize exhibit is the so-called 'Okichi Kannon', a statue of the ill-fated geisha in the guise of the female Buddhist deity. She is nude, which has the unfortunate effect of making her look like a shop-window dummy.

Observing my inappropriate mirth, the wizened museum guide directed me to a small adjoining room dominated by a mural that evidently depicted the horrors of the nuclear devastation at Hiroshima and Nagasaki. The smile was wiped from my face. Figures of women in children, their faces contorted in terror and pain, languished against a flame-red background. On a side wall, pointing towards this distressing, if amateurishly executed scene, was a model of Commodore Perry's Black Ship. The display screamed its message; it needed no explanatory notice. '*Look* what the American presence has done for Japan! *See* what the barbarians did to us!' I remembered Clive James's Tokyo coffee-shop reverie about the pervasiveness of World War II in Japan: 'It's over but it's not over'.

⌘⌘⌘

One childhood Christmas I was given a Viewmaster, a plastic contraption through which one could look at coloured slides.

My favourite was a series of photographs of world beauty spots—Niagara Falls, Fuji, Everest and the Matterhorn, lakes in Scandinavia, the Grand Canyon, tulip time in Holland and a view of the big red monolith, Uluru, or Ayers Rock as it was called then. I remember being fascinated by the clarity and intensity of the focus the Viewmaster afforded. That kind of focus is well suited to Japan. It looks better up close. The panorama of Kyoto from the viewing platform at the Kiyomizu temple is undeniably unattractive—tower blocks and smokestacks vying with the odd pagoda. But down among the gladed neighbourhoods of its shrines and temples the view changes, the beauties of the place reveal themselves.

It would have been easy to miss one of the most memorable things I saw in Japan, located in the small Honen-in temple in Kyoto's Higashiyama district, a temple famous for its Momoyama screens and the fact that Junichiro Tanizaki lies buried somewhere in its graveyard. Placed by the path, in among the moss beds and beyond the raked white sand, lies a perfect little fountain, a small leaf deftly placed so that the thinnest of thin streams of water cascades down the stem to the ground—a soundless waterfall in miniature. When I visited again a year later, the same set-piece was in place and in motion. George Johnston once wrote that, 'like many things in Japan', Mount Fuji is 'enchanting only at a distance'.[8] He might be right about Fuji, but in general it is close up that Japan is at its best.

This is true of the people as well as the landscape. It has often been argued that the famous Japanese courtesies are in fact indistinguishable from bad manners, merely routine, a front, a charade, masking indifference or even contempt. This strikes me as a dumb argument. 'Good manners' are in essence artificial. Of course there is a practised quality to the mechanical

7 BOOMERANG JAPAN

politeness of Japanese shop assistants, bank tellers, waiters in restaurants and people in other public contexts—though not necessarily (and perhaps significantly) in the tourism industry. Japanese propinquity makes for a test of character. Life there is an exercise in rehearsing patience, maintaining equilibrium, keeping a good temper; the place would be unendurable otherwise. My patience, equilibrium and temper were put on trial in a thousand situations, and I too learnt to seethe quietly rather than explode volcanically.

Except once. We had gone to a local restaurant in Kemigawa, a friendly, noisy, inevitably smoky place located above one of the local bakeries where the food was particularly good. These places, called *izakaya*, are Japanese versions of the local Australian pub that offers counter meals. We ascended a rickety staircase, went in and sat down. A pleasant young man, who proudly told us he was a student at Chiba University, took our order and brought us a couple of cold bottles of beer. We drank and we waited for the food to arrive. After half an hour contemplating what a fire trap the restaurant was, having passively smoked half a pack of fags and having drunk another bottle of gaseous Sapporo, we'd had enough. A grumpy inquiry confirmed my worst suspicion—the waiter had innocently forgotten to place our food order. But I didn't think he was innocent. I fumed. At the cash register I paid for the drinks and gave the waiter a burst in lurid Australian, telling him what I thought of him and his ineptitude. As we descended the stairs we passed a chap struggling up to the restaurant carrying a crate of beer. It was the waiter who had taken our original order. I had abused the wrong bloke. I felt like the Australian soldier in the movie *Gallipoli* who realises that he and his mates have trashed the premises of the wrong dealer in fake antiques. I resolved to try to be nicer in future.

A better test of the Japanese character can be found in social, not commercial, contexts. It is true that many of the social contacts we made in Japan were highly formalised, and often developed because of the Todai connection. As a visiting professor at Tokyo University, I was a foreigner worth knowing. It was through my job that I met Masayuki Furuoya, a genial Tokyo travel agent who was a bigwig in the Kawasaki Lions Club. Furuoya-san invited me to several Lions Club functions, sometimes to give speeches to local high-school students, sometimes merely to carouse with his associates. These events were usually held in the outrageous kitsch of the Hotel Ellcy in the unsalubrious environs of Gasoline Street, Kawasaki, as diabolical an urban environment as can be found anywhere. As professional foreigners, Deborah and I (until she started refusing to attend) were invited to participate in various arcane Lions Club rituals, including lending our voice to the club 'ROAR!!!', which in Japlish sounded disconcertingly like a chorus of voices proclaiming 'LAW!!!' Often the evenings would conclude with a visit to a local karaoke bar, where a bottle of very expensive Scotch would be plonked down in front of us and we would be invited to start crooning. But our anxiety not to appear rude did not overwhelm our sense of self-dignity, so we would sit glumly in the darkness pretending to sip our Scotch while watching Furuoya-san and a succession of his mates work their way through a list of numbers, including the Beatles' hits 'Yesterday', 'Norwegian Wood' and—appositely—'Help!'

The *meishi* culture, in strong evidence on these occasions, threw up a succession of unusual contacts. One evening at the conclusion of the annual Lions Club New Year's Party a demure, kimono-clad middle-aged woman offered me her namecard. I tucked it into my coat pocket, to discover the following day that I had been talking to:

HIROKO OZAKI
Chairman
THE EGYPT JAPAN KIMONO DRESS CULTURE
FRIENDSHIP ASSOCIATION
Office: Miyauchi Kimono Institute

Evidently our not being Egyptian was not a problem—Ozaki-san, bless her, was prepared to be friendly to all manner of foreigners. Nor did it stop her, through Furuoya, asking us on several occasions to model kimono in various shopping-centre promotional extravaganzas. Churlish foreigners that we were, we always found a plausible excuse to avoid dressing up and making a spectacle of ourselves for Japanese eyes.

But mixing with the Japanese was not all front, all formality. Far from it. Fleeting social contacts in restaurants, in trains, out walking, were invariably pleasant. Enduring friendships were forged, among them with Teruaki Fujishura, a Kemigawa native whose teenage brother had died of starvation in the aftermath of the war, a gentle and solicitous man as far removed from the stereotype of the raucous salaryman as is possible to imagine. Our neighbours in the Kemigawa apartment block were charm itself, especially Koichi and Akemi Sato and Osaumu and Yuki Chinone. Their generosity, offered naturally, not robotically, was humbling. They were a pleasure to live among; I do not expect to have such good neighbours again. There was only one neighbour I did not take to, a man whose name I have forgotten. During one of our communal summer barbecues (beer, sausages and salad—a disarmingly familiar scene), this fellow informed me that Japanese have 'a problem' with Australia because, unlike Japan, 'it has no history'. He and his sunny-natured wife had three small children; a week or so before she gave birth to their fourth, he woke up one morning with a bad headache, soon collapsed into a coma and died in hospital a few days later, aged thirty-nine. His wife carried on as best she could, with help from family and friends. She and her four fatherless children moved out of her apartment at exactly the same time as I left mine, bound for a new abode nearer her deceased husband's family in central Tokyo. Desperately busy and preoccupied as she must have been, she remembered to knock on my door and present me with a farewell gift.

Each day in Kemigawa brought some small but significant encounter. Working at my computer in the front bedroom of the apartment one winter's morning, I was surprised to hear the front door open and someone walk in. I jumped out of my chair and rushed the few metres to the door, where I was confronted by a woman so old she might have posed for the great Edo-era *ukiyo-e* craftsmen. Clearly disoriented, she had walked into the wrong apartment. Her initial amazement at the presence of some foreign interloper in *her* place soon turned to outrage. Speaking quickly and angrily, she asked me what I thought I was doing, who was I and how dare I. At least that's what I think she said—I couldn't make head or tail of her words, but I got her drift. Trying to appear patient and understanding, the very picture of benevolence, I moved her to the front door, meanwhile explaining as best I could that, yes, this *gaijin* actually did live there. But she remained adamant. Her anger invigorated her, giving her the strength of somebody less than half her age. Grabbing me in a vice-like grip—by which time we looked like a pair of grappling sumo wrestlers—she managed to swivel me around and push me out the half-open front door. Now she was in and I was out, out of my own flat, out in the cold. But I'd managed to wedge my foot in the door, and returned her grip with one of my own.

We both took stock of the situation, eyeing other malevolently, planning strategies, thinking new tactics. This was getting ridiculous. Would I have to flatten this harmless granny to regain my ground? I could see the headline in the *Japan Times*, 'AUSSIE TODAI PROF BASHES OLD WOMAN'. I opted to try to convince her of her error in my hopeless Japanese, but to no avail. Then and only then did I resort to force. Noticing she was tiring, breathing heavily, foaming slightly at the mouth, her grip on my wrist palpably weakening, I made a decisive charge, barging the two of us back into the apartment, down the hall and into the living room. Reeling at the suddenness of the movement, the old lady rested for a moment, then at last, to her horror, realised that the room she was in was clearly not hers. She apologised at such length that I thought both of us would die before the issue was over with. Apparently she'd come down to Tokyo from somewhere north to visit her daughter and grandchildren for a few weeks: as I'd thought, she'd made a simple mistake. We got on famously after that, fellow strangers in the Big Smoke, doing our best to negotiate its vast, intractable wilderness.

Australia receives an indifferent press in Japan, where it is often caricatured as a land of outlandish if good-natured yahoos. Likewise Japan in Australia. Negative stereotypes abound. The Japanese are automata; they are devious; they are innately ruthless. They are fanatical soldiers, fed by bloodlust. They are mercenary businessmen, ripping us off and buying us out. Or they are bloody tourists, great hordes of them, getting in our way and bumping up the prices. One of my favourite moments in Australian travel literature occurs in the narrative of Ethel

Jarman, an obscure woman traveller from Adelaide taking in the famous sights of China in the mid-1930s, who had her trip to the Great Wall ruined by Japanese tourists 'taking "snaps" and surveying the passing country with a proprietary air'.[9] Studies of Japanese culture have so mystified the land and its people that 'Japanese' nature has come to be seen as distinct from human nature. Force-fed elaborations of the gulf between *honne* (the real feelings and opinions of individuals) and *tatemae* (formal, group attitudes), visitors to Japan are constantly wondering what is secretly going on in people's minds, when in fact nothing covert or untoward may be going on at all. Foreigners read signs wrongly or see signs that simply do not exist, always searching for and often finding evidence to support their deep mistrust. World War II has so poisoned Australian attitudes to the Japanese people that it is impossible to regard them 'naturally' at all.

In *The Sword and the Blossom* (1968), the final volume of Ray Parkin's magnificent POW trilogy, an Australian aboard a Japanese prison ship looks out in wonder at the Japanese landscape as the ship nears anchorage 'in a bay that put them right in the middle of a Hiroshige painting', and says, 'There's something about this place that gets you in spite of the little buggers'. It is one of Parkin's great achievements that, after suffering so grievously at Japanese hands for four years, he came to respond to the place because of the 'little buggers' as well. Confronted by the sight of ordinary Japanese people upon disembarkation—women and children, toddlers and teenagers—Parkin does not see 'the spawn of the enemy', and a hated enemy at that, 'but the human family'.[10] These are words that some of today's Australians, with no good reason to harbour brutal racial assumptions about a military enemy of a more than half a century ago, would do well to ponder.

7 BOOMERANG JAPAN

Among the twenty or so students in my weekly Australian Studies lecture at Keio University were two articulate and intelligent young women, aged about twenty I suppose, who always sat together and seemed to take keener-than-average interest in what I had to say, even asking a few questions. Their names were Yumie and Junko. I learnt that in their mid-teens they had both spent time in Australia as exchange students, Yumie in Wagga Wagga and Junko in Armidale—strange and challenging new environments, I would imagine, for Tokyo girls. In one of my classes on Australian immigration I asked them if they had encountered any anti-Japanese feeling during their stay. At first they vigorously denied any animosity, then, after a few moments' hesitation, Yumie volunteered that a group of local schoolgirls had 'slapped and kicked' her one afternoon. 'Nothing much,' she said, a bit embarrassed to be bringing up past unpleasantness. But her candour seemed to encourage Junko. Her host family in Armidale, she said, had treated her kindly, except on one sad day when they locked her in her bedroom. It was 25 April, Anzac Day. In their wisdom her guardians thought that her sweet presence on the streets of Armidale that national day of days, with a procession of war veterans in progress, might incite a few of the less forgiving and more belligerent locals to violence.

⌘⌘⌘

Every way one flies, it has been said, leads inevitably in the direction of home—psychologically as well. To go abroad puts one in mind of the place left behind, as does describing where one has been. Is it possible to write a travel narrative without referring back to where one comes from? Literary travel tends to trace a mental boomerang: the body goes somewhere, but the mind keeps arcing back home. In Italo Calvino's novel *Invisible Cities* (1974), the peripatetic Venetian Marco Polo entertains Kublai Khan with his personal knowledge of the emperor's vast kingdom, but his own tales draw him back into the web of his home town. 'The more one was lost in unfamiliar quarters of distant cities', Polo realises,

> the more one understood the other cities he had crossed to arrive there; and he retraced the stages of his journeys, and he came to know the port from which he had set sail, and the familiar places of his youth, and the surroundings of home...[11]

Some things become clearer, perhaps deceptively so, when seen from a distance. An essential part of the travel experience, 'literary' or otherwise, is that it throws one's homeland into relief. All of us, as we move through foreign places, engage in the act of making comparisons with home. This can lead to the parochialism of travelling Australians who arrive home proclaiming how glad they are to be back 'in the best country in the world'. (But is this a specifically Australian phenomenon?) Travel, the cliché goes, 'broadens the mind'. I wonder. Sometimes it seems the opposite, as if people periodically volunteer to go through some kind of ordeal merely to have their prejudices confirmed or to find further proof that life is immeasurably worse everywhere else. In this sense foreign travel is no voyage of discovery but, as Philip Adams once mordantly put it, 'a ritual of reassurance'.[12] Yet it might just as easily be said that some individuals go abroad to reinforce their personal sense of coming from a place that is unworthy of their citizenship, a dump, a backwater, 'the arsehole of the world'

7 BOOMERANG JAPAN

(to use a not unfamiliar Australianism). It is dangerous to generalise. In some Australians, the long journey overseas and back leads to a renewed insularity; in others the venture abroad leads to reorientation rather than resettlement.

My own time in Japan never looked likely to become a 'ritual of reassurance'. Given my ambiguous situation as a non-permanent resident in the country, someone temporarily living there as a Japanese public servant but with a ticket out of the joint after my time was up, I had an armchair ride in Japan. I never particularly felt that I had to fit in. It didn't bother me much to be regarded as an object of curiosity, though occasionally it could be irritating out in Kemigawa, where foreigners were relatively scarce. I could afford to view a T-shirt ordering me to 'Fuck Off' as a joke. But Japan affected me in ways that surprised me, in ways that are difficult to describe. I felt 'at home' there, whatever that means, even when I was pining for Australia. I could never have proclaimed, as Donald Richie does in concluding *The Inland Sea*, that I 'didn't care' if I never returned to my country of origin.[13] I did care. But I feel now, as I look back at Japan from this antipodean and temporal distance, that I wouldn't mind returning, some day, maybe, as General Douglas MacArthur said of Australia while standing on a rural South Australian railway station.

More than anything, Japan unseated my notion of what—and where—home is, and made me consider the compensations of the state of the outcast. In the end, as a Western interloper, there is not much point reorienting yourself *towards* Japan in some vain hope of 'fitting in'. Fitting in to what? Better to shape the place, or some version of it, to suit yourself. 'A legless body is my kingdom's map', wrote Thomas Middleton nearly four hundred years ago.[14] This is an idea that might properly be applied to a Tokyo salaryman today as he contemplates his nocturnal journey home to somewhere in the suburbs of limbo after a couple of hours' frantic drinking in a Ginza dive; it is certainly a sentiment likely to be understood by the sojourner who finds the cultural and political spaces he is forced to travel inextricable from the personal.

⌘⌘⌘

My last day in Japan dawned damp and foggy. The burst of early spring weather had died, and the leaden skies that greeted me two years earlier had returned. I sent my luggage on to Narita Airport and took the Chuo line from Kichijoji to Kemigawa, ninety tedious minutes away, for a last lunch at Bill's. It was not a journey to make you misty-eyed. The area near Bill's place had changed a bit in the two years we had been in Japan. The vacant lots were being rapidly filled by spruce new double-storey kit homes. A couple of the old huts remained, but not, one suspected, for long. The irony about my two years in suburban Kemigawa still amuses me. I had left Melbourne to live in the world's biggest metropolis, only to find myself in a world created from an A. V. Jennings brochure circa 1965. I had grown up in the 'new' eastern suburbs of Melbourne in the 1950s and 1960s, moving from school to school as my parents kept searching for their dream home. During these itinerant years I formed my first ambition in life. When I was old enough I would flee that 'suburban wasteland', where everything seemed so dull and sterile, and never go back. And here I was, in my mid-forties, surrounded by what could have been the outer-eastern Melbourne of my teenage years. But the Japanese are not stupid. They, of all people, know the consolations of a bit of space and a bit of privacy, those fundamental comforts of the despised suburban way.

In the near distance Tokyo Rose's old studio was still standing, though in a state of advanced decay, boarded up, roped off, abandoned. On one of its grey walls a graffiti artist—perhaps the only one in Japan—had daubed a couple of swastikas, a reminder of old, but now absurd, alliances. Lunch taken, Bill and I headed off to Narita. Still dopey from the midday champagne, we opted for mineral water in one of those desolate airport bars that make you wonder why you have anything to do with air travel. As we moved toward the gate, Bill seemed distracted by the place-names on the departures board, in one of his reveries of escape. Tokyo's hold on him was only tenuous, after all; in his mind he always lived elsewhere, at least some of the time.

As reading material for my flight home, I had a present from Michael Hinds: not a fat John Grisham novel, nor even a *Time* magazine covering the latest comic/squalid instalment in the Clinton–Lewinsky imbroglio. Instead, folded neatly inside a souvenir copy of the race-book for the previous year's Japan Cup meeting, was a single-sheet photocopy of a poem called 'Narita', by the New Zealander Allen Curnow. I read it after take-off, when the plane had levelled out and the tension had evaporated—that moment of elation when one can hear the drinks trolley being put into motion and fantasies of Bloody Marys replace dread spectres of trailing smoke and charred, dismembered bodies. 'Narita' begins:

> Turning its eyes from side to side, inquiring
> brightly, the head of the worm issues
> from the door for arrivals.

> The door for departures is where papers are
> handed in. There are many of these,
> all numbered. Never look back.[15]

I appreciated the unspoken message behind Hinds' gift. He hated nostalgia, indeed sentiment of almost any kind. Too many bombs had gone off in his own back yard for that. Then I read on. The bastard! The poem shifted into a nightmare vision of impending air disaster, its speaker–passenger emotionally oscillating from anxiety to practised but uneasy reassurance. (As in, 'Nothing can go wrong. Can it?') Hinds must have anticipated the grim seriousness with which I would read this. And he especially would have understood how I would respond to the poem's conclusion, where the speaker calms himself with a cosy mind's-eye view of 'small green hills with ginkgo trees', an image that contains within itself the ambiguity of home: the Japanese tree of the country just departed, located on the landscape of home. Michael had suspected that I was a closet Japan-fancier all along.

Eleven hours later I was back in Melbourne—Melbourne, like Calvino's Aglaura in *Invisible Cities*, the city of 'proverbial virtues' and 'proverbial faults'.[16] It felt pretty good to set foot on its familiar, placid earth after Tokyo's tumultuous terrain. I was met at the airport by Deborah, by now hugely pregnant with our made-in-Japan son. In the car on the way home, the newspaper talk was all about Pauline Hanson, the beginning of the football season and the boom in real-estate prices. Apparently even our scruffy inner-city suburb, Brunswick, was going places. But as we swung into our street it didn't look much like it. I must have arrived back on one of those days set aside by the local council to pick up household junk. Piles of tossed-out furniture dotted the streetscape, attracting urban

7 BOOMERANG JAPAN

scavengers of one kind or another. Up the road, a young man struggled to load a dilapidated chest of drawers on to the back of a rusted ute. No economic miracles in Australia either.

We arrived at our house. I was surprised to see it still standing. Deborah had sorted out the Hell's Angels, no worries. A postcard deposited by a local estate agent stuck out of the letter-box in our front door. On one side it listed the name and address of the agency. On the other appeared a photograph of a glowering sumo wrestler caught in the act of going through his earth-trembling preliminaries, preparing to thrust at an opponent represented only by a gigantic flaccid buttock in the corner of the picture. I recognised the thruster as Akebono, the Hawaiian grand champion, who in his prime had taken on and beaten Japan's best in their own sacred sport. Underneath Akebono appeared the word 'STRENGTH'. It was something the bloke trying to make off with the chest of drawers could have done with. I couldn't quite see the relevance of the image to the selling of houses, but I did see that it was going to be hard, very hard, to shake Japan.

Tokyo–Melbourne, January 1998–March 1999

NOTES

PROLOGUE

[1] Arthur Koestler, *The Lotus and the Robot* (Hutchinson, London, 1960), p. 165.

CHAPTER 1: INTO THE INFERNO

[1] Hal Porter, *The Actors: An Image of the New Japan* (Angus & Robertson, Sydney, 1968), p. 14.
[2] Koestler, *The Lotus and the Robot*, p. 169.
[3] See Humphrey McQueen, *Tokyo World: An Australian Diary* (Heinemann, Melbourne, 1991), p. 34.
[4] *Time*, 16 February 1998, pp. 16–18.
[5] *Time*, 9 February 1998, p. 14.
[6] *Time*, 2 March 1998, pp. 48–9.
[7] Alex Kerr, *Lost Japan* (Lonely Planet Publications, Melbourne, 1996), p. 162.
[8] 'What's to blame for the Chuo Line Blues?', *Japan Times*, 8 March 1998.

[9] See Yukio Mishima, *Death in Midsummer and Other Stories* (Penguin edn, London, 1971), p. 186.

[10] See suicide statistics in Ben Hills, *Japan—Behind the Lines* (Hodder & Stoughton, Sydney, 1996), p. 300; see also Russell Skelton, 'Hashimoto pressed to defend yen', Melbourne *Age*, 15 June 1998.

[11] Richard Hughes, *Foreign Devil* (Andre Deutsch, London, 1972), pp. 80–1.

[12] Quoted in Michael Cooper S.J., *They Came to Japan: An Anthology of European Reports on Japan, 1543–1640* (Thames & Hudson, London, 1965), p. 41.

[13] Koestler, *The Lotus and the Robot*, see pp. 178–80; Roland Barthes, *Empire of Signs*, trans. Richard Howard (Hill & Wang, New York, 1982), p. 33.

CHAPTER 2: RIDING SANTA'S SURFBOARD

[1] For those with short memories, Prince Leonard of Hutt is the Western Australian farmer, Leonard Casley, who 'seceded' from the State and federal governments in 1970 in protest over wheat quotas. He turned his property into the principality of 'Hutt River Province' with its own stamps and so on, a kind of Australian Liechtenstein. At the time of writing, Prince Leonard and his consort, Princess Shirley, were still going strong.

[2] George Feaver (ed.), *The Webbs in Asia: The 1911–12 Travel Diary* (Macmillan, London, 1992), pp. 80–1.

[3] Haruki Murakami, *The Wind-Up Bird Chronicle* (Harvill Press, London, 1997), see pp. 74–6.

[4] See 'Artist's Protest Sheds Light', *Asahi Evening News*, 26 February 1998.

[5] See Ivan Hall, *Cartels of the Mind: Japan's Intellectual Closed Shop* (W. W. Norton, New York, 1997).

[6] Koestler, *The Lotus and the Robot*, p. 165.

[7] See Donald Keene (ed.), *Anthology of Japanese Literature* (Charles E. Tuttle & Co., Tokyo, 1956), p. 245.

[8] Clive James, *Brrm! Brrm!, or The Man from Japan or Perfume at Anchorage* (Picador, London, 1992), p. 12.

[9] *Japan Times*, 19 December 1996.

[10] See Colin Simpson, *The Country Upstairs* (Angus & Robertson, Sydney, 1956), pp. 71–2.

[11] Greg Dening, '"Let my curiosity have its little day": a reflection', *Australian Book Review*, no. 180 (May 1996), p. 40.

NOTES

CHAPTER 3: FAULT LINES

[1] Jan Morris, *Among the Cities* (Penguin edn, London, 1986), p. 218.

[2] Roger Pulvers, *General Yamashita's Treasure* (Angus & Robertson, Sydney, 1994), pp. 6–7, 43.

[3] Pico Iyer, *The Lady and the Monk: Four Seasons in Kyoto* (Black Swan, London, 1992), p. 191; Ruth Benedict, *The Chrysanthemum and the Sword* (Meridian, New York, 1946), p. 2.

[4] Marilyn Ivy, *Discourses of the Vanishing: Modernity, Phantasm, Japan* (University of Chicago Press, Chicago, 1995).

[5] Ross Terrill, 'Australia the Ambiguous', *Japan Times*, 24 November 1996.

[6] Fernand Braudel, *A History of Civilizations* (Penguin, London, 1993), p. 276.

[7] See Richard McGregor, *Japan Swings: Politics, Culture and Sex in the New Japan* (Yenbooks, Tokyo, 1996), p. 189.

[8] See Stephen FitzGerald, *Is Australia an Asian Country?* (Allen & Unwin, Sydney, 1997), pp 38, 65.

[9] See McGregor, *Japan Swings*, p. 197, citing W. Macmahon Ball, *Australia and Japan: Documents and Readings in Australian History* (Thomas Nelson, Melbourne, 1969).

[10] See Edward W. Said, *Orientalism: Western Conceptions of the Orient* (Penguin, London, 1991), pp. 206–7, 300.

[11] Quoted in Henry P. Frei, *Japan's Southward Advance and Australia* (University of Hawaii Press, Honolulu, 1991), p. 27.

[12] See figures provided in 'Tourism blow as Asia crises bites hard', Melbourne *Age*, 19 January 1999.

[13] See statistics provided in Japan National Tourist Organization newsletter, June/July 1998; also Australian Bureau of Statistics, *Overseas Arrivals and Departures*, November 1998.

[14] *Japan Times* supplement, 19 September 1996.

[15] A. B. Paterson, *Happy Dispatches* (1934; Lansdowne Press, Sydney, 1980), p. 19.

[16] Robert Strauss, Chris Taylor and Tony Wheeler, *Japan* (Lonely Planet, Melbourne, 1991), pp. 9, 24–5.

[17] Lafcadio Hearn, 'My First Day in the Orient', *Writings from Japan* (Penguin, London, 1984), p. 23.

[18] Basil Hall Chamberlain, *Things Japanese* (Kegan Paul, London, second edn, 1891), pp. 4, 7–8, 220.

NOTES

[19] Chamberlain, *Things Japanese*, p. 127; Isabella L. Bird, *Unbeaten Tracks in Japan* (John Murray, London, 1880), pp. 7, 347.

[20] Donald Richie, *The Inland Sea* (Kodansha International, Tokyo, 1993), pp. 14–16.

[21] See Kerr, *Lost Japan*, p. 226.

[22] 'Goodbye Japan', an interview with Alex Kerr by Ed Gutierrez, *Kansai Time Out*, November 1997, p. 22.

[23] James Hingston, *The Australian Abroad* (Sampson, Low, Marston, Searle & Rivington, London, 1879), vol. 1, pp. 81, 87–91; James Murdoch, *Inaugural Lecture*, School of Oriental Studies, University of Sydney (Angus & Robertson, Sydney, 1919), pp. 16, 28.

[24] See Alison Broinowski, *The Yellow Lady: Australian Impressions of Asia* (Oxford University Press, Melbourne, 1992), p. 103.

[25] Porter, *The Actors*, pp. 6–9, 155.

[26] Porter, *The Actors*, pp. 192, 45, 19, 150.

[27] Koestler, *The Lotus and the Robot*, p. 179.

[28] Clive James interviewed in *Australian Book Review* (December 1996/January 1997), p. 17.

[29] See Humphrey McQueen, *Japan to the Rescue* (Heinemann, Melbourne, 1991), p. 263; Frank Clune, *Ashes of Hiroshima* (Angus & Robertson, Sydney, 1950), pp. 37, 170, 175; Simpson, *The Country Upstairs*, pp. 4, 6.

[30] Norman Bartlett, *Island Victory* (Angus & Robertson, Sydney, 1955), p. 88; Norman Carter, *G-String Jesters* (Currawong Publishing, Sydney, 1966), p. 18.

[31] Porter, *The Actors*, pp. 45, 87.

[32] The cartoons are reproduced in Broinowski, *The Yellow Lady*, p. 9.

[33] See Peter Bowers, *Sydney Morning Herald*, 24 March 1990.

[34] Max Walsh, 'Living dangerously on the fault-lines', *Sydney Morning Herald*, 16 February 1998. See also 'Sayonara', *Bulletin*, 11 November 1997, pp. 24–7.

[35] Hills, *Japan—Behind the Lines*, pp. vii, 415–16.

[36] See Melbourne *Age*, 3 September 1998.

[37] For a lengthy analysis of the bilateral relationship, see McGregor, *Japan Swings*, chapter 7, 'The Odd Couple'.

[38] See Broinowski, *The Yellow Lady*, p. 37.

[39] See Les Murray, 'Aqualung Shinto', in *Lunch & Counter Lunch* (Angus & Robertson, Sydney, 1974), pp. 16–20.

NOTES

CHAPTER 4: THE BIG SMOKE

[1] A reading of Australian literature may give the impression that this procedure is *de rigueur* for male travellers arriving in Tokyo. See stories by John Bryson, 'Our Famous Ladies', in *Whoring Around* (Penguin, Ringwood, 1981) and Robert Drewe, 'Life of a Barbarian', in *The Bay of Contented Men* (Picador, Sydney, 1989).

[2] Paul Theroux, *The Great Railway Bazaar* (1975; Penguin, Harmondsworth, 1977), p. 341.

[3] See Edward Seidensticker, *Low City, High City: Tokyo from Edo to the Earthquake* (Charles E. Tuttle, Tokyo, 1983), p. 8.

[4] Hingston, *The Australian Abroad*, vol. 1, pp. 15–16.

[5] See Hal Porter, 'Rajani in Ueno—a Biography', in *Mr Butterfry and other tales of New Japan* (Angus & Robertson, Sydney, 1970), p. 140.

[6] See Donald Keene, *Dawn of the West: Japanese Literature in the Modern Era* (Henry Holt & Co., New York, 1984), pp. 89–90.

[7] Clive James, 'Postcard from Japan', in *Flying Visits* (Jonathan Cape, London, 1984), p. 49.

[8] See Seidensticker, *Low City, High City*, pp. 14–16.

[9] Hal Porter, 'House Girl', in Ken Goodwin and Alan Lawson (eds), *The Macmillan Anthology of Australian Literature* (Macmillan, Melbourne, 1990), p. 201.

[10] Bird, *Unbeaten Tracks in Japan*, p. 169.

[11] Feaver (ed.), *The Webbs in Asia*, p. 86; C. H. Bertie, *For Pleasure* (Angus & Robertson, Sydney, 1937), p. 214.

[12] Ian Buruma, *The Missionary and the Libertine* (Faber & Faber, London, 1996), p. 37.

[13] Edward Seidensticker, 'Tokyo', in *This Country, Japan* (Kodansha International, Tokyo, 1979), pp. 206–7.

[14] David Malouf, *Johnno* (Penguin edn, Ringwood, 1976), p. 84.

[15] See 'Any Day Now', *New Scientist*, 24 January 1998, p. 20.

[16] Yasunari Kawabata, *Snow Country* (Perigee, New York, 1981), p. 3; Junichiro Tanizaki, *The Makioka Sisters* (Charles E. Tuttle, Tokyo, 1958), p. 530.

[17] Barthes, *Empire of Signs*, pp. 30–2.

[18] Roman Cybriwsky, *Tokyo: The Changing Profile of an Urban Giant* (Belhaven Press, London, 1991), p. 43.

[19] Koestler, *The Lotus and the Robot*, p. 166.

[20] Porter, *The Actors*, p. 85.

[21] Buruma, *The Missionary and the Libertine*, p. 36.

NOTES

[22] The issues of sexual harassment and gender inequality were becoming topics of governmental discussion and analysis while I was in Japan. (See, for example, 'Beef up women's rights, government is advised', *Japan Times*, 16 December 1996; 'Prime Minister's Report: Men not helping around the house', *Japan Times*, 14 January 1998; 'Taking harassment out of the workplace', *Japan Times*, 16 December 1997.) But I wouldn't hold my breath about anything changing in the short term. I am indebted to Philip Brasor's article 'Men make mischief, molehills and a mess', published in the *Japan Times*, 5 February 1998, for its illuminating analysis of sexual vocabulary in the Japanese press.

[23] See D. P. Martinez (ed.), *The Worlds of Japanese Popular Culture* (Cambridge University Press, Cambridge, 1998), p. 92.

[24] Barthes, *Empire of Signs*, p. 38.

[25] For information on the *Meisho Sugoroku*, see Hidenobu Jinnai (ed.), *Ethnic Tokyo* (Bunjo Murotani, Tokyo, 1987), pp. 42–5.

[26] Bird, *Unbeaten Tracks in Japan*, p. 7.

[27] Barthes, *Empire of Signs*, pp. 35–6.

[28] Edward Fowler, *San'ya Blues: Laboring Life in Contemporary Tokyo* (Cornell University Press, Ithaca, 1996), pp. 14–15.

CHAPTER 5: OUT OF EDO I

[1] Paul Theroux, *The Great Railway Bazaar*, pp. 307, 323–4.

[2] See Kerr interview, *Kansai Time Out*, p. 22.

[3] See David Suzuki and Keibo Oiwa, *The Japan We Never Knew* (Allen & Unwin, Sydney, 1997), pp. 246–7.

[4] Ivy, *Discourses of the Vanishing*, pp. 34–7, 46, 65.

[5] Ivy, *Discourses of the Vanishing*, p. 65.

[6] See Theroux, *The Great Railway Bazaar*, p. 69.

[7] *Basho's Narrow Road*, trans. Hiroaki Sato (Stone Bridge Press, Berkeley, 1996), p. 43.

[8] Theroux, *The Great Railway Bazaar*, p. 306.

[9] Suzuki and Oiwa, *The Japan We Never Knew*, pp. 19–20.

[10] I am indebted for this information to Hanzaki Kohei, 'Ainu Moshir and Yaponesia: Ainu and Okinawan Identities in Contemporary Japan', in Donald Denoon et al. (eds), *Multicultural Japan: Palaeolithic to Postmodern* (Cambridge University Press, Melbourne, 1996), p. 120.

[11] See 'Ainu Protection Law is Enacted', *Japan Times*, 9 May 1997.

NOTES

CHAPTER 6: OUT OF EDO II

[1] Bob Dylan, 'Outlaw Blues' (1965), in *Writings and Drawings* (Knopf, New York, 1973), p. 163.
[2] See Roland Barthes, 'The Eiffel Tower', in *The Eiffel Tower and Other Mythologies*, trans. Richard Howard (Hill & Wang, New York, 1979), pp. 3–4.
[3] See 'Fuji-no-Yama', in Hearn, *Writings from Japan*, pp. 168–84.
[4] See James Kirkup, 'Poems on Mount Fuji . . .', *Poetry Australia*, no. 28 (1969), pp. 22–5.
[5] See Simpson, *The Country Upstairs*, p. 91; also p. 82.
[6] June Kinoshita and Nicholas Palevsky, *Gateway to Japan* (Kodansha International, Tokyo, 1992), pp. 122, 124.
[7] Bird, *Unbeaten Tracks in Japan*, p. 81.
[8] Toyofumi Ogura, *Letters from the End of the World: A First Hand Account of the Bombing of Hiroshima* (1948; Kodansha International, Tokyo, 1997), p. 15.
[9] George Johnston, *My Brother Jack* (Collins, London, 1964), p. 300.
[10] See Richie, *The Inland Sea*, pp. 14–15.
[11] See Ian Buruma, 'The Devils of Hiroshima', in *The Missionary and the Libertine*, p. 209.
[12] See Ian Buruma, *The Wages of Guilt: Memories of War in Germany and Japan* (1994; Meridian, New York, 1995), p. 106.
[13] Buruma, *The Wages of Guilt*, see pp. 92–9, esp. p. 92.
[14] Saburo Ienaga, *Japan's Last War* (Basil Blackwell, Oxford, 1979), p. 256.
[15] Okamoto Mitsuo, 'The A-Bomb Dome As World Heritage', *Japan Quarterly* (July–September 1997), p. 43.
[16] Buruma, *The Wages of Guilt*, p. 100.
[17] Rosa Praed, *Madame Izan: A Tourist Story* (Chatto & Windus, London, 1916 edn), p. 180.
[18] Iyer, *The Lady and the Monk*, p. 24.

CHAPTER 7: BOOMERANG JAPAN

[1] See George Sansom, *A History of Japan 1615–1867* (1963; Charles E. Tuttle, Tokyo, 1974), pp. 20, 27.
[2] Emperor Meiji, 'In my garden . . .', in Geoffrey Bownas and Anthony Thwaite (eds), *The Penguin Book of Japanese Verse* (Penguin, London, 1964),

NOTES

p. 157; Miurachura *haiku* in Keene (ed.), *Anthology of Japanese Literature*, p. 431.
[3] See *Hiragana Times*, no. 115 (May 1996), p. 22.
[4] *Japan Times*, 16 December 1997, p. 3.
[5] Kerr, *Lost Japan*, p. 231.
[6] Florence M. Taylor, *A Pot-Pourri of Eastern Asia* (Building Publishing, Sydney, 1935), p. 183.
[7] 'Harold Stewart—An Interview With Richard Kelly Tipping', *Westerly*, no. 4 (1987), p. 198.
[8] George H. Johnston, *Journey Through Tomorrow* (Cheshire, Melbourne, 1947), p. 395.
[9] Ethel Jarman, *Eastern Glimpses: Being the Daily Diary of an Australian Woman on Tour in the Far East* (Vardon & Sons, Adelaide, 1935), p. 71.
[10] Ray Parkin, *The Sword and the Blossom* (Hogarth, London, 1968), pp. 134, 136, 141.
[11] Italo Calvino, *Invisible Cities*, trans. William Weaver (1974; Picador, London, 1979), pp. 24–5.
[12] Philip Adams, *Age Saturday Extra*, 10 September 1983.
[13] Richie, *The Inland Sea*, p. 288.
[14] Thomas Middleton, 'The Wisdom of Solomon Paraphrased', in A. H. Bullen (ed.), *The Works of Thomas Middleton* (AMS Press, New York, 1964), vol. 8, p. 208.
[15] 'Narita', in Allen Curnow, *Continuum: New and Later Poems 1972–1988* (Auckland University Press, Auckland, 1988), p. 15.
[16] Calvino, *Invisible Cities*, p. 54.